Doing Research/Reading Resea

Second edition

This best-selling text enables beginning researchers to organise and evaluate the research they read, and to plan and implement small-scale research projects of their own. It gives structured, practical guidance on:

- the development of a research question;
- techniques of data collection;
- qualitative and quantitative forms of analysis;
- the writing and dissemination of research.

The authors present research as a principled activity that begins with the establishing and structuring of theoretical and empirical fields and research findings as serving to ask questions of educational practice rather than to direct it.

This revised and updated second edition includes a new chapter dealing with the complex issue of research ethics. It also includes consideration of digital technologies and new media, both as settings of research and as research tools, while the chapters on qualitative and quantitative analysis have been expanded and the annotated bibliography updated.

The authors have been active researchers in educational studies for more than twenty years. They have also supervised numerous doctoral and masters dissertations and taught research methods programmes in various higher education institutions around the world as well as in the Institute of Education, University of London.

Paul Dowling is Professor of Education and Director of Postgraduate Research in the Faculty of Culture and Pedagogy at the Institute of Education, University of London. His other publications include *Sociology as Method: Departures from the Forensics of Culture, Text and Knowledge* (2009, Sense) and *The Sociology of Mathematics Education: Mathematical Myths/Pedagogic Texts* (1998, Falmer Press).

Andrew Brown is Professor of Education and Dean of the Doctoral School at the Institute of Education, University of London. He has worked as an international consultant for major education development agencies. His other publications include *Professional Doctorates: Integrating Professional and Academic Knowledge* (with David Scott, Ingrid Lunt and Lucy Thorne, 2004, Open University Press) and *Digital Technology, Communities and Education* (*World Yearbook of Education 2004*, edited with Niki Davis, Routledge).

Doing Research/Reading Research

Re-interrogating education

Second edition

Paul Dowling and Andrew Brown

LONDON AND NEW YORK

First published 2010
by Routledge
2 Park Square, Milton Park, Abingdon, Oxon, OX14 4RN

Simultaneously published in the USA and Canada
by Routledge
270 Madison Avenue, New York, NY 10016

Routledge is an imprint of the Taylor & Francis Group, an informa business

Typeset in Garamond by Prepress Projects Ltd, Perth, UK
Printed and bound in Great Britain by TJ International Ltd, Padstow, Cornwall

British Library Cataloguing in Publication Data
A catalogue record for this book is available from the British Library

Library of Congress Cataloging in Publication Data
Dowling, Paul.
Doing research/reading research: re-interrogating education/Paul Dowling and Andrew
Brown.–2nd ed.
p. cm.
1st ed. entered under: Brown, Andrew, 1956–
Includes bibliographical references.
1. Action research in education. 2. Education—Research. 3.
Education—Research—Methodology.
I. Brown, Andrew, 1956– II. Brown, Andrew, 1956– Doing research/
reading research. III. Title.
LB1028.24.B76. 2009
370.7'2—dc22
2009006961

ISBN 10: 0–415–37601–7 (hbk)
ISBN 10: 0–415–37602–5 (pbk)

ISBN 13: 978–0–415–37601–3 (hbk)
ISBN 13: 978–0–415–37602–0 (pbk)

Contents

Figures

Tables

Acknowledgements

The first edition of this book arose out of our research and research methods teaching during the 1990s. In respect of the teaching, we benefitted enormously from the active participation and criticism of students on doctoral and masters courses at the Institute of Education, University of London, from masters students based in Hong Kong and Cyprus and at the University of Ceara in Fortaleza, Brazil.

Of particular importance was our participation in an Overseas Development Agency sponsored link between ourselves and the Universities of Cape Town and of the Western Cape in South Africa. The remit for the link concerned the development of research capacity in the Western Cape. We are grateful for the active participation of students and staff who attended our sessions at these universities and, especially, to Professor Paula Ensor – now Dean of the Faculty of Humanities at UCT – Professor Joe Muller, also of UCT, and Professor Cyril Julie, then of UWC. The link agreement was Paula's initiative and she was responsible for managing the South African end of it as well as for substantial intellectual input into our project. Parin Bahl attended and contributed to most of our sessions in the Western Cape and also provided continuous critical commentary on both our teaching and the book as they developed. This proved to be invaluable, as did the support provided by Diane Mayers and Michael Brown.

We would like to acknowledge participants on other research methods programmes that we have run individually. We are grateful to members of the Southern African Association for Research in Mathematics and Science Education for inviting Paul Dowling to be a plenary speaker at their 1994 conference and for organising a brief lecture tour of South Africa during his visit. The active participation of staff and students at the University of Transkei, the University of the North, and the University of the Witswatersrand, during this tour, was highly productive. We are also grateful to the participants on the Institute of Education masters programmes directed by Andrew Brown as part of the IBRD Indonesian Primary School Teacher Development project.

We are particularly grateful to Professor Tim Dunne of the University of Cape Town for critical comments and statistical advice on an earlier draft of Chapter 7. Ultimate responsibility for the final version is, of course, ours.

The list of due acknowledgements in relation to our research is potentially very extensive and is dissipated in our research publications. We should, however, recognise our indebtedness to Professor Basil Bernstein, who was the adept in respect to both of our research apprenticeships.

In respect of this second edition, we are indebted to Natasha Whiteman, now of the University of Leicester, for her advice on developments relating to new media and technologies and, in particular, to issues around internet research. Natasha's own work on research ethics – especially in the context of new media – has also informed the new chapter in this edition. We are also grateful to Richard Freeman for assistance in producing the new figures in Chapter 8 and, of course, to the reviewers and users (including our own students) of the first edition of the book, whose observations have contributed to the production of this new edition.

Figure 7.2, 'Barthes's analytic schema', is taken from *Mythologies* by Roland Barthes, published by Jonathan Cape and reprinted by permission of The Random House Group Ltd.

Preface to the second edition

It has now been ten years since the publication of the first edition of this book. Since that time there have been two major developments in educational research, the high profile of which seriously dates the work. The first development is the increasing interest in and formalisation of research ethics by the introduction of Research Ethics Committees. In institutional terms, the origins of this development lay in responses to atrocities committed by Nazi doctors during the Second World War and, more recently, to scandals in medical research in the 1960s and 1970s in the United States (Thrift, 2003). However, although professional associations, such as the British Educational Research Association, the British Psychological Association, and the British Sociological Association have published codes of ethical practice for some time now, it is only in the last five years or so that British Universities have established Research Ethics Committees (RECs) for the purpose of vetting research proposals in ethical terms. The first RECs at our own institution, for example, were set up in 2005 and the Economic and Social Research Council (ESRC) formally introduced its Research Ethics Framework (REF) in January 2006 (ESRC, 2005). The REF required that all research funded by the ESRC must go through a formal ethical review before funds would be released. Research ethics had not been entirely ignored in our first edition. However, under the new regime, it had become clear that far greater consideration was needed. We have, therefore, introduced a new chapter – Chapter 4 – that is dedicated to the issue of research ethics. The chapter draws quite heavily on material produced by one of the authors as part of a module for an online Master of Research programme at the Institute of Education and so this new chapter retains the character of the work as a whole in having developed out of our teaching as well as our own research activities.

The second development has been the explosion in forms and use of new media and, in particular, the internet. We are so familiar with it now that it is, perhaps, surprising to recall that Google was created in the same year in which the first edition of this book was published. Research was being carried out into online communities in the late 1990s; a notable example was Nancy Baym's *Tune in Log on* (2000). But 1998 was arguably the start of the global boom in internet activity, closely followed by a substantial increase in research interest. We had not really dealt with this area in the first edition of this book and, again, it was looking decidedly out of touch in this respect by the mid-2000s. We have addressed this issue, not by adding a new chapter; we felt that this was inappropriate as the internet penetrates all aspects of research methodology, just as methodology is relevant to all aspects of the internet. We have, therefore, added or amended text and added sections where appropriate throughout the book.

A number of other additions and changes have been made and those that are more significant than minor adjustments of style or grammar etc. are generally indexed in the text. Some are not, for example, the introduction of the standard deviation, in Chapter 8 – a small but significant omission from the first edition motivated by space limitations. Also the relationship between the mode of interrogation and Dowling's social activity method (SAM) is made more explicit in this edition and, of course, the annotated bibliography has been updated.

We used bold and italic text to establish a keyword index in the first edition. This apparently irritated some readers, who felt that it made the work look less academic. So we scrapped this facility for this edition; let's see if we get a deluge of complaints. We have also collected together the list of references at the end of the book rather than at the ends of the chapters. Full publication details for the items that appear only in the annotated bibliography are given in the bibliography itself, so we have not included these in the references section.

In the main, we feel that, apart from these key changes, the content of the first edition remains directly relevant to educational research today. So there are a lot of potential changes that we haven't made. We have retained most of our examples, including the small-scale research projects in what is now Chapter 10. We have also retained Alexander Luria's *Cognitive Development: Its Cultural and Social Foundations* (1976) as our central reference text for exactly the same reasons as before; we explain these in Chapter 2. We are also aware that part of the appeal of the first edition was that it was short. This might, of course, be taken to be a negative reflection on our readership; we do not take this view. Rather, we feel that a work of the order of length of a doctoral thesis – the first edition was rather shorter – is about as long as an academic work should be if the authors would like it to be read – at least some of the time – as a single essay. Certainly, research methods books that extend well beyond this length tend, in our experience, to be used more as encyclopaedias; very useful, but not what we are trying to achieve. This being the case, we have refrained from expanding – potentially indefinitely – the range of approaches and techniques that are treated in any detail in the text; there are plenty of alternative works that can satisfy these requirements and a number are represented in our annotated bibliography.

One final change we have made is to reverse the order of our names on the cover. This is not to signify any dramatic change in authorship responsibility between the two versions, but to affirm that both works have been fully collaborative efforts: one name has to go first – the directionality of print can be a curse sometimes – so we've taken it in turns. Perhaps the next edition will be a digital version with names rotating in a cover animation; that'll present a problem for citations, of course.

Paul Dowling
Yokohama

Andrew Brown
London

December 2008

Chapter 1

Introduction

The three Rs of research

This book emerged very gradually out of work on which we have been engaged, individually and collaboratively over a period of ten years or so, prior to the publication of the first edition, and over the ten years since. This work has involved research and research education, teaching about research. The central motivation of the book developed out of two fields of commitment and experiences. These have shaped and been shaped by the general approach to the reading and doing of research that constitutes the principal theme of the book. That is, that research is properly conceived, not, primarily, as a sequence of stages, nor as a collection of skills and techniques, nor as a set of rules, though it entails all of these. Rather, it should be understood, first and foremost, as the continuous application of a particularly coherent and systematic and reflexive way of questioning, a *mode of interrogation*.

Our first commitment is to *research* as a distinctive attitude. The products of educational research are currently being thrust more than ever before into the public domain of political positioning and manipulation. But all too much of this output is interrogated exclusively in terms of its summary conclusions and rarely in respect of its methodological integrity. Under these conditions, 'research' is very easy. Say we want to argue that homework is good for you. Well, all we have to do is select half a dozen schools that have received positive inspection reports and some others that were negatively evaluated. We then count the number of hours of homework that each school sets. A fast piece of arithmetic on the back of an envelope and, lo and behold, we find that the good schools set more homework than the bad schools. Solution: advocate a national homework policy or, alternatively, leave it to the schools to decide, so long as they publish their individual policies (which headteacher is going to declare themself with the baddies?). Both sides of the political game get ammunition for their manifesto and happily sponsor the 'researcher' to keep up the good work. Or they just might employ another one who looks better on the TV – after all, just about anyone can do this!

In the heady atmosphere of serious political debate, no one notices that, since the criteria for positive inspection include setting a lot of homework, the 'research' can hardly be described as adding a great deal to the sum of human knowledge.

Our own experience of research is that it is difficult and frustrating and that it takes a lot of time and brings a lot of tears. But eventually, it can generate ways of looking at the world that you didn't have before and that can motivate real developments in your professional practice as well as spur you on to further research activity.

Our second commitment is to *teaching* as a distinctive attitude. And here, teaching is not to be understood as a relay of performance objectives to be measured by standardised tasks by a functionary whose relation to the content is challenged rather than fostered by bureaucratic authority. Nor is teaching itself to be conceived as a sequence of phases, a set of skills and techniques, or a set of rules, although, again, it entails all of these. We see teaching as the establishment of an apprenticing relationship between a relatively experienced and a relatively inexperienced practitioner. The aim is the transmission of the practice from the former to the latter; we make no apology for the use of the expression 'transmission', though we are not by any means intending that 'transmission' entails cloning; research and research methodology are, at their best, creative and developing fields.

The teaching or transmission of one's practice relates to, but is different from, the doing of one's practice in its own right and for its own sake. We propose that the relationship between a practice and its transmission is to be understood as one of constructive dialogue. This is particularly apposite where the practice concerned is educational research: research and teaching, then, cast their respective interrogative gazes upon each other; each stands as a critic with respect to the other. The motive force of the dialogue is, of course, sustained only so long as the two do not tend to dissolve into each other. In our own research, we describe the distinctions between practices such as research and teaching in terms of the distinctive nature of the structures of social relations that constitute the fields in which they respectively operate. These relational structures include peer group evaluation, in the case of research, and a hierarchical, apprenticing relationship between transmitter and acquirer, in the case of teaching.

As we have announced, our commitments to research and to teaching have shaped and have been shaped by our general methodology. This general methodology begins with an insistence that dialogue is more productive than monologue in generating new ideas. In the next chapter, we shall describe the fundamental dialogue in research as operating between the theoretical and the empirical. More generally, the approach derives from Dowling's *constructive description*, which is presented by Dowling in detail in his own work (Dowling, 1998, 2009). In this work, Dowling also presents his particular organisational language, or theoretical framework, *social activity method*,[1] which has also informed our presentation of the research mode of interrogation.

These commitments to research and to teaching have also arisen from particular sets of experiences during the ten-year period of gestation of the first edition of this book and the further ten years since its publication. We both, for example, benefited enormously from our own research apprenticeships. In both of our cases, this included a substantial period of time working under the supervision of Basil Bernstein, at the Institute of Education, University of London. A dominant figure in educational research since the 1960s, Bernstein was also an inspirational teacher of research. This is not to say that what we are presenting here is fully in accord with Bernstein's own approach. Indeed, Dowling (2009) has marked out a number of quite fundamental points of difference between Bernstein's and his own sociology. However, the mark of a good teacher is the production of constructive practitioners rather than acolytes and, even if he did not dictate this book, he certainly was inspirational in its production.

Our own teaching, over more than twenty years, has included a substantial amount of work on higher degrees programmes, including the supervision of masters dissertations and doctoral theses. We also developed a general course in doing and reading educational research, of which this book is a direct result. The course arose out of teaching that we were initially doing in London, but that has since been taken around the world. In particular, we have taught the course in South Africa, Hong Kong, Cyprus and Brazil. In presenting the course, we have employed a diverse range of pedagogic techniques, including the use of computer-mediated communication modes for the supervision of coursework following the face-to-face components.[2] The interests of course members have varied from a diverse range of curriculum subject and phase specialisms to cross-curricular interests, such as health education, educational media and information technology, and the more general disciplines such as educational management, educational philosophy, psychology, and sociology. Since the publication of the first edition of the book, our research education activities have focused more on doctoral research and we continue – now, mainly individually – methodological courses for a very diverse range of doctoral students and other individuals and groups carrying out personal or collaborative research. In our experience, it is very often the teacher who gains most in the pedagogic encounter. In a very real sense, then, our production of this book owes a great deal to the enthusiastic participation of and critical evaluation by participants on these courses.

Our practice in presenting our original course was to adapt it to the linguistic, national and disciplinary interests of the members of the particular programme that we were running and, naturally, to develop the general structure and specific activities that constitute the course on the basis of experience and feedback each time we ran it. The book, however, represents a transition. Clearly, we cannot target our readership in quite the same way. We do, nevertheless, have an audience in mind.

We envisage that readers of our book will comprise intending producers and consumers of research in the academic and professional fields of education. The kind of producer we have in mind might be someone who wishes to conduct a small-scale piece of research. Commonly, this might form part of an academic course of study, such as a masters or doctoral programme. Alternatively, it might be a response to a problem or a question that arises in the course of the professional educational activity of, for example, a teacher, an educational administrator, or a health educator. Whatever its origins, the research will involve the collection and analysis of data, which is to say, it will be empirical research. The research will also entail a systematic enquiry that attempts to be self-conscious about its assumptions, method of approach, and its limitations.

The producer of research will need to draw on existing work that is associated with their particular interest; that is to say, they will also be consumers of research. Within an academic context, the author is required to situate their work within the field of research. This means that they must make their consumption explicit. Professional research may or may not place a high value on its bibliography. Nevertheless, the professional researcher as well as the academic researcher can gain much from a consideration of previous research, not least in respect of the ways in which other researchers have selected and deployed their methods of data collection and analysis and organised their arguments.

The category 'consumer' of research is, however, more extensive than that of producer. Whereas all producers are (or, at least, should be) consumers, not all consumers are producers. Much of the public output of both academic and professional educational research is aimed at a practitioner as well as a researcher audience. This book, then, is as much about reading research as it is about doing research.

Of course, the producer of research will generally want to address an audience of their own in relaying their work. So, in this book, we shall also address the writing of research. Reading, Researching and Relaying: the three Rs of Research.

Our readership, thus defined, will have diverse interests, backgrounds and needs in terms of research activity. We cannot hope, nor shall we attempt, to meet them all. This book is not, for example, a summary of widely used data collection and analysis techniques. Nor do we spend very much time discussing the metatheoretical (for example, epistemological, ontological) and political debates that take research itself as an object of study. Nor have we compiled a collection of anecdotes on the practical experiences of researchers in the field. There are excellent publications available in each of these categories. We have referred to some of them in our annotated bibliography.

What we have attempted to do can be summarised as four aims. First, and as we have suggested above, this book is not neutral. We approach educational research from a particular position. This position understands research as a particular coherent and systematic and reflexive mode of interrogation. Our first aim is to establish and present this mode of interrogation in a form that is accessible to the beginning researcher, as we have described them. In other words, to apprentice our reader to the research mode of interrogation. We should point out, however, that we have not made major concessions in the sense of diluting the principal ideas in the book. This is a serious position statement as well as a pedagogic resource. Readers will find some, though by no means all, of the book hard work. Second, we aim to achieve this within the context of an introduction to and some development of the language and techniques of research methods. Third, we aim to signal some of the difficulties entailed in research and to provide practical advice on their management. Fourth, we aim to present our approach so that it can be applied in the reading and doing and, ultimately, the presentation of educational research.

The structure of the main body of this book is as follows. Following this introduction, we have included two chapters that focus on the clarification of the context of a research project. Chapter 2 considers the first stages of the development from a general area of interest to the sketching out of relevant theoretical and empirical fields within which the research is to take place. Chapter 3 takes this development further to the sharper delineation of the research problem and empirical setting, including the definition of variables, sampling procedures and so forth.

Chapter 4 is a completely new chapter. It opens up the very important area of research ethics, which was certainly underplayed in the first edition of the book. It is important, again, to understand the content of this chapter and the various guidelines on ethical practice that are associated with the professional research associations as components of a mode of interrogation. These guidelines ask important questions of your research practices; they generally do not provide you with neat answers to these questions.

Chapters 5 and 6 focus on issues of data collection. Chapter 5 focuses on observational approaches and the generation of researcher accounts; Chapter 6 considers the eliciting of accounts from others, including the use of questionnaires and interviews. Chapters 7 and 8 move to issues and techniques of data analysis, Chapter 7 emphasising qualitative analysis and Chapter 8 providing a limited introduction to quantitative approaches. Essentially, although we would like readers to read the book in the order in which it is presented, it is possible to read Chapters 4–8 in any order, making use of the cross-references where necessary.

In Chapter 9 we present the research mode of interrogation in a schematic way, drawing on the discussions of the previous chapters. Chapter 10 focuses on the points of entry to and exit from the research process. In the first half of Chapter 10 we shall revisit the initial phase of the research process that is introduced in Chapter 2. This time, we will be able to make use of some of the terminology that has been developed in the intervening chapters. In the second part of the chapter, we shall give some consideration to the process of writing up one's research. Finally, in Chapter 11, we return to some of the issues raised in this introduction and present our 'manifesto' for educational research.

We contend that, in terms of reading on research methodology, it should be possible for a beginning researcher to produce a good quality piece of work in the form of, say, a masters dissertation without going beyond this book. We would not, however, advise it. We have, therefore, included an annotated bibliography that will enable the reader to broaden their methodological understanding both technically and in terms of general methodology. Certainly, we would strongly advise doctoral researchers to read well beyond this book in terms of research methodology.

So, this book cannot turn you into a researcher. Ultimately, you can make that transition only by involving yourself in the practices of research, preferably alongside a more experienced practitioner – possibly your tutor on a higher degree programme. This is why, whenever we have taught this course ourselves, it has been very much a practical activity and this practical nature also characterises our continuing work in research education. We cannot replicate this practical nature in a book, nor are we attempting to. The book stands in relation to your developing research practice in the same kind of relationship as that which we are claiming obtains between educational research and professional educational practices. That is, as a mode of interrogation. Its fundamental role is to challenge you to greater coherence and systematicity and reflexiveness in the research practice that you are now beginning.

This concludes our introduction, save to say that after Chapter 11 we have included an invitation to send us your responses to the book (and your suggestions for future editions). We are giving advance warning of this here so that you can make notes as you go along ;-).

Chapter 2

Declaring an interest

The empirical and theoretical contexts of the research

Empirical and theoretical domains and the research process

This book is concerned with empirical research within the general field of education. By research, we mean an enquiry that seeks to make known something about a field of practice or activity that is currently unknown to the researcher. In referring to the research as empirical, we mean that the enquiry should, in part, justify any claims that it makes in terms of reference to experience of the field to which these claims relate. We shall refer to this field as the empirical field. By introducing this definition, we are trying to establish an attitude, rather than rule out certain kinds of enquiry. For example, suppose that you are interested in the relation between gender and secondary school academic performance. There is clearly a whole range of approaches that you might adopt in addressing this topic. First, you might go to the library and find a book on the subject. This might qualify as 'research', subject to additional expectations that you may have concerning systematicity and extensiveness. However, it would be difficult to maintain that reading the book gave you any direct experience of secondary schooling. Rather, the author must impose principles of selection and organisation, that is, principles of recontextualisation, upon their own experience of secondary schooling in mediating it to you as reader.

Alternatively, you might consult the published statistical data relating to the GCSE performances of boys and girls in England and Wales in 2004. Clearly, this narrows the field to a national context and also to a particular year. However, it also imposes other principles of recontextualisation that mediate direct experience of this field. For example, it provides a simple binary scale for the category 'gender'. This means that the data treat all girls as the same and all boys as the same. You may feel (and there is evidence to support this) that there are very considerable differences in the dispositions in relation to and experiences of secondary education of girls and boys that vary according to dimensions such as ethnicity and socioeconomic status. Additionally, of course, academic performances do not begin and end with GCSE examination results. However, your data source would make any such differences opaque to your enquiry.

A third approach might be to attempt to get closer to the intended field by conducting interviews with participants, such as students and/or teachers. This narrows the field somewhat further, so that we are now beginning to talk about an empirical setting. In conducting an interview one is often engaging in one setting – that of the interview itself – in order to access information about another – activity in the examination room, for example. As with the library sources, this information is again mediated by principles of recontextualisation that are imposed on their experiences by your subjects. These principles may be imposed self-consciously or otherwise. In either case, you have no clear line of access to them. You may try to overcome the effects of the unknown recontextualisation principles by adopting the position of observer in the intended setting, itself, but there are limits to what you can possibly observe. You will have only so much time available (and you can only be in one place at a time) and you can't observe, far less record, everything that goes on in a particular situation. You must be selective and encode your observations in some way if you are to record them. This is the case even with a video recording. The complexity of even the apparently most simple situation is such that you will be unable to make explicit all of the principles that you impose on your observation and recording activities even if it were possible to be conscious of all of them, which, of course, it isn't. Furthermore, you can rarely discount completely the effect of your presence in a situation as an observer.

Confronted with such apparently insurmountable difficulties, you may be forced to the conclusion that the only settings that you can validly research are those in which you naturally and routinely participate yourself. Unfortunately, this still does not eliminate the impact of recontextualisation. The act of taking up the position of observer or commentator is, of necessity, a shift in perspective from that of participant. This point has been very powerfully argued by the French sociologist Pierre Bourdieu.[1] Whether in prospect or in retrospect, the objectification of your activities is always a different experience from your experience of those activities themselves. You will be familiar with this outside research; planning and evaluating a lesson are very different activities from actually teaching it. We shall refer to this as the epistemological paradox: the act of making your experience explicit of necessity entails its transformation.

There is, then, no position or method that you can adopt that will give you an indisputably clear view of the empirical field (or of any empirical setting within it) that you want to investigate and about which you want to make statements. There is no such thing as the correct method, or even the best method for addressing a particular research interest or question. This does not, however, mean that all methods and positions are as good as each other for the purposes of empirical research. If they were, we could hardly justify writing a book on research methods. A common response to the inevitable shortcomings of any particular approach is to employ two or more approaches to the same problem. This is called methodological triangulation. The term 'triangulation' refers, metaphorically, to the police or military procedure of using geometry to locate an illicit or 'enemy' radio transmission from direction readings at two reception points. In the context of educational research, we might employ a combination of, for example, interviews and direct observation in attempting to gain access to teachers' classroom practices.

There is a fundamental difference, however, between the assumptions that are being made in the radio and the educational research contexts. Essentially, the radio triangulator is making the assumption that there is a unique location for the transmitter and that this will be revealed by the process. This assumption is empirically justified when the illegal transmitter is found and arrested (or shot). The assumption is justifiable because there is already a coordination between the method of finding out and the method of moving to the coordinates of the transmitter. The means of defining the locations of the transmission point and the reception points are coincident. Nothing is being measured that is not already encoded into the practice.

The situation in educational research is, generally, very different. As we have argued, the act of taking up the position of observer entails a necessary break with that which is being observed. The observational 'position' is to be defined in a way that is distinct from the way in which the empirical setting, or observed position, is being defined. If the result of applying methodological triangulation is the production of multiple observational positions, then the research will be incoherent. Reconciling these multiple positions into a single observational position will merely return you to the original problem. Methodological triangulation, then, may be of value in expanding the empirical setting. It cannot overcome the epistemological paradox.

To explain further, we must return to our definition of empirical research. We have already asserted that it must justify any claims that it makes in terms of reference to the empirical field. More specifically, it must justify claims in terms of reference to the empirical setting, which is the local space in which the researcher is working within the empirical field. We must focus on the word 'justify'. Claims must be justified, which entails that the reasoning must be made as explicit as possible. In addition, it will clearly help if the presentation of claims and their justification can be made as systematically as possible so that the lines of argument are visible. This will not only assist the reader, but also enable the researcher to detect faults in their reasoning.

So, you will need to be as explicit as possible about the empirical setting of your research and about the relation to it of any information that you gather. However, this is not enough. We have suggested above that you cannot approach a field or setting without some preconceptions about the nature of that setting. Most obviously, you cannot set out to research the school without having some idea of what you mean by 'school'. Your preconceptions will comprise commonsense knowledge about how schools work and who works in them and about how you can distinguish between good and bad schools and so on. You may also have access to more academic knowledge about the learning and teaching processes or about management practices etc. Furthermore, you may affiliate to moral and political views about how schools ought to work or what they should be aiming to do and so forth. Although these preconceptions will certainly impact upon your observation or interviewing or reading, they will not all be present in your consciousness at the time. You cannot be at all sure, in other words, of your own bias even though you must recognise that it is there. Thus, in justifying the claims that you will make about your empirical territory, you must also try to make as available as possible the conceptual structure that you bring to bear on that territory. This conceptual structure is the theoretical problem with which your research is concerned.

We have now introduced two arenas within which empirical research takes place. The first has thus far been described in terms of two levels, one local and the other general. The *empirical setting* refers to the local region of experience about which you want to make claims – the observed position. The setting is a specified region within a broader empirical field. Thus, secondary school teachers' classroom practices might constitute an *empirical field*; the practices of a small sample of teachers in a sample of their classrooms in a particular school in a particular location, etc., might constitute the empirical setting. We have also introduced two levels of the second arena. The *problem* refers to the conceptual structure that enables you to think about the empirical setting – the observational position. However, this also must relate to a broader field of discourse incorporating, perhaps, academic and professional knowledges and debates. This is the *theoretical field*. Later, we shall introduce third levels in each of these arenas. Research entails the *specialising* of a theoretical framework within a more general field and the *localising* of an empirical setting within an empirical field. It is the bringing to bear of the theoretical framework on the empirical setting that enables you to make both theoretical and empirical claims.

As a beginning researcher, you will probably find it very difficult to give an adequately explicit and coherent description of your empirical setting. You are unlikely to have a clear idea of a problem. You may have initial ideas about an aspect of educational practice or process that interests you. You may also have feeling for the kind of theoretical approach that you are drawn to; whether, for example, the problem is to be conceived of as a psychological or a sociological one, whether it relates to management or health promotion and so forth. But these ideas are unlikely to have been developed very far at this stage. In other words, you are likely to have some initial feeling for your general empirical and theoretical fields. Educational research does not necessarily begin with clearly defined and articulated problems and empirical settings. Rather, we are asserting that the research process itself is properly conceived of as the construction of the theoretical and the empirical as increasingly coherent and systematically organised and related conceptual spaces. It is, in other words, a continuous and productive process. This poses the additional problem of knowing when to stop. We will leave this question for the moment. We will continue this chapter with a discussion on the initial moves in the formation of the theoretical and empirical contexts that constitute the research interest.

Declaring an interest: first steps towards a research question

As we have announced in the introduction and, indeed, in the title, this book is as much about reading research as it is about doing research. In many ways (which we hope will become clear) each of these processes entails the other. We are not, therefore, offering separate sections on doing and reading. Rather, we will be looking at the various stages of the research process in terms of both doing and reading research. Clearly, we need to make reference to publicly available research in considering reading. We have decided to use a very famous and very influential piece of work carried out in the 1930s in the Soviet Union by Alexander Luria and published in English about thirty years ago. Luria was a student and colleague of Lev Vygotsky. Their work is now becoming increasingly influential in the general field of educational research. The particular item that we shall be referring to is Luria's (1976) *Cognitive Development: Its Cultural and Social Foundations*.

Apart from the influential status of this work, its principal appeal for our purposes is its clear definition of its theoretical and empirical contexts. It is, in this respect, a very good piece of research. A third reason for its selection is precisely its time and place of origin. Its distance from us in time and general cultural context gives it a degree of strangeness that makes it comparatively easy to bring into relief the contours of its argument. Vygotsky's and Luria's work also incorporates theoretical ideas, which we shall be referring to at various points in this book. We intend to provide sufficient information about Luria's study to enable the reader who is not familiar with it to negotiate our text. However, we strongly recommend that you read Luria's text for yourself at some point.

In respect of the doing of research, we shall include references to several pieces of small-scale work. Most of these have been carried out by students on diploma, masters and doctoral programmes with which one or both of us has been associated. In referring to this work, we are not seeking, here, to evaluate it. Rather, we are hoping that our discussion of the kinds of questions and approaches that these beginning researchers have adopted will concretise the more general statements that we shall be making. We shall also be referring to work that we have carried out ourselves, individually and jointly. Again, we are not presenting this as exemplary of good (or bad) practice. It is simply providing material for our methodological exposition. We shall begin our discussion of the initial stage of the research process with a brief introduction to the general theoretical and empirical fields that were occupied by Luria's study.

An initial description of Luria's theoretical and empirical spaces

The title of Luria's book gives us a good indication of the theoretical field in which he is working, *Cognitive Development: Its Cultural and Social Foundations*. The main title tells us that Luria is operating within the general field of psychology. The subtitle gives us a clue, should we need one, to the kind of theoretical explanation that he wants to offer. It indicates that he grounds cognitive development in the sociocultural; the level of development of an individual's consciousness is, in some sense, a function of the kind of society in which they live. In his introduction, Luria clarifies his interest:

> psychology has barely begun to study the specific sociohistorical structures of mental processes. We still do not know whether changes in sociohistorical structures or changes in the nature of social practice result only in broadened experience, acquisition of new habits and knowledge, literacy, and so forth, or whether they result in radical reorganization of mental processes, changes at the structural level of mental activity, and the formation of new mental systems. Proof of the latter would be of fundamental significance for psychology as a science of social history.
>
> (Luria, 1976, p. 12)

Here, Luria is indexing a debate within the field of psychology at the time. It was a debate that also held an interest for anthropologists; in particular, Franz Boas and Lucien Lévy-Bruhl. Boas adopted the former of the two positions referred to by Luria. That is, he maintained that the thinking of individuals from culturally different groups varied only in the categories used. Lévy-Bruhl, on the other hand, argued that there were structurally different forms of thought that related to each other in developmental terms. That is, people from 'primitive' societies are characterised by a 'primitive' mode of thought. In the above extract, Luria also hints at his own preference.

There are other dimensions to Luria's interests. Although his work and that of Vygotsky often stood in opposition to the Marxist psychology of the Soviet Union of the day, his general approach must be described as, itself, broadly Marxist. Specifically, his understanding of social development related to the organisation of the relations of production. Luria also adopted Vygotsky's interest in and understanding of language as providing the basis for the structuring of thought. Literacy, in particular, constitutes language as a comparatively context-independent system and thus potentially facilitates a radical transformation in the mode of thinking. Thus, his disciplinary interests were very broad, ranging across psychology, sociology, anthropology and linguistics. So, we can begin to get an idea of the theoretical space within which Luria was working. It is a space that identifies particular discourses and debates within an even broader, multidisciplinary field. It will become more sharply defined in the subsequent chapters of this book. How about his empirical field?

As we have indicated, Luria's interest is in the relationship between social and cultural organisation and cognition. Empirically, Luria wants to look at differentiation in people's productive relations, in their literacy, and in their thinking. The Soviet Union of the 1930s was a society in transition (some might say turmoil). Luria therefore had the opportunity to work in settings that spanned developmental levels. Some of his subjects would be engaged in individualised subsistence production, others might work on a collective farm; some of his subjects would be illiterate, others would have received access to schooling and literacy. He chose to work in 'remote villages of Uzbekistan and also a few in the mountainous regions of Kirghizia' (Luria, 1976, p. 14), where such variations could be found.

Luria's choice of empirical setting was motivated by his theoretical field and, more particularly, by his specific problem. This problem constituted his position within the academic field. The choice also involved taking advantage of an opportunity to study cognition during what Luria conceived to be a particular kind of social transformation. In this respect, the choice was motivated by Luria's contingent location in the Soviet Union in the early 1930s. By definition, beginning researchers have yet to clarify their position within a field of research and the achievement of this clarification will be an important aspect of their research. Very often, however, they will occupy professional positions and will be familiar with and interested in some of the discourses and debates relating to these positions. They will also be immersed in a professional practice within which problems and issues of interest may arise. The initial steps towards a *research question* may well involve the articulating of localised observations and problems with more general professional discourses and debates. We will now consider the inaugural stage of such a study.

Opening your theoretical space: using the library

A primary school teacher on one of our programmes (and more on this study in Chapter 8) claimed that it was her observation of a child's reference to 'a vampire in his or her coffin' that led to her interest in the more general issue of children's use of gender-specific pronouns. The observation indexes the teacher's local professional context as the emerging empirical setting. It also leads to an area of professional literature relating to the issues of gender and language acquisition and use in the primary school. Further, it leads to a more academic literature base in a number of possible fields, including sociology, linguistics and psychology. At this stage, the empirical setting seems fairly well defined, whereas the theoretical space looks dangerously expansive and uncoordinated. It is, therefore, in this space that some initial clarification might be made.

The initial approach might be to try to specify more precisely what aspect of the inspirational observation particularly interests you. This will direct you to relevant areas of the literature. There are a number of possibilities relating to the above example.

For example, your main interest may lie in gender as a structural feature of the primary school and of wider society. In this case, children's gendering of their language would be regarded as instances of a gendered culture. Alternatively, you might be interested in children's language development, either in linguistic or cognitive terms or in relation to children's reading materials. There again, you may be interested in exploring policy in relation to language and gender in primary schooling. Making a decision in these terms is probably about as far as you can go without doing some work in the library.

An academic educational library can be a daunting place for the beginning researcher. It will contain at least seven kinds of resources:

1   The collection of books – including e-books – about education and educational research and associated topics and disciplines. Some of these will be targeted primarily at an academic audience. This category will include 'classical' research in fields such as psychology and sociology as well as work by academic authors focusing specifically on education. Other books will be more deliberately aimed at professionals and, possibly, other groups. This category will include, for example, governmental reports and enquiries as well as books written by professionals for professionals.

2   The collection of journals. Again, both academic and professional journals are likely to be included and these will be in both paper and online media.

3   The archive of dissertations and theses of former masters and doctoral students.

4   Reference materials of various kinds including, for example, statistical data relating to education.

5   A collection of educational materials, such as school textbooks.

6   Various resources that enable the interrogation of the library collection and of educational literature more generally. There will be a library catalogue that, nowadays, will usually include online search facilities enabling users to find specific items or the works of particular authors, or to search using topics or keywords. Most academic libraries will provide online access to indices of educational research, including the British Education Index and the Education Resources Information Center (ERIC). We would also want to extend the conventional boundaries of the 'library' to include other resources of the World Wide Web (WWW), such as Google and Google Scholar, and Web 2.0 environments, such as Wikipedia.

7   The library staff, who will be able to give expert advice on all of the above resources and who are generally rather more tolerant than a computer.

Suppose that you have decided that what caught your attention in the observation about the politically correct vampire was the contrast between this young child's apparent sensitivity to gender as a variable and what you perceive to be a general tendency amongst adults to the use of the masculine as generic. Could it be that there is a difference in the gendering of language by primary-age children and adults? Might any such difference relate to the expressions used or to the intended or perceived meaning of the expressions or both? What might be responsible for any such differences? These questions suggest a sociological interest. That is, they suggest an interest in the structuring of social practices by gender and by age. What is needed, at this stage, is some literature that is directly concerned with sociology, language and gender.

You do not need to carry out a full literature search at the moment. You are not trying to claim that you have read everything that has ever been written on these subjects. Rather, you are trying to make an entrance into this literature in order to define your research question more clearly. A number of strategies are available apart from, of course, asking someone for assistance. The simplest approach might be to look through the contents pages of the available (paper and online) sociology journals covering the past five years or so. Alternatively, you might try a simple computer search, using either the library catalogue – if you want a book – or one of the educational research indices and/or a WWW search engine if you are looking for journal articles. The use of search facilities is particularly useful if you are not entirely clear which journals might cover your particular interests.

In preparation for the first edition of this book, we used our computerised library catalogue at the Institute of Education, University of London, carrying out a keyword search. Initially we entered the terms 'language' and 'gender'. In this kind of search the computer looks for the terms given in the titles, the short descriptions of each book and the keywords appended to each record on the system. It displays those records that contain both terms. Not surprisingly, given that we used just two very broad terms, this search gave us 674 matches. Scanning quickly through some of those identified as close matches gave some indication of the breadth of the field and the types of material available. Some of the work was clearly aimed at the development of classroom practice, for example Goddard, A. (1989), *The Language Awareness Project Years 4 and 5 (Key Stage 2): Language and Gender Pack One* (Lancaster: Framework Press). Although this is of interest with respect to the forms of action teachers might take to address language and gender issues with primary age children, it is of limited interest at this early stage of refining our question and establishing an approach. The existence of this kind of material should reassure us, though, that our general area of interest has attracted the attention of other practitioners.

Some of the references looked more promising. A 1985 collection of papers edited by Steedman, A., Unwin, C. and Walkerdine, V. (*Language, Gender and Childhood*, London: RKP) provided us with an indication of the range of approaches taken to our general area of interest and began to provide possible theoretical resources for the development of our study. A 1983 collection edited by Thorne, B., Kramarae, C. and Henley, N. (*Language, Gender and Society*, Rowley, Mass: Newbury House) fulfilled a similar function, specifically indexing the articulation of gendered language use and wider social practices. Collections like these would help us to develop a better feel for the field in which we are working. Both collections, however, were rather dated, even at that time, and very broad in their concerns. One of the references provided was more recent and more clearly focused: Coates, J. (1993), *Women, Men and Language: A Sociolinguistic Account of Gender Differences in Language*, 2nd edition, London: Longman. This is clearly relevant to our study, although no direct reference was made to the school or classroom in the title or summary.

Rather than plough through all 674 references, we narrowed down our search by including the term 'sociology'. This gave us seventy-one hits. Amongst these we found an Australian study by Evans, T. (*A Gender Agenda: A Sociological Study of Teachers, Parents and Pupils in their Primary Schools*, Sydney: Allen and Unwin, 1988), which was of some interest. The collection by Steadman *et al.* did not appear in the results of this search. This illustrates the importance of carrying out both broad and narrow searches.

The library catalogue is obviously not ideal for locating recent research. For this we need to turn to journals. The ERIC database is particularly helpful because the entries generally include an abstract and sometimes the full text of the items. Again, in our preparation for the first edition of this book, searching the ERIC database using the keywords 'language' and 'gender' gave seventy hits. An attempt to narrow this search by adding the term 'sociology' reduced this to zero hits. As would be expected, many of the seventy references turned up by the initial search were well outside our area of interest. The *Southern Illinois Working Papers in Linguistics and Language Teaching, Volume 1* (Young, 1992), for instance, consisted of five research papers in applied linguistics by members of one university linguistics department. One of these papers concerned gender differences in second language acquisition, hence the appearance of the collection in our search. The use of the abstracts in the ERIC database makes the identification of relevant items straightforward; often the abstracts alone give sufficient detail for you to be able to identify which items are central to your area of interest and which are peripheral. The search facilities are powerful and easy to use. The results of a search can be inspected on screen, printed out or downloaded onto disc. The latter enables the results of a search to be transferred into a bibliographic database, such as Endnote, on your own computer.

Of the seventy references provided by the original ERIC search, eight were in the North American journal *Language Arts*. These papers focused either on children's books or on children's own writing. Although the issues discussed are clearly relevant to our general area of research, the journal is aimed at a professional audience and few of the papers draw on original empirical research. Nonetheless, the eight papers, all published in 1993, demonstrated that there was significant professional interest in the issue of children's gendered language and how this relates to what they read and how they write. One of the papers identified in the search provides a critical review of literature relating to language, gender and education (Corson, D.J., 1992, 'Language, Gender and Education: A Critical Review Linking Social Justice and Power', *Gender and Education*, 4, pp. 229–54.) which is clearly relevant. It also indexes a relevant journal, *Gender and Education*, available in our library and a possible source of additional material.

None of the references provided by the ERIC search directly address our interest in differences in the gendering of language by young children and adults. A number of papers look at the language experience and language use of pre-school children. One questionnaire-based piece of research indicates that the use of gender-specific language is not considered to be an issue in the selection of books to read to pre-school children for the majority of teachers surveyed (Patt, M.B. and McBride, B.A., 1993, 'Gender Equity in Picture Books in Preschool Classrooms: An Exploratory Study', paper presented at the Annual Meeting of the American Educational Research Association, Atlanta, GA, April 12–16). Another strand in the literature addresses shifts that have taken place in the general use of gender inclusive and gender exclusive language (for example, Zuber, S. and Reed, A.M., 1993, 'The Politics of Grammar Handbooks: Generic "He" and Singular "They"', College English, 55(5), pp. 515–30). Searches carried out using the British Education Index, the Australian Education Index and the Canadian Education Index turned up a similar range of references. These indexes do not provide abstracts, which makes it more difficult to evaluate the relevance of the items selected, though nowadays one can often obtain further information using an internet search engine such as Google.

As this reference to Google suggests, there have been considerable developments, over the past decade (Google was launched in the same year as the first edition of this book), in respect of these databases and the general availability of research resources on the internet. We can illustrate this, first, by repeating the search of the Institute of Education catalogue using the new (2007) facility. A repeat of the original, simple search strategy now produced only seventy-three titles; possibly the keyword database had been revised in the interim period, resulting in the reduced count. The items mentioned above were still returned along with some additional and now more up-to-date works. A number of these were textbooks or collections of original or reprinted articles intended for students of sociolinguistics etc. One item – *The Handbook of Language and Gender* (Holmes, J. and Meyerhoff, M. (Eds.), 2003, Oxford: Blackwell) – looked, on the basis of a review in an online journal review by Sara Mills (2006), to be particularly interesting in that it comprises a collection of articles that all 'challenge conventional academic and popular views of the relation between language and gender' (Mills, 2006, p. 297). Another item, also promising and also mentioned in Mills's review was *Language and Gender* (Eckert, P. and McConnell-Ginet, S., 2003, Cambridge: CUP). Refining the search by including 'sociology' as the 'subject' (a facility provided by the new library catalogue) returned just four titles including the Steadman *et al.* collection; changing the terms of the search to return on either keyword, 'language' *or* 'gender', *and* a subject, 'sociology', resulted in a massive, and unworkable, 13,385 items. Further refinement was clearly called for: using three keywords, 'language' *and* 'gender' *and* 'children', returned eight results, some of which had face interest, again including the Steadman *et al.* collection and the second edition of *Shards of Glass: Children Reading and Writing Beyond Gendered Identities* (Davies, B., 2003, Cresskill, N.J.: Hampton Press), which had also turned up regularly and, again, looked to be relevant.

We were assisted, in this new search, by the fact that we can now combine the use of the library catalogue with the use of the WWW and, in particular, a general search engine such as Google in order to locate reviews of items turned up in searches. This is what we did above, finding the review of the Holmes and Meyerhoff book by Sara Mills in a journal to which our institution subscribed.

Repeating the same ERIC search on the revised database (http://www.eric.ed.gov, check the 'advanced search' link) in 2007 yielded 2, 437 hits. We added a third keyword, children, which reduced the count to 586. The ERIC search engine allows searching within the results obtained, so we restricted the search to journal articles only and checked 'gender differences' from the 'thesaurus descriptors' that were offered. This gave forty-nine results, though none of these seemed to have a direct bearing on our research interests, generally lacking a sociological dimension. Replacing 'children' with 'sociology' reduced the number of hits to four, but did not turn up anything that looked directly relevant – not much luck so far. Switching to the British Education Index,[2] selecting 'language-usage' and 'gender' and restricting the search to papers in English returned just five items, one of which – Pauwels, A. and Winter, J. (2006), 'Gender Inclusivity or "Grammar Rules OK"? Linguistic Prescriptivism vs Linguistic Discrimination in the Classroom', *Language and Education*, 20(2), pp. 128–40

– looked relevant, though its focus was on the dilemmas of teachers rather than on the language use of students.

Were we to be continuing with this research, we would clearly need to generate a more extensive range of literature, but we have identified enough to make a start. For books and doctoral and masters theses we will have to make a physical journey to the library (though, if financial resources are available, we might order books online). Books that are not in the library may be available through the inter-library loan system, though we may have to travel to other university libraries for some theses as not all libraries will make them available beyond their own premises. At this stage, though, we do not have to read everything that might appear to be relevant and it's generally better to concentrate on what is directly accessible.

Many journals are now published online. Some are freely available, but most will make articles available only to individual or institutional subscribers. University libraries subscribe to a selection of journals, but, of course, the range is limited by cost. Access to articles in subscribed journals is generally available from any online location using, for example, an Athens password-protected account that is provided by the institution. If your institution does not subscribe to a journal that you want to access, then you can often buy the article that you want, either from the journal site or, for example, from the British Library Direct service (http://direct.bl.uk), which also incorporates a search facility covering its own resources. Buying articles is quickly going to become expensive: British Library Direct will currently charge you £5.00 copyright fee plus a service charge (at least £7.65, depending upon mode of delivery) and VAT (if you are based in the EU) for the Pauwels and Winter article cited above. An alternative is to use an internet search engine to try to find other papers by the same author(s); sometimes authors post articles on their own websites.

As we have pointed out, at this stage, you should focus your attention on what is readily available, rather than spend undue time in tracking down an elusive paper. Your reading will enable you to refine your further search strategies and will also provide you with further items of literature through the bibliographies of the items that you access.

The outcome of this brief literature search indicates that the area that we have identified is worth investigating, though perhaps there is less current interest in this topic than there was a decade or more ago. Nevertheless, a range of relevant work has been identified and professional and academic interest in key issues has been established. By following up the most relevant references we can begin to develop the theoretical framework and state the problem more clearly. At this stage in the development of the research, the review of literature should act as both an inspiration and an affirmation.

We should add a rider. Some proponents of grounded theory – especially Barney Glaser (1992) and see also Corbin and Strauss (2008) – advise against studying in advance the research literature relating to the particular topic that you intend to address empirically. The argument is that this may potentially lead the researcher to preconceptualise their setting and consequently to force theory on the data rather than allowing it to emerge in the analysis. We do not subscribe to this view. Educational researchers inevitably bring prior knowledge and understanding of research to each new research venture and this cannot simply be cast aside. Furthermore, in many instances – for example, in preparing submissions for funding (in respect of scholarships or research grants) – researchers are required to demonstrate the relationship between their proposed project and existing research findings. In our view, some of the proponents of grounded theory underplay the constructive actions of the researcher in the production of theory and sometimes seem to imply that theory is there to be discovered so long as one has an open mind; but can there be such a state? This is not to say that we reject grounded theory as an approach to educational research. It is to say that educational researchers should be given more credibility in respect of the ability to establish a productive distinction between the theoretical and empirical fields that will allow the latter to speak.

The theoretical and empirical spheres

In this chapter we have made a distinction between the theoretical and the empirical contexts of educational research. The theoretical field is the broad area of academic and/or professional knowledge, research and debates that contains your general area of interest. Theoretically, your research will involve the selection and development of a region of this field as a specialised problem. This framework will comprise your theoretical propositions or hypotheses or your research questions and, ultimately, your conclusions. The empirical field is the general area of practice or activity or experience about which you intend to make claims. Empirically, your research must involve the selection and elaboration of a region of this field as a localised empirical setting. This setting will contain the specific site of your empirical work.

We are approaching the reading of research in books and articles in precisely the same way as we are treating the doing of research. It is the responsibility of the critical reader of research to determine the specific problem and local empirical setting of the work. These may be stated, in the book or article, in greater or lesser clarity and detail. They may be described separately or they may be intertwined. They may be given in different forms at different points of the book or article. In particular, the specific problems addressed by educational research are often very hard to pin down in theoretically well-defined terms. Your initial foray into the piece will provide you with a general feel for the theoretical and empirical fields of the research. As you re-read and study the piece, you should begin to formulate a clearer picture of the problem and empirical setting.

The distinction between the theoretical and empirical spheres is crucial in establishing clarity in doing one's own research and in the interrogating of the research of others. However, these spaces are not to be hermetically sealed with respect to each other. As the details of the problem and empirical setting become sharper, they must also be related explicitly to each other. It is to the processes involved in the articulation of the theoretical and the empirical spheres that we shall turn in Chapter 3.

Articulating the theoretical and empirical fields

In Chapter 2 we described two spaces that, we maintain, are the concerns of any piece of empirical research. We have indicated that Luria's theoretical problem emerged within a context of disciplined academic writing and debates. Beginning educational researchers may be interested in similarly academically located debates in respect of their theoretical position. Alternatively, they may see themselves as entering a field of professional debate concerning, for example, curriculum policy or management practice. These are different, but equally valid, starting points. It is not, in our opinion, the particular referential field that defines the theoretical quality of the research. Rather, it is the extent to which the research attempts a systematic and explicit organising of its theoretical space as a theoretical framework.

Luria's empirical setting was, in a sense, an opportunistic one. It is likely that the beginning educational researcher's empirical setting will also be selected on the basis of opportunity. Again, this is unimportant in terms of the empirical quality of the research. What matters is the extent to which the research attempts to make explicit its empirical conditions and the extent to which it justifies the links between its empirical observations and its theoretical categories. Where it is possible, of course, a part of such justification may derive from a more deliberately selected or constructed empirical setting.

In this chapter, we shall make the move to the formulation of specific research questions or theoretical propositions – the problem – on the one hand, to questions about the empirical setting, on the other. We are, then, dealing with the articulation of the theoretical and empirical spaces. However, in this chapter, we are moving from the theoretical to the empirical. Moves in the opposite direction will become important in Chapters 5–8. We do not have the space to introduce alternative theoretical positions. Because of this, we shall refer most of our discussion in this chapter to the work by Luria that we have already introduced.

The problem

Logically – but not necessarily chronologically – the first phase of development of the theoretical field involves making explicit a nebula of debates and theories and, indeed, empirical findings about the area of your concern. These are theoretical because they constitute *general* statements in relation to the local context of your particular empirical setting. This process may be thought of as crystallising out what you will consider to be key pieces of work (in relation to your own) from a more general context. We refer to this key region of the theoretical field as the *problematic* within which you will be working.

Logically, the next phase involves the formulation of more precise statements or propositions or questions in terms of specific concepts. This is where you begin to specify your *problem*. It is important, at this point, to stress that by the expression 'next phase' we are referring to the phase that logically follows the initial marking out of the problematic within the more general theoretical field. In chronological terms, it is sometimes the case that the problem does not emerge in its explicit stage of completeness until the very end of the research. Under such circumstances, the work of data collection and analysis that are the concern of the middle section of this book (Chapters 5–8) may be said to come in between the work of the previous chapter and this one. The point, however, is that data collection and analysis are empty activities unless theoretical development is a constant part of your active engagement with the research. For this reason, then, we must explain and exemplify what is meant by this phase at this early stage of the book.

Theoretical development, then, may occur, chronologically, at various stages of the research process. So, the presentation, in a book or article, of the problem as *propositions* or *hypotheses* to be tested, or as *questions* to be answered, or as observations or *conclusions* may relate more to the form in which the argument is to be made than to the research process as actually experienced by the researcher. The report of the research must be understood as itself a *recontextualising* of this process for the purposes of establishing a case. In his introductory chapter (entitled 'The problem'), Luria presents his problem as both a research question and a hypothesis. In his conclusion, he re-presents it as a *finding*. We will quote from the conclusion, here:

> Our investigations, which were conducted under unique and non-replicable conditions involving a transition to collectivized forms of labor and cultural revolution, showed that, as the basic forms of activity change, as literacy is mastered, and a new stage of social and historical practice is reached, major shifts occur in human mental activity. These are not limited simply to an expanding of man's [sic] horizons, but involve the creation of new motives for action and radically affect the structure of cognitive processes.
>
> A basic feature of the shifts we observed is that the role of direct graphic-functional experience was radically altered in the transition to collectivized labor and new forms of social relations and with the mastery of rudiments of theoretical knowledge.
>
> (Luria, 1976, pp. 161–2)

As is commonly the case in social science and educational writing, the familiarity of many of the terms in this extract tends to conceal the specific and technical way in which they are being used. 'Activity', 'motive' and 'action', for example, are the English equivalents of terms within a particularly Vygotskian theoretical framework. This framework was developed by another of his colleagues, Aleksei Leont'ev, and is now referred to as 'activity theory'. We shall try to make available the general nature of Luria's question/proposition/conclusion without recourse to an extensive theoretical elaboration of this theory.

Other expressions, such as 'graphic-functional experience', possibly, are more obviously technical. Graphic-functional experience is experience structured by the physical nature of the context within which it takes place. It is here being opposed to 'theoretical knowledge', which has the property of generalisability across contexts defined in physical terms.

Essentially, Luria is making the following proposition. First, that societies move between different patterns of *social relationships*. Second, that these movements are associated with developments in *cultural practices*. Third, that these social and cultural developments cause developments to take place in terms of individual cognition. In passing, we should also mention that Luria very much saw these developments as evolutionary in nature.

The basic form of the proposition, then, is that the terminal (i.e. adult) level of cognitive development is a function of the state of social and cultural development. Hypothetically, then, Luria can postulate two societies – respectively, primitive and advanced – for which his proposition enables him to map out their respective social and cultural properties and the levels of cognitive development of individuals within these societies. This has been done in Table 3.1, which presents the proposition in a rather more formal way than Luria does himself.

Table 3.1 Luria's theoretical proposition

Variable	Primitive society	Advanced society
Social relations	Individualised labour	Collectivised labour
Cultural practices	Non-literate	Literate
Cognitive development	Graphic-functional	Theoretical

Levels of measurement

You will note that the first column of Table 3.1 is headed *variable*. A variable is a quality that can take a number of different values or states. The range of states that the variable can take constitute its *scale*. Thus 'gender' is a variable that is generally scaled as masculine and feminine or as male and female. In the case of gender, neither masculine and feminine nor male and female are usually thought of as being organised in any particular order. This kind of scale is called a *nominal scale*.

Luria's scales are rather different. This is because, as we have indicated, he saw social and cultural and cognitive development as evolutionary. Thus, there is a logical ordering of the scales of the three variables in Table 3.1, which places the categories in the second column before those in the third, in developmental terms. Scales that can be ordered in this way are called *ordinal scales*.

Sometimes, a variable is scaled in numerical terms. Thus a time variable may be scaled in terms of the years of the twentieth century: 1900, 1901, 1902, 1903, and so on. On this kind of scale, the intervals between adjacent points are the same everywhere on the scale. In other words, the interval between 1900 and 1901 has the same meaning as that between 1935 and 1936 and that between 1990 and 1991. This kind of scale is called an *interval scale*. Arithmetical operations are permissible with this kind of scale, but not with nominal or ordinal scales. You can calculate the middle year in a scale, but the notion of an average gender or an average in terms of social relations is somewhat bewildering.

Interval scales, such as the calendar years may have a *conventional zero*, for example, AD 1. However, if time were to be scaled in terms of, say, the number of minutes that had elapsed since the start of an experiment (or lesson), there would be an *absolute zero*. That is, the variable is defined in terms of its starting point – the start of the experiment. A scale that has an absolute zero is called a *ratio scale*. It is only on ratio scales that the most sophisticated mathematical operations may be performed.

Nominal, ordinal, interval and ratio are called *levels of measurement*. For most of our purposes in this book, we shall be dealing only with nominal and ordinal levels of measurement in terms of the scaling of *variables*.

Frequency

In addition to the scaling of variables, we will also refer to the measurement of the *frequency* of a category. This means the number of times that the category occurs. Here, we are clearly referring to a ratio level of measurement, since logically (although not necessarily empirically) the minimum frequency is zero.

In determining the level of measurement, it is important to distinguish between the scaling of a variable in terms of its possible values or states and the frequency with which these values or states occur. Thus, supposing you record that your sample consists of fifty-two females and forty-six males. You are recording the *frequency distribution* of the variable, gender, within your sample. That is, the frequency of each state or value of the variable. Gender remains nominally scaled, whereas it is the frequency that is ratio scaled. (See also Chapter 8.)

So, Luria has defined his theoretical proposition as a statement of the relationships between a number of variables, each of which is ordinally scaled with two values. These are theoretical *concepts* or *concept variables*. Where the theoretical proposition is being presented as a hypothesis to be tested in a more experimental mode of design, you may want to refer to these as *hypothetical variables*. Luria's theoretical propositions could easily have been formulated as a question:

What is the nature of the terminal level of cognitive development, in terms of graphic-functional and theoretical thinking, in (a) a society exhibiting individualised social relations of production and a non-literate culture and (b) a society exhibiting collectivised social relations of production and a literate culture?

Whether or not an author presents a theoretical proposition or hypothesis, on the one hand, or a research question, on the other, depends upon the degree of openness that they wish to attribute to their initial predictions. Similarly, in doing research, whether one starts with a hypothesis or a question depends upon how much one knows about the theoretical and empirical contexts in terms of prior work and/or personal experience.

Note that the movement from theoretical proposition or hypothesis to research question does not entail any loss of precision. Just because it's a question does not mean that you should feel entitled to be vague. Theoretical development is precisely the generation of explicitness and systematicity in the definition of one's variables and the statement of the relationships between them. Naturally, this precision develops with the research process, but at the point of writing up it should have been achieved and can be demanded in your interrogation of other people's research reports.

Having tightened up the theoretical space somewhat, it is now time to move towards the empirical setting.

Operationalisation: the empirical measurement of theoretical propositions

Luria's theoretical propositions clearly make certain demands of his empirical setting. However, they do not, as they are formulated, immediately specify exactly how the empirical work is to be carried out. It is clear that Luria needed to be able to access individuals in a way that allowed him to measure their cognitive level and the nature of the society in which they lived. He also needed to draw samples from each of the two kinds of society. But what counts as evidence that an individual's cognitive processes can validly be described as 'graphic-functional'; what are the principles whereby the samples should be drawn? The move from the statement of a theoretical proposition to its empirical measurement is called *operationalisation*. We shall now consider how Luria facilitated the movement between his theoretical framework and his empirical setting. We shall begin with the empirical measurement of the theoretical propositions.

There are three concept variables that must be measured: social relations; cultural practices; and cognitive level. The first is scaled as individualised as opposed to collectivised production; the second as non-literate as opposed to literate. Luria worked with five groups of subjects, which he describes as follows:

1.   Ichkari women living in remote villages who were illiterate and not involved in any modern social activities. [. . .]

2.   Peasants in remote villages, who continued to maintain an individualistic economy, to remain illiterate, and to involve themselves in no way with socialized labor.

3. Women who attended short-term courses in the teaching of kindergarteners. As a rule, they still had no formal education and almost no literacy training.

4. Active *kolkhoz* (collective farm) workers and young people who had taken short courses. They actively involved themselves in running the farms – as chairmen, holders of kolkhoz offices, or brigade leaders. They had considerable experience in planning production, in distributing labor, and in taking stock of work output. They dealt with other kolkhoz members and had acquired a much broader outlook than had the isolated peasants. But they had attended school only briefly, and many were still barely literate.

5. Women students admitted to a teachers' school after two or three years of study. Their educational qualifications, however, were still fairly low.

(Luria, 1976, p. 24)

Luria classifies these groups as follows:

> Only the final three groups had experienced the conditions necessary for any radical psychological change. There now existed new motives for action, and also new forms of access to a technological culture and mastery of mechanisms such as literacy and other new forms of knowledge. The transition to a socialist economy brought along new forms of social relations and, with them, new life principles. The first two groups were much less exposed to the conditions for any such fundamental shifts.
>
> (ibid.)

The principles whereby this classification is made are, essentially, encoded into the descriptions of the groups in the first extract. Subjects in the first two groups are simply asserted to be illiterate and not to be involved in collectivised relations of production. No further information is given, presumably because Luria considered these features to be self-evident properties of the subjects. The subjects in the third and fifth groups are described as having been exposed to schooling and, therefore (presumably), to literate culture. The fourth group had additional and active exposure to collectivised relations of production on a collective farm. Luria is careful to point out, however, that none of these subjects could be described as having had more than rudimentary schooling. The difference between the two groups is described in terms of zero as opposed to some exposure to modern society. Luria is hypothesising (at this stage) that only a small amount of exposure is needed in order to trigger the expected psychological advances.

Now, you may feel that the description of the activities of the fourth group of subjects is sufficiently detailed to provide a plausible case that they are involved in collectivised relations of production. It is less clear, perhaps, that the description of the first two groups is sufficient to justify their social categorisation, although you may be content to accept Luria's assertion that they were illiterate. The women in the third and fifth groups had participated in schooling, but not necessarily in collectivised relations of production. Is this important? These issues concern the *validity* of Luria's operationalisation of the two variables, 'social relations' and 'cultural practices'.

Validity and reliability

Validity concerns the relationship between theoretical concept variables (or concepts) and empirical *indicator variables* (or *indicators*). For example, supposing that your problem includes the variable 'gender', scaled 'feminine' and 'masculine'. Suppose, further, that your empirical setting includes a written list of the names of school students in alphabetical order of family name. You may decide that their given name provides a valid indicator of their gender, because you are confident that you can recognise girls' and boys' names. You, therefore, expect to be able to *code* each student correctly as either feminine or masculine. This would be an assertion of *face validity*; the given name is a plausibly valid indicator of gender.

There may, however, be ambiguities, such as names which may be written in abbreviated form (Chris, Pat, and so on), names with which you are unfamiliar by virtue of their and your ethnic origin etc., and names that are commonly associated with one gender but which may, contingently, be associated with the other (the actor, John Wayne's given name was Marion, for example). In coding the list, you will have to make a decision, in the first two cases; you may not notice the third. These ambiguities weaken the validity of the variable 'given name' as an indicator of the concept variable, 'gender'. Validity, then, is a measure of the extent to which you are measuring what you think you are measuring.

In addition to relying on face validity, the results of coding according to one indicator may be compared with the results of coding according to another indicator that has previously been demonstrated to be valid. A statistical measure of the agreement, or *correlation*, between the two coding results provides a measure of the *criterion validity* or *convergent validity* of the new indicator.

Alternatively, you may be able to demonstrate that coding according to your chosen indicator bears out an already known relationship between two theoretical variables. This comparison provides a measure of the *construct validity* of your indicator.

Reliability is a measure of the consistency of a coding process when carried out on different occasions and/or by different researchers. As a test of reliability, a researcher may produce instructions for coding a set of information. The rules and the information (or some of it) are then given to two coders and their results compared. A measure of the correlation between the two coding results provides a numerical measure of reliability.

Luria is far more elaborate in describing his principles of recognition of the

variable 'cognitive level'. For example, in his introduction to his findings on generalisation and abstraction, he describes the previous findings of Goldstein in order to illustrate in concrete terms the distinction between responses in the two levels of cognition:

In abstract or categorical classification, the normal subject forms a distinct category by selecting objects corresponding to an abstract concept. This kind of classification yields instances of abstract categories such as *vessels, tools, animals,* or *plants* in an appropriate group, no matter whether the particular objects are ever encountered together. An ax, saw, shovel, quill, and a knitting needle are all assigned to the category *tools* [. . .] Subjects who gravitate towards [concrete or situational thinking] do not sort objects into logical categories but incorporate them into graphic-functional situations drawn from life and reproduced from memory. These subjects group together objects such as a table, a tablecloth, a plate, a knife, a fork, bread, meat, and an apple, thereby reconstructing a 'meal' situation in which these objects have some use.

(Luria, 1976, pp. 48–9)

Luria then provides his readers with examples of his experimental *protocols*, which is to say, transcripts and notes from his interview work:

Subject: Rakmat., age thirty-nine, illiterate peasant from an outlying district; has seldom been in Fergana, never in any other city. He was shown drawings of the following: *hammer–saw–log–hatchet.*

'They're all alike. I think all of them have to be here. See, if you're going to saw, you need a saw, and if you have to split something you need a hatchet. So they're *all* needed here.'
Employs the principle of 'necessity' to group objects in a practical situation.
[. . .]
Which of these things could you call by one word?
'How's that? If you call all three of them a "hammer," that won't be right either.' *Rejects the use of general term.*
But one fellow picked three things – the hammer, saw, and hatchet – and said they were alike.
'A saw, a hammer, and a hatchet all have to work together. But the log has to be here too!'
Reverts to situational thinking.
Why do you think he picked these three things and not the log?
'Probably he's got a lot of firewood, but if we'll be left without firewood, we won't be able to do anything.'
True, but a hammer, a saw, and a hatchet are all tools.
'Yes, but even if we have tools, we still need wood – otherwise, we can't build anything.'
Persists in situational thinking despite disclosure of categorical term.
(ibid., pp. 55–6)

By presenting this lengthy extract, together with his commentary (in italics), Luria is attempting to mark out resonances between this subject's responses and the description of situational thinking in the illustration involving the reconstruction of the meal situation. In this way, Luria is presenting an argument for the validity of his coding of the subject as employing situational or graphic-functional thinking. You will notice that no clear distinction is made between the concept and the indicator variables. This is because Luria has elaborated his theoretical propositions through the use of concrete illustrations and he has described his empirical data directly in terms of the concepts. In this way he brings the theoretical and empirical spheres closer together and this constitutes his argument in respect of the validity of his coding. We shall refer to this approach as *elaborated description*.

Elaborated description constitutes the apprenticing of the reader into Luria's coding principles. This apprenticing, together with the very substantial number of protocols that Luria provides may be taken to stand in the place of a formal test of the reliability of the coding principles. Had Luria given only one or two examples, you might feel entitled to ask him to demonstrate that one or more of his colleagues also coded the subjects in the same way as he himself did. Failure to employ one of these approaches might encourage the suspicion that he had selected only those cases for which the coding was clear and that these may not be representative of the sample as a whole.

One alternative to elaborated description is to provide explicit rules for the recognition of indicators. An example of this approach is discussed in Chapter 8, where we consider Dowling's use of textual 'icon' as an indicator for his concept 'localising strategy'. Where the statement of the rules is sufficiently explicit to persuade the reader of the reliability of their application, there is clearly less need to provide large numbers of examples. Rather, the data can be summarised in quantitative terms. The quantitative representation and analysis of data is discussed in Chapter 8.

A second alternative to elaborated description is to *precode* the data. This would be appropriate in the use of a questionnaire that is designed so that the respondent makes their response by selecting from a range of possible responses. Precoding clearly addresses the issue of reliability. However, there remains the question of the validity of the precoding. The scaling of questionnaire items must be justified in terms of the theoretical variables that they are intended to measure. We shall include some discussion of the use of questionnaires in Chapter 6.

In this section, we have looked at the empirical measurement of theoretical propositions. Our particular concern has been with the issue of the validity of the relationship between theoretical concept variables and their empirical realisation. In the case of Luria's work, the distance between theoretical and empirical variables has been reduced through his use of elaborated description. In the next section we shall look at the issue of sampling, which is concerned with another aspect of validity.

Operationalisation: sampling procedures

We have described the empirical setting as a localised region of the empirical field. Luria's empirical setting in Uzbekistan and Kirghizia was a localised region of the empirical field of social relations, cultural practices and cognitive processes in which people were engaged in the Soviet Union and globally. The setting also localises the empirical field in terms of time, that is, during the period of Luria's fieldwork in the 1930s. Luria's report of his fieldwork incorporates claims about this particular setting. However, Luria also wants to make claims about the empirical field more generally in bringing together his theoretical and empirical spheres. This being the case, the nature of the relationship between the local setting and the general empirical field is crucial.

Luria had also to act selectively on his empirical setting. There was clearly a limit to the amount and nature of information that he could gather in terms of both subjects and situations. Again, the principles of his selection procedures become important to the extent to which he wants to generalise beyond the information actually gathered.

The relationship between setting and field and between information actually gathered and information potentially available is concerned with *sampling procedures*. All empirical research involves drawing a sample. Attention to the sampling procedures is a necessary prerequisite to establishing or questioning the validity of claims that generalise beyond the sample itself. We shall describe three main categories of sampling procedure: opportunity sampling, theoretically informed sampling, and random sampling.

Opportunity sampling

The selection of empirical setting is very often a matter of seizing an *opportunity*. A secondary school teacher, for example, wanted to observe the processes of marking and moderation whereby examination coursework was graded. As head of department, he had access both to teachers' written evaluations and to their discussions at a moderation meeting. A primary school teacher was interested in the possible impact that media images of politics and politicians might have on children. Fortunately, she was conducting her research across the period of a general election and so was able to compare students' political knowledge before and after the event. Robert Lawler (1985) wanted, for his doctoral research, to observe the cognitive development of young children across as wide as possible a range of contexts over an extended period of time. Luckily, he had a six-year-old daughter. He took her with him just about everywhere he went (or went with her wherever she went) during a period of six months. Conducting such a programme with someone else's child would clearly have been awkward.

An interesting example of an opportunity sample was provided by Howard Becker (1953) in his study of marijuana users in Chicago in the early 1950s. The practice that Becker was studying was (and still is) an illicit one. This clearly presented him with difficulties in respect of drawing his sample of subjects. As it happened, however, Becker was himself involved in a practice which brought him into routine contact with marijuana smokers – in addition to being a social psychologist, he was a jazz musician. He therefore decided to interview his friends and colleagues whom he knew to be marijuana smokers. He also asked them to refer to him other smokers whom they knew, acting as guarantors of confidentiality, as it were. These new contacts were similarly asked to refer additional subjects and so forth. For obvious reasons, this kind of sample is called a *snowball sample*.

Commonly, educational researchers attempt to put a gloss of deliberation onto their opportunity samples by referring to them as *case studies*. We have difficulties with this expression either when it is reified as a specific technique or method or when it is used to fudge the issue of validity in respect of generalisation. Essentially, all research is case study research in so far as it makes claims about one or more specific cases of or in relation to a broader field of instances or phenomena. All research seeks to relate its own local findings to this more general field in one way or another. Where the empirical setting is defined by an opportunity sample, the validity of generalisation relies on the researcher marking out the continuities and discontinuities between the setting and the empirical field in an *ad hoc* manner. The resulting presentation will bear some similarity to the *elaborated description* employed by Luria in validating his empirical measurement of his theoretical proposition. We shall return, briefly, to the issue of case study research in Chapter 11.

Theoretically informed sampling

The proposition that no sampling procedure can be independent of theoretical considerations follows from our discussion of the theoretical and empirical fields in Chapter
2. However, the extent to which theoretical considerations explicitly operate in the
construction of the sample does vary. For example, although Luria's research involved
the grasping of an opportunity, it was only recognisable as an opportunity in terms
of Luria's well-developed theoretical framework. The societies in Uzbekistan and
Kirghizia were recognised as transitional in terms of social and cultural development.
Luria was thus able to recognise them as *critical cases*.

The study of a critical case must be opposed to an approach that attempts to draw
a *representative sample*. In making this distinction in relation to Luria's research, we
need to introduce another expression, the *unit of analysis*. This refers to the object that
is to be described in terms of the research variables. Thus, Luria describes societies in
terms of the variables, social relations and cultural practices. Focusing on the society
as the unit or level of analysis, we can describe the Uzbeki society as a critical case.
However, the variable 'cognitive level' describes individual human subjects. When we
focus on the human subject as the unit of analysis, it is less clear that Luria is looking
for critical cases. He wants subjects that he can locate within one of his two categories
of society. One group must be clearly located within 'primitive' society. His selection of
subjects must result in representatives that can unproblematically be described in this
way. The other group must be describable as having some measure of participation in
'advanced' society. The subjects who are chosen are thereby taken to be representative
of this group as a whole.

The second group of subjects, but not the first, are closely associated with the
critical nature of the societal case – they have only limited participation in 'advanced
society'. They are, then, representatives of a critical class of subjects. Thus critical and
representative cases are not necessarily mutually exclusive categories.

A third method of theoretically informed sampling is referred to as a *quota sample*.
This approach is commonly used in market research; however, we will illustrate it
using a hypothetical educational context. Suppose that a researcher wishes to investigate teachers' experiences of appraisal. Suppose, further, that they have decided to
conduct interviews at a teachers' conference. It might legitimately be hypothesised that
these experiences will depend on, amongst other variables, the subject's professional
position defined in terms of, say, years of experience and position in the career structure. If the researcher wanted to make claims about the teaching profession as a whole,
then it might be important that they select subjects who are representative in respect
of each of these variables. The two variables might be scaled and *cross-tabulated* to
produce a matrix similar to that in Table 3.2.

The next stage would be to determine how the teaching profession as a whole was
composed in terms of the matrix. That is, the table would be completed in terms of
the number of teachers in each cell of Table 3.2. Suppose that the researcher has the
resources to interview a sample of 100 teachers. A representative sample (in numerical
terms) would be obtained by dividing the 100 subjects between the cells of the table in
the proportions of the teaching profession as a whole. This would give a quota for the
number of subjects to be interviewed in each cell. The sampling would then proceed
as follows. The researcher would approach a teacher at the conference and ask their
number of years in teaching and their career position.[1] This would locate them in the
matrix. The interview would proceed only if the quota had not yet been filled.

Table 3.2 Quota sampling matrix

Years teaching	Career position		
	MPG	Middle management	Senior management
0–4			
5–9			
10–19			
20+			

MPG = main professional grade.

Critical, representative and quota sampling procedures are not mutually exclusive. In particular, quota sampling is clearly one method of attempting to produce a representative sample. They have in common that they all depend upon a degree of theoretical development being done in advance of the definition of the empirical setting; hence the term *theoretically informed sampling*.[2] The level of theoretical development may be very advanced, as with Luria's work. Alternatively, it may hardly seem to merit the term 'theory', as in the illustration of quota sampling. Nevertheless, theoretically informed it is, because it consists of general conceptualisings of the empirical field. It is to be hoped, of course, that theoretical development does not end at such a preliminary stage.

Random sampling

The final category of sampling that we shall refer to is *random sampling*. Like quota sampling, this set of procedures is a strategy for achieving a *representative sample*. There has been a considerable amount of mathematical and statistical development in the theory of probability in relation to random sampling. This means that the use of random procedures can potentially allow the use of very sophisticated statistical tools in the analysis of the data. We have included in the book a chapter on quantitative analysis (Chapter 8). However, we shall not be able to get very far at all into probability theory. You are strongly encouraged to follow up our references to statistical manuals if your interest lies in that direction. Here, we shall simply describe some of the simpler techniques in drawing a random sample. At the outset, we must emphasise that 'random' certainly does not mean 'unprincipled'. Random sampling is a highly technical and theoretically informed and deliberate procedure.

The production of a random sample involves attempting to ensure that each member of the *population* that you are sampling has an equal chance or *probability* of being selected as a subject. The population is the notional class of possible subjects. It may be defined at any level of analysis. For example, your population might comprise all secondary school teachers in the UK, all secondary schools in the UK, or all local education authorities in the UK. In practice, the researcher will often not have immediate access to a complete list of the whole population. They will therefore have to draw up such a list as best they can. The list may be an approximation to the notional population as, for example, the electoral register may be taken as an approximation to the list of the adult population of a political constituency.[3] When the list is drawn up and arranged in alphabetical order, it is referred to as the *sampling frame*. In practice, then, a random sample is one that ensures that each member of the sampling frame has an equal probability of being selected.

Suppose that you wish to draw a 10 per cent random sample of the students of a particular university. Suppose, further, that you have an alphabetical list of registered students that you are going to use as a sampling frame. Your procedure is as follows. You first find a list of random numbers in a book of statistical tables. You then take a pencil, close your eyes, and stab the random number list. If the digit nearest the pencil point is, say, 7, you take the seventh student in your sampling frame as your first subject. Thereafter, you select every tenth name on the list, that is, the seventh, seventeenth, twenty-seventh, thirty-seventh . . . names. This gives you a sample of one of every ten students, that is, a 10 per cent sample.

The procedure just described is used to draw what is called a *simple random sample*. Now it may be that you want to combine the statistical potential of randomisation with the representative features of quota sampling. For example, suppose that you want your sample to consist of students of different genders and different courses of study in proportion to the representation of these groups within the sampling frame. You can achieve this by reorganising or *stratifying* your sampling frame. You would first organise the frame in terms of the various courses – anthropology, biology, chemistry and so on. Within the frame, each course list should be arranged as consecutive, alphabetical lists of female and male students. You would then proceed as before, using a randomly selected digit as the starting point. The stratification of your sampling frame would ensure the kind of quota representation that you want, provided, of course, that the number of students in each category was sufficiently large. If any of the groups are small in number, then your procedure might result in a sample of greater than or less than 10 per cent of these groups; a very small group (fewer than ten in number) might be omitted altogether.

The *stratified random sample*, as this procedure is called, deviates somewhat from the principle of randomisation. This is because two elements of the sampling frame that occur sufficiently near to each other cannot both be selected. In the case of a 10 per cent sample, two elements must be separated by a multiple of ten if they are both to be selected. Applying a principled organisation to the sampling frame clearly alters the nature of the sample by putting together elements sharing particular properties; it imposes a *bias* upon the sample. You might argue even that simple alphabetical organisation may not be entirely free of this kind of bias because of the ways in which different ethnic groups distribute family names differently within the alphabet. This is certainly a valid point. All you can do, however, is try to be aware of possible sources of *unintentional bias* and, if you can't eliminate them, at least try to take account of them in qualifying any inferences you may make on the basis of your analysis.

In some cases, the sampling frame may be so extensive that you cannot, in practice, compile it. Under such circumstances, it may be possible to *cluster* it. For example, suppose that you want to draw a random sample of all students currently registered in universities in the UK. The compilation of the sampling frame is clearly a major task in itself and may be beyond your resources. An alternative would be to compile a preliminary sampling frame that consists of the universities rather than the students. You could then draw a simple or stratified random sample of universities from this sampling frame. This would leave you with the task of compiling sampling frames of registered students for only each of the universities in your sample.

This approach is also useful if you actually intend to visit the subjects in your sample personally. Drawing an unclustered sample from the UK electoral register, for example, would be very likely to result in an enormous amount of travelling between your subjects' locations. Alternatively you could cluster the sample by constructing a sampling frame comprising all of the electoral constituencies in the UK and draw a random sample from this. You could then compile sampling frames comprising all of the postcodes for each constituency in your sample and draw a random sample of postcodes from each. Finally, you could compile sampling frames of electors for each postcode in your sample and draw random samples from these. This would generate clusters of subjects with the same postcodes and clusters of these clusters each within the same constituency.

You would certainly save petrol by using such a cluster sample. Again, however, your reorganisation of your ideal sampling frame will have resulted in deviations from the principle of randomisation. As is commonly the case in educational research, your decisions are likely to be compromises between ideals and practicalities. What is important is that they are considered compromises and that you take into account any deviation from the ideal in your conclusions.

Moving into the field

In this chapter we have discussed, first, the development of the problem in the formulation of research questions or theoretical propositions in terms of theoretical concept variables. We then considered the development of the empirical setting and its articulation with the problem. We were concerned, initially, with the measurement of concept variables in terms of empirical indicator variables. Key issues here were validity and reliability. Finally, we looked at the issue of sampling.

Many of the terms and strategies that we have discussed in this chapter – terms such as 'validity', 'reliability', 'concepts and indicators', 'random sampling' – are commonly associated more with quantitative research than with qualitative research. However, we take the view that the kind of interrogation of research that the use of these terms facilitate is appropriate for all modes of educational research. Ultimately, the researcher will be making claims (theoretical field) in relation to an empirical data set or object (empirical field); some researchers may prefer to rephrase this as making interpretations. In either case, it is at least interesting to consider the relationships between the data set or object and the claims or interpretations that are being made. For example, establishing a distinction and then exploring, explicitly, the relation between the concepts that form the claims or interpretations and the organisation of the data into instances (indicators) of such claims is, we feel, an important process in qualitative research.

We have not finished with any of these topics. They will feature throughout the rest of the book. However, the discussion so far has been strongly led from the theoretical side of things. Our consideration of ethical issues in educational research in the next chapter is also informed by the theoretical field. However, our approach to research ethics is to give primary consideration to the specificities of the empirical setting in terms of expectations in respect of, for example, privacy. So there is a move towards the empirical in Chapter 4 that will be continued in the subsequent four chapters, which deal with data collection and analysis.

Chapter 4

An ethical dimension to research

The side effects of research activity

Many of us, nowadays, have access to very sophisticated digital technologies that enable us to communicate with family, friends and colleagues in text, sound, image and video and that bring to our desktop, laptop or even mobile phone the seemingly infinite resources of the World Wide Web – many of us, but, of course, not everyone. Some people tend to shy away from technology, but very many others just could not possibly afford even a low-end computer and telephone internet connection. How would such people, having no real experience of this kind of connectivity, make use of it? Wouldn't it be a good idea to run a research project to see? If we found that it substantially improved people's quality of life, then we could perhaps agitate for government support to increase internet access provision for low-income groups. In order to run the research project we might apply for funding for the purchase or hire of equipment and, say, six months' internet access for several volunteer families. We might arrange for technical support etc. And we might interview family members at various points during the period of the research. We would obviously need the consent of the families taking part; what would we tell them?

Melinda Bier and colleagues (1996) conducted a very similar research project to the one that we have described. It is not irrelevant that it was carried out over ten years ago, when internet access was far less common than it is today. The researchers were very careful in ensuring that their participating families were fully informed about the project and their part in it; presumably they would have explained about the processes of data collection and, most importantly, how their privacy would be maintained both during the project and afterwards, especially with the publication of results and so forth. Unfortunately, something happened that the researchers had not anticipated. Essentially, the lives of at least some of the participants became very substantially changed for what they saw as the better. However, this involved the development of a dependency upon the technology, which, come the end of the project, they were expected to return. Being low-income families, they were certainly in no position to replace it:

> As one participant put it, only half tongue-in-cheek, 'Oh yeah, you university people are worse than the dope peddlers; now that we're hooked, you're going to take it away.' They feared they would not be able to maintain the daily routines they

had established on this ideal Internet access. In addition to losing Internet access, they feared the loss of positive personal transformations they had undergone as a result of their Internet experiences. Specifically, participants feared losing their newly acquired sense of identity, education, and community.

(Bier *et al.*, 1996, pp. 146–7)

This story had a happy ending, in the sense that the researchers were able (and will-ing) to extend indefinitely the loan of equipment and the provision of internet access.

The principles of *informed consent* and *avoidance of harm* are well enshrined in the tabernacle of research ethics. There is a clear basis for this in the 'human subjects' interpretation of research. This interpretation subordinates the rights of the researcher to those of the researched subjects (see, for example, Basset and O'Riordan, 2002). Deciding just what 'rights' human subjects should be able to claim is itself not without its problems. But, as the illustration suggests, whatever one decides, there remains the difficulty that researchers cannot guarantee to be able to anticipate all possible implica-tions of their research activities, however well-intentioned they may be. Indeed, even the most routine of guarantees offered to most participants in research – the guarantee of anonymity – may be impossible to deliver and may be seen to be substantively undermined at every stage of the research process (see, for example, Van Den Hoon-aard, 2003).

Furthermore, social – and this includes educational – research clearly feeds on the lives and activities of people who are not themselves always in a position to benefit from it and, even if they are, may not feel that the ends justify the means. Academic careers are routinely measured by the number and academic influence of publications, rather than by their contributions to individual or social quality of life, however altru-istic researchers may consider themselves to be. Clearly, something similar might be said of any social activity: professional footballers are, presumably, in it for themselves – the elaboration of their skills, glory in competition, financial gain – and not for the general benefit of society. It is also the case that everyday life encounters frequently involve hidden motives, routine deception, and taking advantage of opportunities (see Goffman, 1990) very often (and very often deliberately) at the expense of others. Should educational researchers be concerned to behave more righteously than other people?

There are at least three kinds of answer to this question: moral, legal and collegiate. A moral argument would simply assert that educational researchers should uphold certain values and may go on to delineate what these values are. The Ethical Guidelines of the British Educational Research Association (BERA, 2004) state that:

The Association considers that all educational research should be conducted within an ethic of respect for:

- The Person
- Knowledge
- Democratic Values
- The Quality of Educational Research
- Academic Freedom

(BERA, 2004, p. 5)

There are, of course, a lot of other items that might have been added to this list. It doesn't mention animals or the environment, or the law (although this area does get in elsewhere), or society, or God(s). Even so, who could possibly disagree with the BERA list? Well, anyone who considers that 'democratic values' signifies little more than an excuse for powerful nations and international organisations to interfere in the affairs of less powerful ones, for a start. The point is that 'values' expressed like this either are too vague to determine action or, if rendered precise, are certain to invoke opposition within any group of any size.

The legal argument has rather more force, because, generally speaking, the law is rather more specific and comparatively non-negotiable. The BERA guidelines, for example, draw attention to the Data Protection Act. There is also the more general Civil Law and the possibility of litigation if a research participant considers themself to have been harmed or libelled by a researcher. One difficulty, of course, is that very few educational researchers are trained in the law or have routine access to expert legal advice. So, following a code of practice that will have been constructed with the benefit of such advice is probably not a bad idea if we want to protect ourselves and our institutions from prosecution and lawsuits.

The collegiate argument proposes that researchers have responsibilities to the community of researchers that include the need to avoid bringing educational research into disrepute or making it more difficult for colleagues to gain access to research settings by virtue of one's own research practices. Some time ago, for example, a piece of research carried out by a student at our own institution was interpreted as claiming that teachers do not do what they say they do. There was a degree of outrage on the part of teachers in London as a result and university-based educational researchers were pretty much debarred from carrying out research in inner London schools until the Inner London Education Authority was abolished in 1985.

We should also mention the general interdiction on plagiarism – also an ethical issue – that relates to both the legal and collegiate arguments through the concept of intellectual property rights. The policing of this interdiction is also an important plank in the maintenance of the value or educational qualifications, which would be seriously undermined if it became generally suspected that the award of a bachelors degree, for example, was not necessarily predicated on the work of the individual to whom it was awarded.

The dramatic rise in the availability and use of the internet over the past decade has also seen a rise in instances of plagiarism, at least on taught courses. Instances of this phenomenon range from the cutting and pasting of sections of articles digitally available on the WWW, through the copying of essays written by other students and posted publicly for discussion purposes, to the purchasing of bespoke essays from a variety of online sources offering such services. We should perhaps point out that these strategies are countered by anti-plagiarism resources, such as turnitin (www.turnitin.com) that allow submitted material to be compared with digital material already on the WWW. These facilities can even counter the bespoke essay services as it seems that the essays that are claimed to have been tailored to the requirements of an individual client are frequently re-sold as generic essays.

The legal and collegiate arguments are sufficiently compelling to give us confidence in asserting that a serious consideration of ethical issues should be part of all research activity.

A framework for the ethical review of educational research

In 2005 the Economic and Social Research Council (ESRC) – the largest single funder of educational research in the UK – published a *Research Ethics Framework* and adopted a new policy that, from January 2006, all research projects funded by the Council would be required to comply with this framework. In anticipation of or in response to this policy, most centres of educational research established Research Ethics Committees (RECs) to ensure that they would be able to comply with the ESRC requirements. Now it is unhelpful to attribute any single motive to these developments, which are probably better described as being overdetermined, that is, the outcome of multiple developments in political and legal practices and discourses. Whatever the roots of this development, we consider it to be a positive one, because it brings the careful consideration of ethical issues right to the forefront of the practice of educational research. Those of us who are involved with education are, of course, generally concerned that our professional actions should bring about positive outcomes, if possible, but should certainly avoid any negative impact on participants. In our experience, however, research in this field has all too often been carried out without a systematic and objective interrogation of its procedures in ethical terms. Of course, research ethics is not just about doing good and avoiding bad. It is also concerned with being aware of and responsible to the implications of the law, including civil law and the possibility of litigation. And it is concerned with the professional status and responsibilities of researchers and their relationships with other researchers and professionals in associated fields. This clearly raises a very complex nexus of questions to be put to any research project and bad decisions may potentially lead to quite disastrous results. The six key principles of the ESRC framework should give us a start; they are:

- Research should be designed, reviewed and undertaken to ensure integrity and quality.
- Research staff and subjects must be informed fully about the purpose, methods and intended possible uses of the research, what their participation in the research entails and what risks, if any, are involved. Some variation is allowed in very specific and exceptional research contexts for which detailed guidance is provided in the policy Guidelines.
- The confidentiality of information supplied by research subjects and the anonymity of respondents must be respected.
- Research participants must participate in a voluntary way, free from any coercion.
- Harm to research participants must be avoided.
- The independence of research must be clear, and any conflicts of interest or partiality must be explicit (ESRC, 2005).

Unfortunately, it seems, a close look at these principles suggests that they raise more questions than they answer, in terms of both what they mean and how they might be implemented. 'Integrity' and 'quality' sound very good, but how do we measure them? How much understanding of the research do subjects, or participants, need to have in order that 'voluntary' participation is meaningful? The authors of the ESRC framework recognise that these are not simple questions and that there can be no straightforward list of rules that will guarantee that research is ethically conducted, not least because local conditions must be understood and taken into account, but also because there are divergent views on research ethics. The review of a research project in ethical terms is itself something of a research activity.

This being the case, we might appropriately approach the ethical review of a research project in the same way as we are approaching research more generally in this book. The mode of interrogation that we have introduced centres on a methodological apparatus that first establishes a division between a theoretical field and an empirical field and proceeds to articulate them in a systematic way. When it comes to ethical issues, the methodological apparatus should be thought of as the procedures of ethical review that are in place in the institution in or under the auspices of which the research is to be conducted. But, whatever these are, they will of necessity involve reference to precedents, in terms of studies that bear relevant similarities to the one being reviewed, in terms of literature directly addressing research ethics, and in terms of the codes of practice of the various professional associations, such as the British Educational Research Association (BERA), the British Psychological Society (BPS) and the British Sociological Association (BSA); this is the *theoretical ethical field*. The review procedures will also be concerned with the local, empirical specificities of the project and this is the *empirical ethical field*. We shall consider each of these fields in turn, the latter in a little more detail than the former.

The theoretical ethical field

The theoretical ethical field is established by addressing questions such as these.

1　To what code of ethical practice does the researcher subscribe?
2　What general interpretation of research ethics is being taken?
3　How do relevant, methodologically similar studies highlight ethical issues and/or provide precedents for the kinds of decision being taken in the current project?
4　What other sources of ethical advice are available?

The various codes of practice – all available on the WWW – present a more complex array of questions than can be introduced here. What they do not do, by and large, is provide simple answers. In considering the general interpretation of research ethics, the researcher will need to consider what is the appropriate balance between the interests of the researcher, the interests of research participants, and, indeed, the interests of society in general: are there situations in which the outcomes of the research are potentially of such great importance that a reduction in the attention placed on individual 'rights' is justified; or is this never the case? The literature, of course, provides a diversity of opinion and debate.

The third question invites the researcher to consult the archive of past research experience in relevant areas. The literature search described in Chapter 2 will almost certainly identify some suitable material. However, the theoretical *ethical* field is to be constructed with a somewhat different motive from that generating the theoretical field referred to in other chapters of this work. This is because relevance is determined not only in respect of the substantive research question that is to be addressed, but also by the methodological choices that are being made. For example, from an ethical point of view (and, indeed from the point of view of methodology more generally) any research that has involved interviewing young children may potentially (though, of course, not necessarily) be of relevance to any project involving interviewing young children, whatever the topic of the interview. The review of a project involving covert observation of internet activity (lurking) might reasonably involve the consideration of covert research projects more generally.[1]

The final question relating to the theoretical ethical field is intended to refer most directly to the procedures and personnel involved in the ethical review policy of the institution under the auspices of which the research is to be carried out. However, one should take advantage of expertise and experience wherever it is to be found, and research and masters students, for example, should certainly be discussing their projects in ethical terms (and more generally) with their colleagues as well as with their tutors.

The empirical ethical field

As will be apparent, the construction of the theoretical ethical field cannot be achieved without reference to the empirical setting of the research. But is it also necessary to scrutinise this setting rather more closely in establishing the empirical ethical field. These are some of the questions that we might need to ask:

1 Does access to the setting involve negotiating with a 'gatekeeper'? Can the gatekeeper provide legitimate access?
2 Does the research involve collecting data from people, directly or indirectly? Who are the people? How will they be recruited? How will the data be collected?
3 How will the informed consent of those from whom data is to be collected and relevant others be obtained or, if informed consent is not to be obtained, on what basis is this justified?
4 What level of confidentiality is to be promised, to whom? How is this to be guaranteed?
5 Whose rights or interests might potentially be compromised by the research? How is this to be obviated?
6 How is the ongoing scrutiny of ethical issues to be managed?

It will be apparent that the questions to be put to the empirical ethical *field* are generally answerable only by direct reference to the empirical *setting*. However, as, for example, the research participants will be members of broader categories, cultures etc., reference to the wider empirical field will be necessary. In reflecting on one's responsibilities in respect of a group of school students, for example, it's not just these particular school students that one needs to consider – though this is of course crucial – but expectations regarding school students generally within the culture in which one will be working. This is, of course, especially important if the culture is other than one's own.

The first question is primarily to do with access; not just access per se, but access in order to conduct the research. 'Gatekeeper' is a term referring to an individual who is in a position to provide access to a site. The school principal is one obvious example.

The ethical issues, here, include a consideration of the extent to which the gatekeeper is in a position to provide *legitimate* access for the purposes of the research. In the case of the school principal, for example, is their permission sufficient; if they do not insist that parental consent should also be sought, should the researcher seek it anyway; if not, why not? Internet research raises interesting questions here. Many discussion boards are, of course, open to anyone to view and post to – does this entail that they are fair game to be used for researchers' own purposes? Others require the user to set up an account name and password, some requiring personal information, such as name and email address. This registration process is, metaphorically, a gatekeeper. It would seem to stand as a regulating strategy – albeit one with minimal force – does this entail that the researcher should be rather more circumspect in terms of the use they make of data collected in these more 'private' sites, and how about sites that members pay to enter? Essentially, the researcher needs to make and defend their decisions in terms of the theoretical ethical field in much the same way as they do for more conventional research sites.

It is worth adding that, because the internet is a comparatively new site for research, questions about what is private and what is public and about property and ownership are still being hotly contested.

Associated with the question of initial access is the issue of recruitment procedures (question 2). It is widely considered, for example, that it is not appropriate to pay research participants anything other than reasonable compensation for their time and travel expenses etc. In ethical terms, inducements may be interpreted as unreasonable persuasion, inhibiting the freedom of choice that research participants should express. In methodological terms more generally, it might be claimed that participants who are in the pay of the researcher are more likely than volunteers to attempt to cooperate with the researcher in ways that do not assist the research – providing answers to interview questions that they think the researcher wants to hear, for example. But, turning this whole issue around, why shouldn't the research participants directly benefit from the research? As Anne Oakley (1976) famously argued, a principal problem with male-dominated social research is that it regards its subjects in the same way as male-dominated natural science research – as objects. Oakley's approach was very much to involve the participants in her study of housework in her research and, indeed, involve herself in the lives of some of her subjects by becoming friends with them.

The issues of informed consent and confidentiality (questions 4 and 5) are highly complex and, as with so many other ethical issues, are generally characterised by disagreement. We have already mentioned that some consider that an absolute guarantee of anonymity is all but impossible in much qualitative research (in quantitative research, individual responses are generally anonymised by aggregation). If absolute anonymity cannot be guaranteed, then participants will need to be apprised of the risks to their privacy that this might entail. Similarly, some researchers argue that there are circumstances in which obtaining the informed consent of participants may be impossible or impractical. With internet-based research, for example, it may not be possible to determine even who the participants are. If obtaining the informed consent of research participants is taken to be an absolute requirement, then some kinds of research – research into criminal activity, for example – may very well become impossible to carry out. It is also argued that there are circumstances in which the knowledge that a setting is being researched or even the knowledge of the possibility that would result from seeking informed consent may itself be damaging to participants who would, for example, consider themselves to be under scrutiny in an activity that they had believed to be private, whether or not this belief is realistic. There is, of course, also the question of the meaning of 'informed'. Clearly, the research participants are unlikely to be able to attain the same level of understanding of the research as that of the researcher; so how much do they need to know?

Most codes of ethical practice – including the ESRC framework – allow for covert research provided that it is fully justified. The BERA code proposes that informed consent should be sought *post hoc* if obtaining prior consent is deemed to be inappropriate. This strategy, however, clearly does not address all of the concerns mentioned here. Some authors argue that there are no circumstances under which covert research is justified; cases for both sides are put by Homan (1980) – for – and Herrera (1999) – against.

In his argument defending the use of covert methods, Roger Homan draws attention to a very important mode of research that many of us are involved in routinely:

> I and many sociologists spend available Saturday afternoons observing professional football: as far as we are aware we hope for skilled and creative performances, an enjoyable match and possibly a victory for the favoured side, and are much less motivated to attend matches by the opportunity to observe crowd behaviour or interaction between professionals. Inevitably, however, there are moments when one's observation is guided by sociological principles and I have even recorded notes after a match. It would be absurd to announce that there was a sociologist on the terraces making casual observations and to explain his purpose and methods. For those who pay their money at the turnstile sociological observation is, unlike throwing beer bottles or running on to the pitch, an acceptable and unobtrusive activity.
>
> (Homan, 1980, pp. 56–7)

Homan is referring to informal or opportunistic research. Homan makes the point that sociologists (and presumably educational researchers as well) often regard the world with a researcher's gaze even when they are not on duty, so to speak.

There is a long tradition of informal research in which researchers have observed their own children. Jean Piaget (1932), for example, observed his own children at play in formulating his early ideas on moral development; Gunther Kress (1993) has used his own children's drawings in his work on social semiotics; Robert Lawler (1985) studied the cognitive development of his own six-year-old daughter over a six-month period of intensive observation. Each of these and many other studies has produced important educational research results, though it is not clear to what extent informed consent was formally sought or obtained; certainly, the children are not anonymous.

The issue of rights more generally (question 5) also raises tricky questions. For example, many researchers approach their research with the intention of effecting change at some level. In the field of educational research, this is certainly characteristic of *action research*. Here, a practitioner-researcher, such as a school teacher or educational manager, seeks to develop or improve their own professional practice through a process that involves surveying the current situation and identifying problems, designing and implementing an innovation, evaluating the outcomes and, possibly, reformulating the innovation for a second and subsequent cycles. A key feature of this kind of research is that the principles of evaluation of the impact of the innovation are highly local to the research setting. However, whereas, in many other approaches to educational research, the intention is to minimise the impact of the research on the participants, action research, in a sense, aims at the opposite outcome. From an ethical perspective, then, particularly in respect of question 5 put to the empirical ethical field, the researcher would have to take into account that there may be local disagreement on just what constitutes an 'improvement'. Risks here may be minimised if the evaluation principles can be tied directly and explicitly to the institutional objectives that guide the researcher's professional practice as practitioner, but any change to an accepted routine is likely to be resisted by someone. Surprisingly, perhaps, it is not necessarily clear that action research, described in this way, actually counts as 'research' according to the ESRC definition, which is, 'any form of disciplined enquiry that aims to contribute to a body of knowledge or theory' (ESRC, 2005, p. 9), though action researchers can reasonably claim that the accumulation of disseminated cases in publications itself constitutes a 'body of knowledge', as does the development of action research methodology.

An interest in change is not confined to the social sciences. Stanley Fish (1995), for example, is very concerned about what he perceives to be a prominent line in literary criticism that is concerned to effect political, social change. The kind of work that he is referring to is the new historicism of Louis Montrose:

> On its face he seems to be saying something like this: 'I have surveyed the various approaches to Shakespeare and Spenser now in play and have decided to employ in my own work those (like gender studies) that will be the most subversive of the political powers oppressing us.' But when I read Montrose I find his analysis informed by a conviction that the accounts he offers of Shakespeare and Spenser are true. He may believe that by producing these true accounts he will be participating in the reformation of contemporary society, but his belief in their possible political efficacy is independent of his conviction that they are true. Were he to be persuaded that there was no particular political benefit to be had from putting forward these views of Shakespeare and Spenser, they would still be his views, and they would remain so until they were changed by the usual kinds of argument one associates with literary studies. It is surely the case that his views of Shakespeare and Spenser could change, but one thing that won't change them (if they are really his views and not merely politically convenient sentiments) is the realization that they aren't doing the kind of political work he hoped they would do. (What might change, if he experienced that realization, is his determination to remain a professional reader of texts; he might get into another line of work.)
>
> (Fish, 1995, pp. 47–8)

Fish believes that no one outside literary studies will be very interested in what Montrose has to say *qua* literary critic and so his political will is, in so far as he is performing literary criticism, impotent. The danger, however, seems to be that Montrose and the other new historicists may succeed in transforming the practice of literary criticism out of all recognition. This is possible, because, in Fish's view, literary criticism is as it is by convention and, this being the case, is vulnerable to collective transformative acts:

> A conventional activity [. . .] lives and dies by the zeal with which we ask its questions and care about the answers. A conventional activity is one whose possibility

and intelligibility depend on a specialized and artificial vocabulary which is genera-
tive of the phenomena it picks out, in this case the range of verbal nuances that
emerge when one takes up the tools of close reading, semiotics, and poetics. If that
vocabulary falls into disuse, the facts it calls into being will no longer be produced
or experienced. If no one any longer asks 'What is the structure of this poem?'
or 'What is the intention of the author and has it been realized?', something will
have passed from the earth and we shall read the words of what was once literary
criticism as if they were the remnants of a lost language spoken by alien beings.

> (Fish, 1995, p. 70)

The supposed political gains of a shift in the discipline towards new historicism are,
therefore, imagined rather than real, whereas there is a very real danger in the loss of
what, to many now working in the field, is a worthwhile activity.

The dispute between Stanley Fish and the new historicists really highlights the fundamental dilemmas that are at the base of all of the assertions, challenges, rationalis-
ings and decisions that constitute the agonistic discourse of research ethics: just to
whom does the researcher have responsibility and just precisely what are those responsibilities? Fish may be sympathetic to the new historicists' claim to have responsibility
towards oppressed groups, but he questions whether the nature of that responsibility
should lie in the transforming of literary criticism on the grounds that this cannot assist
the oppressed or in any way deter the oppressors. On the other hand, Fish might say,
these wayward colleagues do have a responsibility to others in the field, who, after all,
are likely to constitute their biggest audience. And the nature of this responsibility lies
in treating the traditions of the discipline with greater respect, especially since these
traditions – concerning the grounding principles of questing for meaning and the truth
– can be revealed as the real basis of even new historicist criticism.

We have introduced this consideration of the field of literary criticism precisely
because it does not, in general, involve collecting data from human subjects – at least,
not directly. Indeed, the ESRC appears not to regard literary criticism as 'research' at
all (ESRC, 2005, p. 10), though this seems to represent a narrow-mindedness that is
not characteristic of the ESRC Framework more generally. The point that we want to
make is that there are ethical issues to be considered in all research, even in those areas
that appear to be most insulated from direct human contact. Given that research is of
necessity a social activity, such insulation is, ultimately, never a possibility.

The final question in the ethical review concerns the expectation that the review
process is to be continued throughout the research and, indeed, beyond it during the
dissemination of research findings and archiving of data. The UK Data Protection Act
Eighth Principle provides that:

> Personal data shall not be transferred to a country or territory outside the Euro-
> pean Economic Area unless that country or territory ensures an adequate level of
> protection for the rights and freedoms of data subjects in relation to the processing
> of personal data.
>
> (http://www.opsi.gov.uk/acts/acts1998/ukpga_19980029_en_9#sch1)

Many of us now routinely carry our computers with us when we travel to confer-
ences and even on holidays; our computer hard drives presumably often contain data

collected in the course of research. How many of us can affirm that we are never break-ing the law purely by travelling from one place to another?

The mode of ethical interrogation

In this chapter, perhaps even more so than in the others, we have generally not felt able to provide clear answers to the questions that we have raised. Of necessity, decisions on issues relating to ethical practice in research potentially affect individuals other than the researcher and groups beyond the community of educational researchers. In coarse terms, there are: human research participants and others, such as parents and teach-ers, who may be closely associated with them; colleagues and, where the researcher is a student, tutors; the community of educational and social science researchers; the institutions of the law and educational policy and practice; and society more generally. Even within each of these categories there will be fundamental disagreements on gen-eral ethical principles. And, having established one's general ethical principles, these must be operationalised in terms of the local context of the empirical ethical field of the research.

We have proposed that a rigorous ethical review is a vital component of all educa-tional research and, indeed, such reviews are fast becoming mandatory and increas-ingly formalised processes. We have offered in this chapter an ethical analogue of the more general mode of interrogation that we have described in this book. This consists of a methodological apparatus that establishes and articulates a *theoretical ethical field* and an *empirical ethical field*. In the context of a given research institutional setting, this methodological apparatus will be dominated by the procedures for the ethical research that are in place. This apparatus is likely to include a committee structure, pro formas, procedures for submitting project proposals and so forth. Here, we have indicated some of the questions that are likely to be involved in formulating a review and that we consider should be addressed even where a formal ethical review is not required. Addressing these questions should enable a clear statement of the ethical issues that are expected to arise in undertaking the research project, the clear delinea-tion of decisions that have been taken, and the clear defence of these decisions in terms of the nature of the research and the literature that constitutes the theoretical ethical field. Expressed in these terms, the ethical review of a research project takes much the same form as the more general statement of its methodology. Exploring the ethical dimension of research is not only an essential part of research; it is, in a sense, in itself a complete research activity.

In the next four chapters, we shall move further into the empirical setting and on the collection and analysis of data. Chapters 5 and 6 are concerned with data collec-tion; Chapters 7 and 8 deal with analysis. We have designed these chapters so that they can reasonably be read in any order.

Chapter 5

Experience and observation

The collection of first-hand data

In previous chapters we have stressed that empirical educational research must be involved with both empirical and theoretical development. We have also suggested that, at different stages of the research, one or other of these spheres may move into the foreground of attention and the other may be temporarily backgrounded. This is also the case in our consideration of the research process. In this chapter we are moving into the (empirical) field, as it were. Therefore, although we will try not to lose sight of the theoretical problem, we shall be foregrounding issues relating to the empirical setting and its management. In particular, we shall be focusing mainly (but not exclusively) on operational issues relating to the measurement of indicator variables rather than on their theoretical conceptual development. This is a pragmatic choice. In order to survey a range of approaches to research we shall need to draw on a wide empirical field. Unfortunately, we do not have the space to develop these empirical resources to a theoretically sophisticated level.

In this chapter we are going to look at a number of ways of collecting first-hand data, that is, data obtained through the researcher's direct experience of the setting being explored. This covers a wide range of techniques, from the systematic observation of behaviour in the context of a highly structured, experimental study through to making incidental fieldnotes as a participant in an everyday setting. Our intention is to outline the major forms of observational data collection, to consider why a researcher might select a particular way of collecting data, and to develop the means to evaluate both other researchers' and one's own practice. In describing different forms of observational data we shall focus on, first, the degree of manipulation by the researcher of the context within which the observations are being made and, second, the extent to which structure is imposed on the observations and the point at which this happens. As we discuss different forms of data collection, we shall also consider the question of research design.

Manipulation of context: from experiments to participant observation

Experimental research design

Researchers adopting an experimental approach attempt to establish a relationship between *variables* by exercising very tight control over key aspects of the setting with which they are concerned. The simplest form of *experimental design* would enable the researcher to manipulate one variable (known as the *independent variable*) and to observe the effects that this has on another variable (the *dependent variable*). For example, a researcher wishing to explore whether the adoption of a particular teaching strategy has a positive effect on children's scientific reasoning might conduct a simple experiment. The teaching strategy would be the independent variable and the children's scientific reasoning the dependent variable.

As they stand, neither variable is sufficiently well defined. In order to construct an experiment, the teaching strategy in which you are interested has to be translated into an explicit procedure, which can be repeated with a high degree of consistency. This constitutes the *experimental treatment* you are to carry out. You also need to be clear about how you will gauge any changes that occur in the children's scientific reasoning, the dependent variable. You thus require an *indicator*, or cluster of related indicators, of the quality of children's reasoning in order to render this visible and measurable. Having clarified what you mean by 'scientific reasoning', and how you might recognise different levels of this, you could measure each child's level of scientific reasoning using a test of some sort. Alternatively you could devise some tasks for children to carry out, and make an assessment of their level of scientific reasoning on the basis of your observations of their performance on the tasks. Whatever form of measurement of 'scientific reasoning' you choose, it is essential that you can establish both the validity and reliability of the judgements you make.

In order to investigate the relationship between the dependent and independent variable, you have to decide on the form that your experiment will take. There are a number of alternative designs from which to choose. You could select a group of children, administer the treatment (i.e. teach them using the teaching strategy in which you are interested) and see what effect this has had on their scientific reasoning. To do this you would need to test the children before and after the treatment. This design is known as the one group *pre-test–post-test design*. A design such as this would be adopted in an attempt to establish causality; in this case, to establish that the use of a particular teaching strategy causes the observed changes in the scientific reasoning of the children.

There are, however, a number of possible influences on the performance of the children that you would be unable to control. This is particularly acute if your treatment takes place over an extended period of time, say over a series of science lessons covering a school term or semester. In this case you would not know whether the observed changes were due to the treatment or to activities that were taking place outside the experimental session. Even the general maturation of the children over the period of time may be important. Although these factors cannot be directly manipulated, an attempt can be made to *control* for their effects through the design of the experiment. The introduction of a second group of children, who do not receive the treatment, into the design is one way of doing this.

In a *pre-test–post-test control group design*, an *experimental group* and a *control group* are selected. The members of the experimental group, but not those of the control group, receive the treatment. In all other respects, the two groups should have, as far as possible, the same characteristics and experiences. Both groups are tested before and after the treatment is given to the experimental group. These pre- and post-tests enable us to compare changes in the performance of the subjects who receive the treatment with those who do not.

If the two groups are actually *matched* in terms of their characteristics and experiences, then, once any differences in performance on the pre-test have been allowed for, differences in post-test performance can be attributed to the treatment received by the experimental group. The matching of the groups is vital as the design is based on the assumption that the effects of all the non-manipulated factors can be accounted for by making a comparison between two groups with as near identical characteristics as possible.

The *random* selection and allocation of individuals to groups is one way of achieving this. In randomly selecting subjects from a population there should be nothing motivating the selection and allocation of a particular person to any particular group. With a numerically large sample, the profile of each group should be similar to that of the population from which the sample is drawn. There are, of course, limits to what random allocation can achieve, especially where numbers are small. Mark Warschauer (1996), for example, was interested in whether college students participate more equally in small group discussions held in computer-mediated mode than in face-to-face mode. He was also interested in how the differences in participation related to other factors, such as gender and nationality. Warschauer randomly assigned students to four discussion groups for his experiment, varying the order of discussion mode and discussion theme between the groups. However, there were only sixteen participants altogether, only two of whom were men. There were five Filipinos, five Japanese, four Chinese and two Vietnamese. Clearly, there was no possibility of any of the groups being representative of the group of students as a whole (far less students more generally) and it would not have been possible to distribute students in a way that produced groups that were matched in terms of nationality or gender, so it is not at all clear that random allocation achieved anything at all. With such small numbers, we might reasonably expect that individual differences within nationality groups might be at least as significant as differences between these groups. The problem was compounded by Warschauer's use of quantitative techniques, which effectively rendered invisible the details of the interactions in discussion, which may well have been far more revealing than the statistics. This is not in any way to devalue the use of random allocation and quantitative approaches to data analysis, but, in general, these approaches are not best suited to research in which sample numbers are small.

An alternative strategy is to *pair* subjects with similar characteristics and to assign one person to the control group and the other to the experimental group. In this way it is possible to construct two groups that are similar in particular ways. To do this one has to be clear about which characteristics of the individual matter with respect to the study being carried out. If we are examining teaching strategies in science, it is unlikely that we will feel that it is important to match individuals in terms of hair colour, but we might feel it is important to match them in terms of attainment in science. Producing matched groups in this way requires reference to prior research and/or theoretical development relating to the object of our study. Confidence that matched groups can be produced by random allocation, on the other hand, is based on probability theory. Matching would not have worked well in the case of Warschauer's experiment; he might have been better advised to use just two groups (although this would have negated the aspect of his design that attempted to control for order of discussion theme) or to construct four groups based on nationality (although this would have resulted in one group of just two students), or, perhaps, tried alternative groupings and a more qualitative approach.

The strict demands made by experimental designs create a number of problems for educational research. Randomly assigning pupils to groups is disruptive and likely, in many, if not most circumstances, to be impractical. The conditions necessary to construct groups in this way, and to be able to manipulate the treatment received by these groups with sufficient precision, leads us away from the classroom and towards tightly controlled experimental settings. This raises questions regarding both the typicality of behaviour within experimental contexts and the transferability of treatments from an experimental setting to the classroom. These questions relate to concerns about the *ecological validity* of experimental research in which phenomena are explored in contexts other than those in which they naturally occur.

There are also potential *ethical* problems in the manipulation, for the purpose of research, of the circumstances in which school students are taught. It is obviously important not to embark on a course of action that, it is thought, could be harmful to the educational progress of a group of school students. Similarly, one has to take care that the research design does not lead to beneficial forms of action being withheld from particular groups for extended periods of time. If teachers and/or children are participating in an experiment, it is important that they be aware of this. On the other hand, this awareness might itself compound the research by what is known as the Hawthorne effect.

The Hawthorne effect

Influenced by the 'scientific management' techniques of F.W. Taylor, the management of the Western Electric Company plant at Hawthorne, USA, set out to determine which working conditions were most conducive to high productivity. In a series of studies conducted in the 1920s and 1930s (reported at length by Roethlisberger and Dickson, 1939) researchers attempted to investigate the effects on the productivity of workers of changes in variables such as the length of the working day and the level of heating and lighting in the plant. The results were highly ambiguous.

In the 'Illumination Study' they attempted to find out if increasing the level of lighting would cause workers assembling electrical relays to produce more. As the lights grew brighter, productivity increased, suggesting a relationship between level of illumination and productivity. However, when the lighting intensity was subsequently reduced, productivity remained high. In response to this, the researchers attempted to take into account both physical and economic factors and to conduct the investigation in more tightly controlled circumstances. In the 'Relay Assembly Room Study' they selected six workers to work in a special observation room. They varied wage incentives, heating, lighting and other working conditions. Irrespective of the conditions, the output of the workers increased steadily over the two-year period of the study. On the basis of their observations the researchers hypothesised that the changes in productivity were the result of the special attention being paid to the workers as the subjects of a research study. In this case the effects of 'being researched' far outweighed the influence of any of the physical and economic factors the researchers were exploring. This phenomenon clearly has implications for all forms of observational research. The possible effect on behaviour of being studied has subsequently come to be known as the *Hawthorne effect*.

These kinds of effects can be controlled for in a laboratory setting. Outside the laboratory this is more difficult. In the testing of new drugs, an experimental group can be given the drug being studied and the control group given a *placebo*. This is a treatment that appears to be similar to the test drug, but which has no physiological effects. The research subjects do not know whether they are in the experimental group or the control group. In this way allowance is made for the effects of participation in a study. It is of course possible that the person administering the treatment will behave differently according to whether they are administering the test drug or the placebo. For this reason a double-blind design is generally used. In this design, neither the person administering the treatment nor the subject know whether the test drug or placebo is being used.

In an attempt to overcome the problems associated with experimental designs when applied to the study of complex social contexts such as schooling, some researchers adopt compromise, *quasi-experimental designs*. Rather than making a comparison between two groups constructed for the purpose of research, comparison can be made, say, between two classes within the same school, one receiving a particular treatment, the other acting as a control group. There is no pretence here that precise matching of subjects can be achieved in this way and thus the researcher cannot make inferences about the effects of the treatment with the same degree of confidence as would be possible if the groups were matched in the ways described above. It becomes increasingly difficult to establish a clear relationship between the independent variable and the dependent variable, as it is no longer possible to say that the effects of the multitude of non-manipulated variables are the same for the two groups. In other words, the quasi-experimental design makes the control of these non-manipulated variables more difficult.

In the discussion of experimental studies thus far we have made the assumption that the treatment that takes place is a purposive, pre-designed intervention of some form. This need not be the case. We could, for example, use a simple experimental design to examine the effects of a 'natural' event that is beyond our direct control. The event would be the independent variable and the researcher would need to gather data relating to the dependent variable before and after the event.

An example of such a 'natural experiment' is one of the studies referred to in Chapter 3. This study was carried out by a primary school teacher. She had a particular interest in the political knowledge of young children and how this relates to representations in the mass media. She took advantage of an imminent general election to explore the effect on children's knowledge of high levels of media coverage of national politics. In order to do this she had to test the political knowledge of a group of children (in this case the children in her own class – an opportunity sample) before the lead-up to the election and again after the election had taken place. She used a questionnaire of her own design for data collection.

Here, a kind of single group pre-test–post-test design is being used, but the form of intervention (increased media coverage of politics) is beyond the control of the researcher. Being a single group study makes it difficult to establish that any differences found in the children's political knowledge has been caused by the 'intervention'; no control for other variables is being exercised. The use of the pre-test (essential if the logic of the design of the research is to be followed) might indeed have a profound effect. It could sensitise the children to political issues and make them more likely to pay close attention to political coverage in the media. The sensitising effects of pre-tests are recognised by experimental researchers. In order to account for these effects, additional experimental and control groups are added. These groups match the original groups closely but are not given the pre-test. By administering the post-test to all groups, the effects of the pre-test can be estimated. In the case of the study of the children's political knowledge this would mean the administration of the post-test questionnaire to another class of children whose characteristics matched those of the teacher's own class.

It is also possible to explore the effects of a treatment that has already taken place. This is known as *ex post facto research*. Here the researcher explores the possible causes, or influences upon, a currently observable state of affairs by looking back at antecedent conditions. You might, for example, wish to examine the proposal that the earlier introduction of a staff appraisal scheme in a school has produced a high level of teacher involvement in continuing professional development (CPD) activities. A study exploring the relationship between a past event (the independent variable in this case) and a current situation could also take the form of a comparative study. You could, for instance, compare levels of CPD involvement in a group of schools in which formal staff appraisal had not been implemented with a group of schools where formal staff appraisal has been established.

In ex post facto research, the adoption of a quasi-experimental design in a natural setting allows the possibility of making comparisons between similar groups that, for some reason, are already receiving different forms of treatment. An interest in the effects of whole-class teaching on primary school children's attainment in mathematics might lead you to look at two samples of primary school classes. You might take one set of classrooms in which whole-class teaching is used in the teaching of mathematics and another in which there is no formal whole-class teaching. Teaching method is the independent variable (the treatment) and is scaled according to the presence or absence of whole-class teaching. Attainment in mathematics is the dependent variable. In lieu of a specifically designed pre-test you could use already available data on the children's mathematical performances at a particular point in time and measure changes in this performance over a given period.

Here we have moved away from the artificiality of direct manipulation of contexts and planned interventions, and towards the investigation of more 'natural' phenomena. Whereas an approximation to an experimental design has been retained, the compromises regarding sampling and procedure that have been made have, to an extent, undermined the logic of the design. This weakens its potential to provide support for a causal relationship between the variables. It also weakens the potential for the generalisation of the results.

This is often forgotten. Seductive accounts of, say, the apparent success of whole-class teaching in countries on the Pacific rim may be compared with the apparent failure of individualised methods used in the UK. These comparisons may be based on descriptions of teaching methods observed in classrooms and on the attainment of school students based on international tests. However, there are clear difficulties in matching samples. There are also difficulties in control. An adequate comparison would seek to take into account variables relating to differences in the social and cultural relationships between, for example, the state, the family, schooling and employment. The incommensurability of societies at such macro-levels makes it impossible to establish that the teaching methods observed cause, or are even a major influence on, the observed differences in attainment. Unable to support a causal relationship, we are left with a correlation between the use of a particular teaching method and high attainment. Our data will not enable us to rule in or out a possible third variable, or cluster of variables, that lies behind the observed association between whole-class teaching and high attainment. In passing, we should also point to the difficulty of constructing a valid and reliable cross-cultural measure of attainment, especially given the lack of theoretical development that generally characterises international surveys.

In this section we have illustrated how the basic experimental design may be adapted in addressing concerns regarding ecological validity and the ethics of manipulation. In these kinds of study an attempt is made prior to the conduct of the research to isolate key variables and to organise these in the form of a possible causal relationship. For the design to be tenable we must be able to measure the variables with a degree of precision. In many cases it may not be desirable or possible to preconceptualise and/or organise the phenomena in which one is interested in this way. The difficulties involved in the application to complex social settings of an experimental logic, inspired by research design in the physical sciences, has led some researchers to reject this model. One result of this is the growth of ethnographic studies of education.

Ethnographic research

Ethnographic approaches draw inspiration from anthropological research, in which the researcher sets out to understand and describe a setting with which they are, in most cases, initially unfamiliar. The development of this understanding involves the immersion of the researcher in the practices in the empirical setting and sustained interaction with participants. The predominant means of collecting data is through highly detailed observation. In the classic social anthropology of the early twentieth century, the researcher would have been a Western academic and their object of study would have been a distant 'exotic' culture (see, for instance Malinowski, 1922). Through direct experience, the researcher would collect detailed information about the society, or a particular segment of the society, and generate a description of this 'novel' setting. Minimally, this enterprise would involve learning the language of the people being studied, observing what they do in a variety of situations and, from this, constructing an account of how the society works.

The legitimate site for anthropological work was originally the distant, 'exotic' culture. Over time the number of little-known distant cultures about which to 'bring back news' has reduced. The association of this kind of work with the self-assumed colonial authority to produce accounts of 'other' cultures has also made it less acceptable. As a consequence ethnographers have brought their investigations closer to home, for instance the study of AIDS support groups, weight watchers, wholefood cooperatives, parent–teacher associations and even groups of ethnography students (see Burawoy *et al.*, 1991). Ultimately we can look to our own lives and the contexts within which we operate as settings for ethnographic research. Rather than entering an unfamiliar setting as an outsider and attempting to make sense of this, we are in the position of already being a participant in a familiar setting. The challenge is to be able to strip away our assumptions and everyday understandings to render the world around us 'anthropologically strange'. For the educational researcher the adoption of an ethnographic approach makes possible the exploration of the processes of teaching and learning in the classroom, the 'lore' of the playground, power relations amongst school staff, the relationship between the home culture of children and the culture of the school, and so on.

The immediate appeal of this kind of approach is that the actions of participants are studied in the context in which they naturally occur. Furthermore the researcher is making no attempt to manipulate what happens, but merely observing and recording. The fluidity of the research process also allows the researcher to analyse data as they collect it and thus to refocus their study as they go along and specifically seek out particular information or look for counter examples. There are, however, a number of issues about this method of collecting data and conducting research that need to be addressed.

First, as we pointed out in Chapter 2, data collection and description inevitably involves a process of recontextualisation. This process includes the imposition of principles of selection or recognition. For the ethnographer the process of selection of what counts as relevant information starts very early in the research process and the principles of this selection are often not made clear. Why have they chosen a particular empirical setting for their research? Why have they chosen certain people as guides and informants? How do they establish the genuineness and typicality of what they see and what they are told? When the researcher observes, why do they notice some features of what is around them and not others? How do they decide what to record from their observations?

The researcher must also impose principles of interpretation or realisation. Ironically, perhaps, the more familiar a setting may seem, the greater the danger of bringing your own unexamined interpretive frameworks in making sense of what you see. Educational practitioners researching educational practices are clearly vulnerable in this respect. The following extracts are taken from a study that included classroom observation in three schools in Brazil; they refer to pedagogic practices in two of the schools:

> The process of creation, re-creation and discovery of concepts and principles was emphasised to the detriment of the mere storing of facts and information. Correspondingly, experimenting and investigating, observing and drawing conclusions, and organising results and reporting, were used more often than filling in textbooks or worksheets of factual and fragmented questions. The purposes and

procedures of every activity were fully presented to the children, and they also had opportunity to discuss them.

(da Silva, 1988, p. 61)

The extensive use of solitary drills and exercises excluded the use of other modes of teaching and types of activities. There was an impressing sameness to the type of work in these classrooms. Besides children working individually at their desks, short presentations of new topics by teachers and occasional dialogues between the teachers and the pupils, little else, as far as schoolwork is concerned could be seen there.

(ibid., p. 62)

The descriptions of these two modes of pedagogic practice are quite clearly coloured by the researcher's preconceptions of what constitutes appropriate pedagogy. However, although an educationalist might recognise constructivist and behaviourist pedagogies in the respective descriptions, the researcher does not explicitly theorise pedagogic practice. To do so would require some theoretical articulation between, shall we say, transmission and acquisition. In the absence of such clarification in the area of the problem, nothing is learned by the observation. This kind of reporting of observational data may be little more than the rehearsal of one's prejudices.

This is not to suggest that there should be a circular relationship between theory and data. If our theory predicts precisely what it is that we will find when we enter the field then, again, there would be little point in conducting the research. What theory provides here is a way of making visible how, why and with what consequences we make particular decisions in the various phases of the design and conduct of the research. In this way the integrity of the process of collecting and analysing data is open to scrutiny by others. Similarly, as readers of ethnographic work, we need to be able to see how selections and interpretations are made and how conclusions are drawn in order to be able to evaluate the research.

The second issue concerns the scope for a tension between extremes of 'objectivism' and 'subjectivism' Some ethnographers may regard the above description of the approach as unduly 'objectivist'. The ethnographic researcher may legitimately be concerned with the meanings that events and phenomena within a particular setting may have for participants in that setting. The object of study becomes the means by which the symbolic world of the participants is produced and maintained. From this perspective, the observer cannot simply record what they see and present this record as a set of facts.

However, this concern carries the attendant danger of abdication from one's responsibility as an analyst, of ignoring the principle of recontextualisation. Having collected detailed notes from numerous observations and discussions, there is a temptation to present participants' own accounts of what they are doing as explanations of social and cultural phenomena. This is inappropriate. Neither the rules for producing acceptable performances nor the wider significance of particular practices are necessarily explicitly available to the participants. The ultimate responsibility for analysis lies with the researcher. In this sense, research is simply not a democratic activity.

This apparently obvious point is worth remembering. Commonly, the accounts of participants are indeed inappropriately presented as analysis rather than as data. Collecting together and summarising the views of teachers on, say, the appraisal process and presenting these as research findings, although possibly making interesting reading, contributes little to our understanding of teachers and schools.

A third cluster of related problems concerns the extent to which the ethnographic observer is also a participant and the consequences of different levels of participation. The options for an observer are conventionally marked out on a continuum from complete participant to complete, non-participant, observer (see, for instance, Robson, 2002). Both ends of this continuum are problematic. Limits are placed on the possibility, and desirability, of being a complete participant by the necessary differences between taking part in an activity, on the one hand, and the production of an analytic account of that activity, on the other. To become a participant an outsider has to learn to how to recognise and produce legitimate performances within the setting they are investigating. As every setting has associated with it a number of legitimate identities that can be ascribed to and achieved by human subjects, the researcher has to learn to 'be' one of these. This entails coming to be recognised as a legitimate participant by the other participants.

This is more than taking on a 'role'; one cannot be who or what one wants independently of who one is seen to be by others. Let's say that we wish to conduct an ethnographic study of homeless people who live on the streets in London. There are a number of possible identities to which a researcher could aspire. There are the police officers who attempt to regulate the activity of homeless people, and social services and charity workers who attempt to provide support for them, there are the 'passers-by' who might act as a source of income, there are the homeless people themselves and so on. Each group can be distinguished and can distinguish themselves from the others. There is also variation within each group. Each group member has some common expectations of others in their own group and of members of other groups. Clearly for the researcher, achieving membership of the 'homeless' group is likely to be more fruitful than becoming a 'police officer' or a 'passer-by' (they are probably already a member of the latter group). Thus it is vital to be aware of both the work involved in 'becoming' a participant and that the account produced will be dependent upon where one places oneself with respect to the range of possible identities. If you wish to study the culture of disaffected youths at school, whether you participate as a disaffected youth (few educational researchers have this option) or as a teacher will clearly affect the data you collect and the account you produce.

Being seen as 'a researcher' will also affect what you are able to achieve and may affect the manner in which people behave. This raises the issue of whether one operates as an overt or covert researcher. There are clear weaknesses in adopting the former position, not least that you are immediately seen as not being a 'real' participant. These are counterbalanced by the obvious ethical problems associated with covert observation, some of which were discussed in the previous chapter. These issues demand careful consideration before embarking on a piece of research, and our considered responses are likely to limit what it is possible to research and the ways in which research on certain topics can be approached.

The practitioner-researcher, who might be studying an aspect of their own workplace, will not have to address the question of coming to be seen as a legitimate participant and producing contextually acceptable performances. They will, however, have to consider carefully the question of what they tell their colleagues, pupils and others about what they are doing. It is generally preferable to be open and honest. Nevertheless, care must be taken not to transform the behaviour of others by the manner or detail of your representation of your study

Careful consideration also has to be given the relative status of the observed and the observer. What children do in front of parents will differ from what they will do in front of teachers or peers. The way teachers act may, similarly, be different when observed by an inspector, their headteacher, a colleague, a trainee teacher and so forth. Whatever form of observation one adopts, there will be a range of possible observer effects that will have a bearing on what happens (see also discussion of the Hawthorne effect, above). It is important to take these into account in both your own work and your reading of other people's work.

As we pointed out in Chapter 2, the act of taking up the position of observer necessarily transforms the practice being observed. We referred to this as the epistemological paradox. This impacts on the ethnographic researcher whether they are an outsider negotiating a 'participant identity' or a practitioner-researcher studying a familiar, everyday setting. In particular, in producing an analytic account as a researcher, both the descriptive resources upon which you will draw and the criteria by which your account is evaluated will, at least in part, originate outside the activity that is the object of your study. In our view, this is a positive feature of research as a distinctive activity in itself. It encourages us to stand outside our everyday practices and to scrutinise them in terms of what we have described as the research mode of interrogation. We shall return to this issue in Chapter 11. It will be clear already, however, that we view as highly questionable the proposition that an observer can be a full participant.

The notion that one can be a complete (non-participant) observer also presents difficulties. Researchers who aspire to being non-participant observers usually do so in an attempt to minimise the impact that the presence of an observer has on the setting. This involves keeping some distance from the activity in question and minimising interaction with the participants. An observer in a classroom might, for instance, sit in the corner of the room, away from the pupils and the teacher, and make notes on what they see. They might have particular strategies for avoiding any discussion with participants and have previously prepared answers to anticipated awkward questions. Although it is obviously reasonable in some forms of work to attempt to minimise observer effects, it is not possible to eliminate them altogether. Some form of identity will be ascribed to the researcher by the participants, no matter how unobtrusive they attempt to be. What is important is to be as aware as possible of the effects that one's presence has on participants and how these affect the integrity of the data. This directs us away from trying to be 'invisible' and towards thinking carefully about the image that we project in a given situation. The performance of a teacher will be affected in particular ways by the presence of someone they think of as a school inspector or if they feel that information gathered by the observer will find its way to someone who is in a position of authority with respect to the teacher.

You will need to design your observation fieldwork so as to minimise effects that may compromise your study. You will also need to be able to judge the extent of the influence of those factors that you cannot control. One technique used by observers is to habituate participants to the presence of an observer. This involves entering the setting (in whatever position one has decided to adopt) a number of times before the collection of data begins. In this way participants become accustomed to the researcher being around. Although behaviour will initially be affected by the presence of an outsider, it is hoped that this will settle down into customary forms once the observer becomes familiar.

A similar technique can be used if an audio or video recorder is used. Some teachers or pupils might find being recorded in this way inhibiting. Habituation would involve introducing the recording device into the setting before actual data collection begins. If, for instance, you wish to study the discussions that take place when children collaborate on science investigations, you might record their conversations over a period of weeks but not use, say, the first three recorded sessions for your analysis. In a study similar to this, a teacher used an audio recorder as the means by which children routinely made a record of what they had done. In this way they became used to the presence of an audio recorder that could then be used as a means for the collection of data for analysis.

Not all researchers employing participant observation as a method for collecting data wish to minimise their impact on the setting. Ethnomethodologists, for example, have sometimes employed techniques that are specifically designed to disrupt the smooth running of everyday interactions and activities (see Garfinkel, 1967). Ethnomethodology is concerned with gaining an understanding of the manner in which everyday life is accomplished. The empirical work carried out sometimes attempts to identify the taken-for-granted assumptions that operate in particular social situations by asking the researcher to behave in an unusual manner. The intention here is to break with some of the shared, but usually unstated, conventions that operate in everyday interactions and to examine the ways in which people respond. Through the disruption of social order, at the level of the everyday and the commonplace, the ethnomethodologist hopes to gain access to the manner in which the social reality of participants is achieved and maintained.

The disruptive techniques used are usually simple. For example, consistently using very formal modes of address when talking to friends or family, or constantly asking people 'what do you mean' when engaging in everyday conversation. Here the researcher is a participant in everyday settings but is engaging in a form of social experiment. By 'being strange' they are manipulating the context in particular ways and producing uncharacteristic behaviours and forms of interaction between themselves and others. Their own experiences and observations constitute their data. As with any manipulation of context, there will be ethical issues to be addressed: to what extent and under what circumstances can we justify sitting down at the dinner table and addressing a parent as Mrs Dowling or Mr Brown, rather than mum or dad?

Observation online

The very rapid development of the internet over the past decade or so has provided researchers with what is, in effect, a new empirical field. It is also a very diverse empirical field: there are online worlds, such as Second Life (secondlife.com/); gaming environments, such as World of Warcraft (www.worldofwarcraft.com); online gambling sites, such as Texas Holdem (www.texasholdem-poker.com); sites for fans and fanfiction writers and readers relating to literature (for example, www.sugarquill.net), TV shows (for example, sword.borderline-angel.com) and other cultural phenomena; social networking sites, such as Facebook (www.facebook.com); marketplace sites, such as eBay (www.ebay.com) and of course Amazon (www.amazon.co.uk); broadcasting sites, such as YouTube (www.youtube.com); blogs; institutional (www.ioe.ac.uk) and personal websites (homepage.mac.com/paulcdowling/ioe); etc., etc. Some of these are Web 2.0 sites that are interactive, others simply provide access to information and products, and there are other online communication resources and environments such as email and Skype (www.skype.com) and, of course, there are the search engines, such as Google. Interaction between users of these environments may be exclusively online or may also involve other channels of communication such as phone and face-to-face (f2f). All-in-all, it would be a mistake to think of either 'online' or 'offline' as single entities. However, whereas different empirical settings perhaps highlight different methodological questions, upon reflection, the general issues tend to be quite consistent.

Online environments clearly offer very extensive opportunities for research of both experimental and ethnographic design. Natasha Whiteman (2007; in press; forthcoming) conducted a study of two online sites, one for fans of a horror TV series and the other for fans of a survival horror video game. The study was primarily ethnographic in nature; however, a part of the study was concerned with the effects of dramatic events, such as the cancelling of the TV show, the release of a Hollywood movie adaptation of the video game, and the hacking of one of the sites. This aspect of the study, taken as a whole, might be construed as quasi-experimental in nature. Students of ours have established online discussion groups in the context of teacher development and teacher education or the evaluation of web-based learning environments and so forth. Others have made use of email voice attachments and blogging environments to bring together learners of English with native speakers of English in action research projects. This is clearly interventionist research. Others have acted as participant or non-participant observers of forums that had already been established in a more ethnographic mode.

In general terms, the issues that we have raised in previous sections of this chapter are all relevant to online research. It is worth pointing out, however, that it may still be that the familiarity of 'real world' settings and the comparatively long history of research activity in such settings may tend to make research seem to be more straightforward than in the comparatively unfamiliar (and very rapidly changing) online environments. Some have argued, for example, that the narrow range of cues available online, which often eliminates, for example, physical gesture and vocal intonation, renders interpretation particularly problematic. On the other hand, some students in f2f classrooms may also give very little away in these terms. We would argue that it is generally the case that the range of cues is likely to be different rather than narrower when considering online as compared with f2f interactions. Even in an exclusively textual environment, playing around with upper and lower case and non-standard punctuation, non-verbal symbols, emoticons, texting conventions, the use of quotations and, in an asynchronous setting, varying the timing of responses provide rich semiotic apparatuses that are no more problematic in terms of interpretation than, for example, facial expressions. We should recall here Gilbert Ryle's observations on winking and blinking:

Two boys fairly swiftly contract the eyelids of their right eyes. In the first boy this is only an involuntary twitch; but the other is winking conspiratorially to an accomplice. At the lowest or the thinnest level of description the two contractions of the eyelids may be exactly alike. From a cinematograph-film of the two faces there might be no telling which contraction, if either, was a wink, or which, if either, were a mere twitch.

(Ryle, 1968; no page numbers)

What is needed in order to differentiate between a wink and a blink or, indeed, between different modes of winking is, as Ryle and, following him, Geertz (1973), note, *thick description*, which is to say, the kind of description that seeks to capture as much as is possible of the context of any particular action. Ultimately, in both online and f2f situations, the description that is produced by the researcher is always going to be partial and selective – is always going to be a recontextualisation of the setting; there is nothing, in essence, that renders this more or less problematic in the online context. We should emphasise, perhaps, that the fact that covert research by *lurking* is often so easy online does raise additional ethical concerns; we have discussed some of these in the previous chapter.

   Now one area of contention that does seem to generate a good deal of interest is the question: to what extent can one be sure that one knows with whom one is interacting in an exclusively online environment? Again, however, we maintain that this issue is not one that is specific to online research. In much survey research, for example, the researcher cannot be entirely sure who completes their questionnaires. In observational research that involves f2f contact between researcher and research, there may be an assumption that being able to identify a real, physical person enables one to make valid judgements about key identity markers, such as age, gender and race. By contrast, in online interactions it is frequently not possible to make such judgements with the same kind of confidence; certainly, there is plenty of evidence to the effect that internet users play around with identity markers; Brenda Danet (1998), for example, reports evidence that many MUD[1] players were effectively 'cross-dressing'; this would clearly be rather more difficult to achieve in f2f interactions. It is often suggested that the solution to this is to conduct offline, f2f interviews with the participants in one's online empirical settings. However, the extent to which this is necessary, or even desirable, is going to depend on one's research interests. Many activities on the internet take place exclusively online and participants never meet f2f. If one's research questions are concerned with practices within such environments, then it is not clear how offline data might contribute to this; after all, none of the non-researcher participants have access to such information other than about themselves, so the researcher, as participant observer, is in the same position by limiting themselves to online interactions (see Hine, 2005). The question at issue is: is the research concerned with connecting offline with online life? Research that seeks to compare online activity between adult men and women would need to take steps to confirm the age and gender of research participants; a study that seeks to establish the gendering of online performances, that is, how gender is produced online, may not.

   Of course, some online activities do spill out into the 'real world' in various ways. T.L. Taylor (2006), for example, conducted an ethnographic study of the MMOG[2] *EverQuest* and begins her book with a narrative description of her first attendance at an *EverQuest* convention, having been participating in the online environment for the previous three years. Albeit originally an exclusively online environment, *EverQuest* is clearly an activity that, for at least some participants, involves both online and offline interaction and it is, therefore, entirely appropriate that Taylor's ethnography explored both.

In this section we have discussed variation in the extent to which the context in which first-hand data is collected is manipulated by the researcher. To do this, we have counterpoised experimental designs and ethnographic work and given some particular consideration to online settings. We hope to have illustrated that, although experimental and ethnographic forms of research design are quite distinct, a clear contrast between high levels of manipulation and control in experimental studies and the apparent 'naturalism' of ethnographic studies is difficult to sustain. Relatively non-intrusive comparisons can be made between settings using a quasi-experimental design and such comparisons are common in ex post facto research. Conversely, the aspirations of some ethnographic studies to describe 'natural' settings 'as they are' have been shown to be problematic. Like experimental work, participant observation can be used to achieve a variety of ends, including the testing of hypotheses.

Structure: from schedules to fieldnotes

As we have been stressing throughout this book, conducting research involves recontextualising the world in various ways. In Chapters 7 and 8, we shall be looking at the recontextualisation of data constituted in and by analysis. Here and in the next chapter we are focusing on the methodological process. Essentially, the production of data involves acting selectively on the observable world; it is clearly not possible ever to record everything that might be going on in a particular setting, and the act of recording anything generally involves some kind of transformation of it, for example, a change of mode such as between speech and writing or the elimination of gesture in audio recording; even a video recording is transformative, as Ryle's comments on blinking and winking illustrate. Our position is that educational researchers should seek to make explicit the principles of both analytical and methodological recontextualisation. This is necessary if researchers are to be able to justify the decisions that they make and communicate to others precisely what they are doing and why; only in this way can educational research be fully open to interrogation.

Observation schedules

In the conduct of research based on observation, the extent to which and the point at which observations are structured may vary dramatically between studies. Take, for example, an observational study exploring possible differences in the ways in which teachers interact with girls and boys in the classroom. We could, on the basis of previous research on classroom interaction, adopt a highly systematic approach to the collection of data by using an existing observation schedule. An observation schedule provides, first, a number of categories that the researcher uses to record their observations. Second, it includes a set of instructions describing the manner in which the schedule should be used. The categories relate directly to the phenomenon being investigated. The schedule should enable all forms of the phenomenon, in this case different forms of interaction, to be categorised. Clearly, a decision must be taken on whether this should be limited to verbal interaction or should include non-verbal interaction as well. The descriptive power of the categories is a key element in establishing the validity of the schedule as an instrument for collecting data.

An observation schedule can be relatively straightforward, with just a handful of categories. One widely used schedule, the Flanders' (1970) Interaction Analysis Categories, for example, has just ten categories for the classification of both teacher and pupil talk. In order to achieve such brevity, the schedule must either be narrow in its focus or have categories that are very broad. The former will provide us with detailed but specialised data, the latter will provide a wider-ranging picture of the events observed but expressed in less precise terms. Having a small number of categories makes the schedule easier to use in practice. It is, for example, easier for the observer to learn the category descriptions and this makes recording quicker and more reliable. For the ORACLE study of primary school classrooms (see Galton, Simon and Croll, 1980), more complex observation schedules were designed in order to construct a finer-grained picture of teacher and student behaviour (and to examine the relationship between these). Two schedules were developed for the observation of teacher and students respectively. The categories used make fine distinctions between, for example, the kinds of questions asked (five forms of teacher questioning are listed), the types of statements made (nine forms of teacher statement are given) and the kinds of non-verbal interaction observed.

The attractions of a complex observation schedule are clear. The researcher has just one opportunity to record events and commonly wishes to bring back from the field as detailed an account as they can. However, making a distinction between, say, 'open' and 'closed' teacher questions is not always easy, particularly when under the strict time pressures of filling in an observation schedule. Recording using the ORACLE schedules, for example, takes place at 25-second intervals; using the Flanders schedule, they take place every 3 seconds. The more detailed the schedule, the more difficult it is to be consistent in making distinctions between one category and another. This in turn has an effect on the reliability of the schedule as an instrument for collection of data.

The sample for the ORACLE study was large and a team of observers was used to collect data. To ensure that similar interpretations of events were being made by all the observers, careful attention had to be paid to training people to use the schedule and to align their judgements. As an observer uses a schedule over a period of time, the interpretations made may change slightly, that is, there may be *category drift*. With multiple observers it is clearly important to ensure that everyone continues to be consistent in their use of the schedule. It is also important for the lone researcher to guard against this. The consistency of the use of a schedule can be checked using video extracts. By coding the same material at different points in the data collection process, the researcher can check to see if there have been any changes in interpretation over time.

To make it possible for an observation schedule to be used consistently across a number of contexts and, perhaps, by a number of different people, it is obviously important that the categories are clearly and unambiguously defined. In addition to a set of categories, an observation schedule must have a set of explicit instructions for its use. The instructions will include details of the frequency with which one records events. This is a question of sampling. How often does one need to sample events in the classroom to be able to record them in a way that retains the distinctiveness of the distribution of events within different settings? Attention also needs to be given to the format in which recording takes place. The use of a grid, with the categories along one axis and a scale marked out in the time intervals being used along the other, enables a record of the sequence of coded events to be made. It then becomes possible to examine the characteristics of different phases of a lesson, or to look at the points at which particular behaviours or forms of interaction occur most frequently. It is also possible to explore the occurrence of particular pairs, or longer sequences, of coded events.

If the sequence of events is of central importance to the researcher, *interval sampling*, as used by both the coding systems discussed so far, may not be appropriate. By coding at regular intervals one gets an impression of the distribution of events across periods of time. However, because there may be other, non-recorded events between one recorded event and the next, some patterns or sequences may be missed. The alternative is to record specific events as they happen, rather than wait for a fixed period between the coding of events. This is known, not surprisingly, as *event coding*. In this way we could investigate, for instance, what kinds of interactions take place when a teacher asks an open question. Event coding can be very effective for gathering data on the relative frequency of particular events. Closer attention has to be paid to the definition of the unit that is being recorded and to recognition of the beginning and end of a codable event. These are less important issues for interval coding, whereby the observer need only consider, at the moment at which the coding is to be done, 'what kind of event is occurring now?'

In designing an observational study it is unlikely that an off-the-shelf schedule will do precisely what you want it to do. The two schedules mentioned above were both developed for specific purposes and are thus limited in their scope. The Flanders schedule, for example, was designed at a time when teacher-centred, whole-class teaching was the predominant mode of organisation. Consequently, it does not work well in classrooms where alternative modes of classroom organisation predominate. The schedule would be difficult to operate, for example, in a classroom in which the teacher moves between groups of students and interacts sometimes with individuals, sometimes with groups and sometimes with the whole class.

Further, as each schedule is developed from a particular theoretical perspective, its form and content will be based on a set of assumptions that might not be shared by other researchers. An alternative is to develop your own observation schedule. This is most appropriate if you are exploring an area in which some previous research has been carried out, or if you are working from a well-developed theoretical position. Working with a clearly articulated problem will enable you to show how the categories of your schedule – your indicator variables – are derived from your concept variables.

Of course, the schedule must also be designed with direct reference to the empirical setting. It should provide a range of categories that enable all forms of the phenomenon in which you are interested to be easily classified, that is, the categories should be *exhaustive*. In addition, each coded event should fall into just one category, that is, the categories should be *mutually exclusive*. The schedule should be easy to use. It should have full descriptions of the categories and clear instructions for use. To maximise consistency in the use of the schedule, the coding of events should require a minimal amount of inference on the part of the observer. The more contextual information needed to make judgements and the more the observer has to make inferences from what they see in order to code an event, the greater the necessity for training in the use of the schedule to ensure that it produces data with a high degree of reliability.

A new observation schedule has to be piloted and any necessary changes have to be made before it is used for the collection of data for analysis. The reliability of the schedule can be tested by employing two independent observers to code the same sequence of events, either from live action or from a video recording. You will then need to consider the level of agreement between the two observers. This provides a good indication of the extent to which the categories are adequately defined. This procedure for checking the *inter-coder reliability* can be used wherever schedules or coding frames are used to categorise events. Not only does it test the explicitness, coherence and clarity of the framework, it also helps to identify any unintentional bias that might creep into the researcher's own coding.

As a way of collecting data, structured observation has both strengths and weaknesses. A major strength is that a well-designed schedule allows data to be collected from a variety of settings and for comparisons to be made with a high degree of reliability. However, in describing a complex social setting in terms of a pre-formed set of categories much information is lost. This can be either a positive or a negative feature, depending on the priorities of the researcher. On the one hand, making meaningful selections is what category systems are designed to achieve. They serve as effective focusing devices at the stage of data collection. On the other hand, your observations are available only in terms of these categories. No other information from the event can be reliably reclaimed. For this reason, systematic observation has been criticised for producing static representations of phenomena (see Hamilton and Delamont, 1974). Clearly, using this technique for the collection of data in a classroom misses much of what goes on. There may be important but subtle features of classroom life that cannot be recorded using a schedule, no matter how detailed. Furthermore, the observer has only limited knowledge of the particular setting and can work only on the basis of what can be seen. The significance to participants of certain events, for instance the use of in-jokes, may not be immediately accessible to the observer. Misinterpretations, with respect to the meanings ascribed by participants, can thus occur.

Fieldnotes

An alternative to the highly structured approach is to engage directly in the setting being explored and to make in situ *fieldnotes* on what is experienced. This resembles an anthropological or ethnographic approach to educational contexts. Here the researcher enters the setting with a range of questions, interests and orientations. A description of the setting is developed through the successive compilation and analysis of fieldnotes. As with the use of observation schedules, the result is a *biased* account in that it constitutes an imposition of recontextualising principles of recognition and realisation. Consequently, as with the use of observation schedules, it is essential to make explicit the basis on which these selections and interpretations are made. There is, however, an important difference between the use of schedules and the use of fieldnotes. The schedule constitutes a pre conceptualisation of the empirical setting (particularly in the sense that only that which can be categorised can be recorded). With the use of fieldnotes, on the other hand, the structuring of the empirical setting can occur progressively across the period of the fieldwork as successive sets of notes are analysed and the researcher returns to the setting with more finely developed foci for their observation.

In other words, the distinction between structured and unstructured approaches refers to the point at which selection and structuring information from the empirical setting takes place. Bringing back fieldnotes, photographs, or even video or audio recordings of what has happened in the classroom defers the production of a structured account. This deferral can allow a more open exploration of a setting. Ultimately, however, a structured account of the empirical setting and associated phenomena has to be constructed. Without this we have nothing to say; we have no research findings.

There are important methodological and technical issues to be addressed when working with fieldnotes, just as there are with the use of schedules. The researcher will carry with them a number of presuppositions about what is being investigated. The fact that the observation process is not being prestructured in a rigid way does not mean that preconceptions can be ignored. On the contrary, there is a sense in which the interrogation of the researcher's preconceptions forms as important a part of the research process as does the direct observation of the empirical setting. Unfortunately, in many cases researchers do not examine their assumptions carefully, and consequently they themselves are unaware of the presuppositions that are guiding their work. It is not that fieldnotes are unstructured but that, often, their structuring is not made explicit.

Working with fieldnotes, and other information and documents gathered when conducting fieldwork, requires a high level of administrative discipline. For instance, in making fieldnotes it is helpful to distinguish between the different kinds of information that one wishes to bring back from observation episodes. In our own study of three secondary schools in South Africa (Dowling and Brown, 2007) we followed classes of school students for entire days and took fieldnotes in all the lessons we attended. Our initial aim was to examine how pedagogic texts, very broadly defined, were used by teachers and pupils across a range of school subjects and in different kinds of schools. To guide the production of fieldnotes and to facilitate comparisons between the notes made by the three fieldworkers, we drew up a set of fieldwork guidelines. These included guidance on the format of the fieldnotes. For each lesson we recorded, at the head of the first page, contextual details, such as the number of children, the arrangement of the furniture, the manner in which the pupils were organised, the resources available and so on.

Underneath this opening section, the fieldnotes were divided into two columns. On the left hand side a chronicle of events was written. Each fieldworker kept a running record of what they observed including accounts of the teacher's actions, interactions between the teacher and the pupils, verbatim speech extracts, a record of what was written on the chalk board and so on. To speed up the process of recording, the use of abbreviations was useful. In the right hand column the fieldworkers made a note of their own ideas, links with other data and thoughts about preliminary analysis. At the foot of the fieldnotes for each lesson, a note was made of any additional information collected, including information gathered from conversations with the teacher and school students at the end of the lesson. Following each day's observations, we each read through our fieldnotes and added any additional information that we had not been able to note at the time. This included the addition of references to other material collected, such as copies of worksheets used. We also began to develop our analysis.[3]

A potentially very useful device, not available to us when we conducted this fieldwork, is the digital pen. The Livescribe Pulse Smartpen, which one of us now uses, will work with Macintosh and Windows operating systems and enables handwritten notes to be kept in special notebooks and transferred to a computer. The paper notes can be updated or annotated and the pen will update the computer files when next docked. This pen will also record stereo audio and coordinate this with the handwritten notes: touch the page with the pen and it will play back what was recorded at the time that the particular inscription was made. If you are going to use audio recording, of course, you will need to obtain appropriate consent from the participants in the activity being recorded.

In making fieldnotes it is important to have a system that enables a clear distinction to be made between the notes that constitute the raw data (albeit already highly selected) and the emerging analysis. It is also vital to have a cross-referencing system that allows information to be easily recalled and for links to be made with other material collected. The adoption of the form of fieldnote organisation described above enabled us to keep different forms of information separate. The event chronicle acted as a reference back to what we had observed in the classroom. This is a record of what, from our perspective, had happened, and it effectively acted as the empirical basis for our subsequent analysis. As all three fieldworkers observed the same lessons and were using a common fieldnote format, we were able to compare notes and reach a common account of the lessons we observed. Often one observer had been able to note down some details of a lesson that the others had not included in their notes. It is neither possible nor desirable to 'get it all down' and produce a completely unbiased account. Being able to compare notes does, however, help to guard against the dangers of inadvertent selective attention, recording and memory lapses. Contextual information was also shared and checked with the other fieldworkers. Our preliminary analytic notes, often just hastily scribbled ideas, were made in the right hand column and acted as a reminder of lines of enquiry that might prove to be fruitful. In this way analysis proceeds alongside the collection of data.

The form of recording we have described provides greater flexibility than the use of a schedule, and was more appropriate for the type of study we wished to carry out. The notes taken can provide an image of the classroom and the activity within it, remind us of key events, and provide us with information for use in the development of our analysis and in writing this up. They do not provide us with quantitative data, nor can they be used as the basis for generating data of this sort. Our subsequent analysis does, however, impose structure on what we have observed. In developing and writing up our analysis we have to be every bit as clear, and explicit, about how we move from our observations to our results as the researcher using systematic observation has to be about the design and use of their schedule and the interpretation of the information gathered.

It is not always possible to make fieldnotes as the activity being investigated is taking place. Sometimes, especially in covert observation in sensitive settings, writing may not be an appropriate activity. Furthermore, when the observer is personally involved in the activity, for instance, a teacher observing interaction between children in their own class, taking notes may not be physically possible. In these cases notes have to be made as soon after the event as feasible. Under these circumstances, having some means of remembering information, such as the use of mnemonics, is particularly useful.

Whatever the form of record that is made of an event, and whatever the circumstances, it is necessary to be clear about the status of the record – what precisely can the notes, or the completed schedules, tell us about the object of our investigation? This concerns the relationship between the theoretical and empirical contexts of the research, in particular the validity of the findings in relation to the problem.

The structure of online data

In most observational research the phenomena that we are observing are ephemeral. Rather than relying on our memory, we generally attempt to produce a permanent record of events as we have discussed above and, as we've indicated, this always involves a recontextualising of the phenomenon. Now with some internet research the situation is different. Natasha Whiteman – whose study we have introduced above – had access to all of the posts on the fan community sites that constituted her empirical setting. In effect, this amounted to a complete archive of the totality of interactions on these sites (though we shall have more to say about this below). Whiteman reports that the smaller of the two sites, at the point of its closure, had '1,450 registered users, 495 threaded discussions (threads) and 19,183 posted messages (posts)' (Whiteman, 2007, pp. 54–5); the larger site had, at the time of her writing, '6,492 registered users, 7,830 threads, and 175,685 posts' (ibid., p. 55). As well as these forums, both sites contained a range of other content and activities. Clearly, this is an unmanageable amount of data and sampling strategies had to be deployed.

All of the sampling strategies that we introduced in Chapter 3 are potentially relevant to research on this kind of site. Whiteman's strategy was 'theoretically driven'. She was particularly interested in destabilising events and actions and this guided her selection of threads and posts for analysis. For example, one of her areas of focus was the discussion on one of the forums during the run-up to and release of a movie adaptation of the video game series that was the object of one of her sites. In the end, Whiteman's analysis was based on 149 threads containing 3,253 posts, from one site, and 140 threads containing 4,092 posts, from the other; still a substantial amount of data.

Now, although this kind of internet activity is not ephemeral in the sense of f2f interaction, neither is it permanent. The owners and managers of sites do reorganise them from time to time, sometimes removing content and sometimes closing down a site altogether; this happened with one of Whiteman's sites; her other site was hacked, at one point, resulting in the permanent loss of all of the discussion data up to that point. So WWW sites offer a limited degree of stability. In order to insure against the possible disappearance of your empirical setting before your research is completed, it is clearly a good idea to archive it in some way. Various strategies are available; each has advantages and disadvantages.

1 Saving individual web pages or using screenshots:

- these approaches are useful if you need to record the visual appearance or layout of a page;
- a screenshot will not capture the movement of moving images or animations;
- saving the page source (html) is likely to result in a change in appearance of the page and the loss of some images etc.;

- saving as a Web Archive file generally leaves the page looking as it did originally, though the links from the page may suffer 'linkrot', i.e. disappear.

2 Using archiving software:

- this kind of software enables researchers to download and store archives of individual websites; examples are WebWhacker (free trial available at www. bluesquirrel.com/products/webwhacker) and Offline Explorer Pro (www. metaproducts.com);
- the benefit of this kind of software is that it achieves a replication of sites as a whole, capturing content and moving images and enabling offline 'surfing';
- you need to set the number of levels of the website to archive otherwise the program may try to save the entire internet;
- some sites block the use of this software;
- you will need to consider the ethical issues relating to ownership and storage of web content before using this kind of software.

3 Saving text files:

- this might involve archiving individual forum threads as text files as you read through them;
- this is clearly much less demanding, in terms of memory space, than the other strategies, but it is also likely to be more time-consuming;
- one benefit of this 'manual' approach is that it allows you to get to know the data as each thread is looked at, copied, pasted into a text file and then saved individually.

Clearly, archiving of any form stops the action at the point that the archive is made. It is, therefore, important in any kind of longitudinal study that the archive is frequently updated (and, of course, that backup copies are kept).

Experience and observation: conclusion

The focus of this chapter has been on the details of the empirical setting. We have turned our attention to the specifics of the collection of first-hand data in order to raise what we feel to be important methodological and practical issues. We have not attempted to provide a comprehensive survey of methods, nor have we dealt with any of the approaches in great detail. There are numerous general research methods texts and more specialised works to which the beginning researcher can turn for further advice. We have included those we feel to be the most useful in our annotated bibliography.

We initially distinguished between approaches in which manipulation of the research setting is paramount and those in which the researcher attempts to minimise their effect on the research setting. Both positions present problems. In social and educational research it is rarely possible to establish the high degree of control that is required in experimental designs. As a result, compromises are made and the experimental design logic on which many forms of educational research are predicated is weakened. On the other hand, it is also impossible for a researcher to have no effect on the settings in which they are working. The very presence of a researcher, indeed the knowledge that a setting is subject to study, will affect activity within that setting. This provides a challenge to the notion that it is possible to conduct a fully naturalistic enquiry. Once it is constituted as the object of research, a setting is transformed and can never be precisely what it was before. The situation may seem to be different in respect of internet settings that facilitate covert research by lurking. However, although, in covert research, the researcher may be able to avoid impacting on the setting itself, they are nevertheless taking up a position that is other than that of normal participant and this is transformative in terms of their principles of selection in respect of what they attend to and the ways in which they interpret what they see.

Furthermore, the production of an account requires choices to be made with respect to both what is described and how it is described. The claim that one is presenting a situation 'as it is' or 'as it is construed by participants' obscures the principles by which such selections are made and accounts constructed.

Our second distinction focused on the point at which structure is placed on the information in the production of data. We have argued that all forms of data collection and analysis involve the imposition of structure – this is fundamental to the conduct of research. The use of a structured observation schedule imposes structure at a very early stage in the research process. Once the schedule has been designed, data can be collected only in terms of the categories of the schedule. The structuring of data is less obvious in the use of fieldnotes, particularly in the early stages of research. This more open form of data collection allows the possibility of developing a focus as the research progresses. In the analysis of the data the researcher must identify patterns and relationships in the data. If the data remain unstructured, they have not been analysed. We have also drawn attention to the the need to archive internet data in the case of some forms of online research and to some of the ways of approaching this.

We have chosen not to present the choice of a particular way of collecting data as indicating a strong affiliation to a specific epistemological position. In our view these associations are commonly *post hoc* and are of limited help in either the design or interrogation of research. It is of greater importance to ensure that, in deciding how to collect your data, you ensure that the methods you choose are consistent with the general theoretical framework within which you are working. It is also important that you are clear about the status of your data with respect to your study. As we have argued, there is a great difference between the manner in which observations made in an experimental setting and narrative description brought back from the field can be used within a study. You have to take care to treat different forms of data in an appropriate manner and to be clear what your data represents. These issues will be taken up again in Chapter 6, in which we turn our attention to the collection of data from the accounts of others.

Gathering information and asking questions

Questionnaires, interviews and accounts

In Chapter 5 we discussed ways of generating data by recording first-hand experience, either by directly manipulating a setting and observing what happens, or by motivated observation of social interaction in a 'natural' setting. In this chapter we turn our attention to the ways in which other people's accounts, rather than the direct observations of the researcher, can be used as the main source of information. We have made a distinction between these two modes of data collection for pedagogic reasons. Researchers often employ complexes of methods so, in practice, it is often difficult to maintain the distinction. As we have already seen, an ethnographic approach to research can involve the use of informants from whom details of local practices are obtained. Discussion with participants can inform the development of an understanding of how they make sense of the world. Questionnaires and interviews can also be incorporated into experimental designs, for example to gauge changes in attitude associated with a particular intervention. It is thus possible that, in both reading and doing research, you will encounter data produced from a combination of both observational sources and personal accounts, questionnaires and interviews.

Many of the issues discussed in the previous chapter are relevant here. The contexts within which accounts are produced, for instance, can vary from settings created specifically for the purpose of direct questioning through to documents, such as diaries or perhaps blogs, that may be an incidental outcome of everyday activity. As with observational methods, the stage at which structure is imposed upon the accounts of others can also vary. Self-completion questionnaires distributed by post are usually highly structured, with respondents being asked to select answers from a predetermined list of possibilities. In contrast, some exploratory face-to-face interviews may resemble a conversation with little apparent prestructuring of either form or content by the researcher. In considering the different approaches, we will look first at variations in the extent to which the researcher manipulates the context before moving on to discuss variations in the structuring of data collection.

Researchers clearly enter the field with different objectives, and select their data collection techniques accordingly. In considering observational techniques we had to take care to establish, for instance, the extent to which the researcher may be attempting to retain and describe the 'natural qualities' of the settings being observed and the activity taking place within them. We must address similar questions when considering the status of accounts. In general terms, we might distinguish between five broad categories of interests in terms of gathering accounts. That is, the researcher may be interested in what people know; what people do or have done; what people think or feel; how people think; and/or how people construct meanings. In practice, however, these categories are rather more problematic than they may at first appear.

Manipulation of context: from clinical interviews to diaries

Clinical interviews and elicitation techniques

The purpose of a *clinical interview* is to probe beneath the surface of events (such as the behaviour, including utterances, of an individual) in order to explore the underlying processes from which these events arise. It is concerned with *how people think* or *how they construct meaning*. In a clinical setting, the therapist organises a context specifically for the examination of a client's condition. The ultimate aim is not only to explore possible causal relationships and develop a better understanding of the condition, but also to bring about a transformation, to alleviate the condition.

The manner in which the therapist makes sense of what the client says or does and the way in which they manage the interview procedure depend on the theoretical perspective from which they are working. The therapist has a particular way of 'reading' what the client says and does (a theory) and way of proceeding in terms of eliciting forms of behaviour that can be read in this way (a method). In some forms of therapeutic encounter the therapist is in clear control, asking specific questions, reacting to the client's responses in particular ways and guiding the course of the interview. In others, such as Rogerian approaches, the therapist responds in as neutral a manner as possible and attempts to put the client in control of the encounter. In both these types of approach, the clinical interview constitutes a specialised context, a setting that has been created, and is being manipulated, for a particular analytic purpose.

The aims of therapy and of research are clearly different. A form of clinical interview has, however, been fruitfully adopted by some social researchers. Luria, for instance, does more than just ask his interviewees a series of questions to which they are expected simply to give answers. Working from an initial stimulus, such as a syllogism or a classification problem, Luria confronts his subjects, probing and asking supplementary questions in order to explore the form of reasoning they employ. His theorising of the relationship between forms of social organisation and modes of human cognition leads him to explore whether or not his subjects are capable of particular ways of reasoning.

How a person reasons is not open to direct inspection. Luria thus needs to be able to recognise, from what his subjects say and do in particular situations, when they are engaging in certain types of reasoning. The probing that takes place in these interviews is thus designed to examine the way in which each subject approaches the problem given and to offer them every opportunity to look at the problem in an alternative way. The extract from the interview with Rakmat, discussed in Chapter 3 (see p. 25), illustrates Luria's technique. Having explained the task and given a detailed example, Luria uses a set of cards with drawings of familiar objects on them to initiate a classification activity. On being shown the collection *hammer–saw–log–hatchet* and asked which ones are similar, Rakmat gives the following response:

> They're all alike. I think all of them have to be here. See, if you're going to saw, you need a saw, and if you have to split something you need a hatchet. So they're *all* needed here.
>
> (Luria, 1976, p. 55)

Rakmat has clearly failed to produce the 'correct' answer. Luria interprets Rakmat's response as indicating that he 'employs the principle of "necessity" to group objects in a practical situation' (ibid). Rather than simply record Rakmat as having produced a particular type of response when set a certain kind of problem, Luria pursues the matter further. As it is possible that Rakmat simply does not understand what is being asked of him, Luria attempts to explain the task by using a 'simpler example':

> Look, here you have three adults and one child. Now clearly the child does not belong in this group.
>   'Oh, but the boy must stay with the others! All three of them are working, you see, and if they have to keep running out to fetch things, they'll never get the job done, but the boy can do the running for them . . . The boy will learn; that'll be better, then they'll be able to work well together.'
>
>   (ibid.)

As the subject once again applies the same principle of grouping, Luria explores this further by providing more examples and additional prompts before returning to the original problem. He approaches this by continuing to probe with additional questions and statements. The transcript extract, which is reproduced on p. 25, illustrates the method.

This form of interview does not consist of a set of standard questions that are given to all interviewees in a fixed order, nor does it consist of a task at which the subject is judged to have succeeded or failed on the basis of a single response. Instead Luria has a range of tasks specifically designed to explore particular forms of reasoning. In administering these tasks he has a general strategy to guide the manner in which the interview is conducted. Through the exploration of the responses of the subjects, Luria tests and develops his own theory.

Probes and prompts

A *probe* is a question used in an interview to gain further information, clarification, or which seeks to access underlying causes or reasons for a particular response. A *prompt* involves suggesting possible responses. The use of both probes and prompts interrupts the spontaneity of the response. This does not mean that they should be avoided; the use of probes, in particular, is a crucial strategy in many kinds of interview. You should, however, give careful advance consideration to the kinds of probes and prompts that you are prepared to use.

Luria made extensive use of both probes and prompts because his method involved trying to nudge his subjects into what he classified as a higher mode of cognition. Luria reasoned that if a subject failed to do so, despite his probing and prompting, then this indicated that the subject was unable to operate at the higher level.

Jean Piaget (for example, Piaget, 1953) used a similar form of clinical interview to examine children's reasoning, that is, to examine how children think. Piaget and his colleagues designed a range of tasks and problems to be given to individual children by a researcher. How the children made their judgements or solved the problem was explored through extended questioning. For Piaget, it was not enough to ascertain whether or not a child produces the 'correct' solution to a problem; one must look at the form of reasoning that took place in producing a solution or making a judgement. Each task provides a research context. The responses to the task and to the subsequent probing enable the researcher to make and support theoretically informed judgements.

Piaget's tasks, usually in modified form, have subsequently been used by other researchers as the basis for their own experimental research designs (see, for example, Donaldson, 1978). Here samples of children are set tasks under tightly controlled conditions. Rather than acting as the initial stimulus in a detailed exploration of forms of reasoning, the tasks are used as tests. It is certainly legitimate for researchers to draw inspiration from the work of others. Nevertheless, this recontextualisation of Piaget's work is open to question. In particular, the probes used by Piaget and his colleagues are entirely or substantially eliminated in much of this subsequent work, Arguably, the researcher is thus more concerned with *what* children think than with *how* children think.

The starting point for the form of clinical interview conducted by Luria and Piaget is a task of some kind. The nature of each task relates to the substantive focus of the research (e.g. the exploration of generalisation and abstraction in the work by Luria discussed above) and the theoretical standpoint adopted by the researcher. These also guide the form that the interview will take. Although there are clearly criteria for evaluation of the suitability of the task and the ultimate form of realisation of each individual interview, there are no fixed techniques or procedures that are common to all interviews. George Kelly (1969) developed both a theory of personality and specific techniques for the elicitation (and analysis) of theoretically relevant information from interviewees. As a school psychologist, he worked initially from a clinical perspective. Kelly's prime interest was in the way in which individuals made sense of the world around them, that is, in how people construct meanings.

Kelly proposed that individuals come to a personal understanding of the world through attempts to predict and control events. Each individual, he argued, comes to conceptualise the world in terms of a limited number of *personal constructs*. These are conceptual dimensions marked out in terms of bipolar oppositions, such as 'strong'/'weak' or 'good for me'/'bad for me'. These constructs are used to make sense of and evaluate phenomena with which the individual comes into contact (e.g. people, events, objects). These phenomena are referred to as *elements*.

Kelly's method is designed to identify the personal constructs by which individuals make sense of their world. This can be done by, first, eliciting key elements from the interviewee. The person might be asked, for instance, to note down, in a list or on cards, the people who are significant to them. Having produced a set of elements, the interviewee is asked to form groups of three in which two of the elements are the same in some way but differ from the third element. The way in which these elements are similar or different should be expressed as a bipolar opposition, such as friendly/hostile, honest/dishonest, competent/inept. These are the constructs. The way in which two elements resemble each other is the *similarity pole* of the construct; the way in which these two elements differ from the third is the *contrast pole*. By working through the elements in this way a number of personal constructs can be elicited. Once this has been done a grid is drawn up. Each row of the grid represents a construct and each column an element. The interviewee is asked to take each construct in turn and indicate whether each element lies at the similarity pole or the contrast pole. The completed grid, known as a *repertory grid*, can be used to explore both how each construct is used and how the interviewee construes each element.

There is substantial debate amongst researchers drawing on Kelly's work regarding the process of constructing the repertory grid and its subsequent analysis. Engagement with these debates is beyond the scope of this book. For our purposes, Kelly's work offers an example of an empirical technique that is derived from theory. Personal construct theory provides principles for the construction of a particular kind of encounter and techniques for the analysis of information collected. It is potentially applicable either in a therapeutic/diagnostic setting or a research setting.

Diaries and documents

The approaches discussed above involve a high degree of manipulation of the context within which an enquiry takes place. The interview is separated from the everyday activity of the subject and involves engagement with tasks designed specifically for the purpose of research. Accounts relating directly to everyday activity can be collected with less direct manipulation. In some forms of activity, accounts of various kinds are produced routinely by participants. Teachers, for instance, produce policy documents, teaching plans, student evaluations and so on. A researcher wishing to study, for instance, the relationship between school policies and the form of planning carried out by teachers could do so on the basis of the analysis of policy documents and examples of teachers' long-term and short-term planning drawn from a sample of schools.

As with all the forms of study we have discussed, there is a need for clarity about what constitutes relevant information and explicitness concerning the manner in which the information is organised and analysed as data. It is also important to be clear about the conditions under which the information has been produced and the status that is being accorded to it. In designing your study you will have to attend to questions of sampling and comparability. Whether or not you are manipulating the context in which the source information is generated, you still need to attend to fundamental issues in the design and conduct of research.

Brown (1993, 1994, 1999; Brown and Dowling, 1993) analysed documents produced incidentally by primary school teachers in the everyday activity of attempting to involve parents in the mathematical education of their children (these were schools taking part in the IMPACT project, see Merttens and Vass, 1990, 1993). These included examples of school mathematics activities sent home by teachers, booklets produced by teachers for parents and comments about mathematics tasks made by parents in IMPACT diaries (see Chapters 7 and 8 for some further details of this work). Sampling is clearly an issue here. Writing to schools and asking for, say, any booklets they have produced for parents is a viable approach to information gathering. However, when the booklets are analysed it is important to be quite sure what the sample that has been drawn represents. You cannot, for instance, claim that a sample collected in such a non-systematic manner is representative of booklets produced by schools. In fact,

Brown chose to analyse all of the booklets in use in one Local Education Authority in one particular year. This avoided the possibility of being inadvertently selective. It still left unanswered the question of the extent to which the booklets analysed could be taken as representative of a wider population.

Although the manipulation of settings is minimal in the collection of incidental or 'found' information, there are ethical considerations that you must address. This is because the information may originally have been generated for purposes that were quite different from those of your research. The producers of the information may be in no position to give consent to its recycling as research data. Consideration, then, must be given to anonymity. In most cases this is easily achieved by the use of fictional names and the exclusion of collateral information that would enable institutions and/ or individuals to be identified. Particular care has to be taken over the use of confidential information. Schools, for example, keep much information that has a limited circulation and some that is highly confidential. Researchers have to consider carefully whether such information should be used at all and, if it is, how it should be treated and represented. Although you are not directly manipulating a setting, you are intervening. Here our discussion converges with the consideration of observation in the previous chapter and with the discussion of research ethics in Chapter 4.

In order to follow the activities of participants in their everyday lives you may ask them to keep a diary of events. This would enable you to look, for instance, at the proportion of time spent on various kinds of tasks. For example, you might be interested in the manner in which headteachers allocate time to different aspects of their work. To do this you could provide a number of categories of the types of activities that you feel typify the work of headteachers. A sample of headteachers could then be asked to keep a diary showing at what times during the day they took part in these activities (event sampling). Alternatively they could be asked to record what they are doing, in terms of the categories you have provided, at particular times of the day (interval sampling).

This kind of diary is a form of self-administered, structured observation schedule. It thus has both the strengths and weaknesses discussed in the previous chapter with respect to observation schedules. The categories have to be clearly defined and relatively unambiguous in order to be consistently applied by the members of the sample. With each person mapping out their own daily activity, you face all the difficulties of having multiple observers, with no automatic guarantee that everyone is interpreting the category descriptions in the same way. As with the construction of observation schedules you also have to have a fair understanding of the activity being investigated in order to construct a set of categories that have the potential to describe the activities adequately.

Diaries can be used in a more exploratory manner. Headteachers could be asked to keep unstructured, freeform notes on their activities as they take place or to look back on and describe the work they have done at the end of each day. This would not give the neatly categorised information of the structured diary but could give the researcher insight into the manner in which headteachers construe their work. In effect the subjects of the research are being asked to make fieldnotes on their own day-to-day activities. Although no observer is present, this kind of research is not free from observer effects. The awareness that one's behaviour is under scrutiny, even if the details of this are self-reported, can affect what one does (see the discussion of the Hawthorne effect in Chapter 5). With self-reporting techniques we also have to be aware that subjects might present idealised accounts of what they do.

Structure: from questionnaires to conversations

Questionnaires

Self-completed *questionnaires* hold a number of attractions for the researcher who wishes to collect information from a large number of people but has limited time and resources. On the surface the process of construction, distribution and analysis of questionnaires appears to be straightforward. The appeal of the questionnaire is that, once the information required by the researcher has been identified, it appears to be relatively easy to construct a list of questions that get straight to the heart of the matter, to be delivered directly to chosen respondents to complete and return in their own time. There are, however, severe limitations on what can be achieved using a questionnaire. Even once these limitations are taken into account, the design of effective questionnaires is fraught with technical difficulties. Excellent advice on the construction of questionnaires is readily available (see Oppenheim, 1992, for instance). Even so, in our experience, beginning researchers frequently run into serious problems in the use of questionnaires and many invest a lot of time collecting information that is ultimately of little or no use to them.

As is the case with the use of structured observation schedules (discussed in Chapter 5), the strengths and limitations of the questionnaire are closely related. For instance, if information is to be of use to the researcher, it is necessary to standardise the questionnaire to ensure that the responses received are comparable. This entails more than simply giving the same questions to all respondents. The researcher has to be confident that each question will be interpreted by each respondent in a similar manner. The questions thus have to be as free as possible from ambiguity. The researcher must take care to keep the questions short and ensure that there are no double-barrelled questions (i.e. single questions that ask for two items of information). Questions must be checked carefully to ensure that they are free from bias and that they do not lead the respondent towards a particular answer. Technical language that may not be understood by all respondents should be avoided. Care has to be taken even with common, everyday terms. In cases where it is not clear that an important term will be understood in a similar manner by all respondents, a definition can be provided. This also carries problems.

To illustrate this difficulty we can consider the use of a questionnaire, distributed to school students, to investigate the incidence of bullying in a school. Although the terms relating to bullying are used in everyday speech, it is not clear that they are used in the same way by everyone. The question 'how many times have you been bullied this month?' becomes problematic if, across the sample, there is wide variation in what respondents consider bullying to be. Some students might see a single incidence of name calling as bullying whereas others view bullying as occurring across extended time periods and involving physical threat.

In response to this, the researcher might choose to include a definition of bullying in the questionnaire. This imposes a particular understanding of what it means to be bullied. The danger here is that by presenting bullying as an objectively defined phenomenon, the researcher is no longer gathering data on the extent to which people subjectively feel that they are being bullied. The provision of a definition might lead some respondents who feel they are, by their own definition, being bullied to indicate that, by the definition provided, they have not been bullied. Similarly, students who previously have not seen themselves as the victims of bullying might, in the light of the definition provided, indicate that they have been bullied.

The alternative is to accept the definition of each respondent and focus the research on the subjective feeling of being bullied, whatever this might mean to each individual. If relevant, the researcher could include items in the questionnaire that are specifically designed to draw out what each respondent understands by the term bullying. The decision to either include a definition of a key term or not, in this case, fundamentally affects the nature of the study. This decision is clearly not a technical issue. It relates back to the theoretical framework from which the problem being addressed is derived.

Whichever approach is adopted it is vital to carry out a pilot study with a sample that matches the profile of the sample for the main study. The questionnaire items can be trialled with the specific intention of gaining feedback from the respondents concerning their interpretation of the questions. This can be achieved through the addition of some open, free-response questions asking respondents to reflect on how they interpreted the questions. Alternatively, a brief interview focusing on the questionnaire might be conducted. Attention also has to be paid to the ordering of questions, the division of the questionnaire into sections, and the format of the questionnaire. All these aspects can be modified on the basis of the feedback obtained from a pilot study.

Difficulties with regard to interpretation can be exacerbated by the mode of delivery of the questionnaire. If questionnaire forms are sent out by post, the researcher has no opportunity to correct any obvious misunderstandings, probe, or offer help, as they would in an interview. Consequently, forms might be returned with some sections not completed or incorrectly completed. Questionnaire forms might be passed on to other people to complete, or they might be consigned to the wastepaper basket. It has been found that response rates to some online surveys may be particularly low, as low as 10 per cent; this compares poorly with other forms of unsolicited survey, where a response rate of 20 per cent is not uncommon, whereas traditional survey research will commonly take 50 per cent as the minimum level that is acceptable (see Witmer *et al.*, 1999, p. 147). Low response rates and idiosyncratic responses do more damage than just reducing the sample size. They can also be a source of unintentional bias to the extent that there is a connection between the reasons for non-response and the topic of the research. There are no straightforward ways for correcting for sample bias caused by non-response. You simply have to do everything you can to foster a good response rate.

Improved response rates to questionnaires distributed by post can be obtained by taking such measures as inviting respondents to participate in the survey (either by phone or by letter) or by providing advance warning of the arrival of the questionnaire form. Explaining why the respondent has been selected and describing the nature (and importance) of the research also helps to allay fears and engender personal commitment. This is easier if the topic is likely to be of interest to the respondent. It also helps to let the respondent know who you are and what you intend to do with the results. The promise of confidentiality and the anonymity of each respondent (if you are able to make such assurances) can also have an effect. The appearance of the questionnaire form is also important. It must not look as if completion will be an onerous task nor that it will take a long time. The inclusion of a stamped addressed envelope can also encourage people to return the completed questionnaire. If responses are slow in coming in, a reminder can be sent. If anonymity has been promised, the reminder will have to go to the whole sample. Attention to detail in both the design and the use of the questionnaire will all enhance the quality of the study.

The researcher can enhance response rates by more closely supervising the administration of the questionnaire or by becoming more personally involved in its distribution and completion. The questionnaire may be given to a group of people (such as a class of children or a group of teachers attending a training course) who are asked to complete the questionnaire at a specific time. The completed questionnaires can be collected from them immediately. This, of course, increases the researcher time required and thus reduces one of the attractions of the questionnaire.

If we follow this path, the researcher could, ultimately, administer the questionnaire to each individual in the sample, either in person or by telephone or by using a synchronous online facility, such as chat or Skype, or an asynchronous mode, such as email. This overcomes some of the disadvantages of postal distribution, but negates a prime advantage. We effectively have a form of very structured interview and this significantly increases the amount of time required for data collection over, say, the self-completed questionnaire. The forms of direct administration mentioned have sampling implications. The f2f and telephone modes allow the inclusion of people who are unable to read or write. The telephone interview obviously excludes those people who are not accessible by telephone and online modes exclude those without internet access: you will obviously need a list of phone numbers, email addresses or Skype names of people who are contactable in these ways. Of course, even personal administration of the questionnaire does not guarantee a 100 per cent response rate; people can always refuse to take part.

It may be that, despite your efforts, the response rate is low. You may also be aware of a bias in the distribution of your responses. For example, you may have received very few responses to a questionnaire on school-based teacher training from headteachers of inner-city schools. Under such circumstances, it is important to state this bias and consider any implications it might have for your findings.

In using postal questionnaires or online modes the researcher operates at some distance from the respondents. This impersonality can lead to researchers making unwise decisions. No matter how interesting it might appear to investigate the views of people who have recently suffered a bereavement in their close families, they are unlikely to appreciate receiving a postal questionnaire or emails probing at their feelings when they may still be experiencing great distress.

Questionnaires are particularly useful for gathering simple information on what people do or have done (although care must be taken to allow for the limitations of memory in the questions asked) and what people know. Details of a person's educational qualifications or of their reading habits can be gathered by using either closed questions with carefully selected alternatives to choose from (*precoded* responses) or simple open questions. In the latter case, the responses will have to be coded by the researcher after data collection. On the other hand, questionnaires are not always good for exploring how people think or how people construct meanings. It is possible to use a questionnaire to explore what people think or feel, although this requires great skill in the design of items. With this in mind, we shall now look at techniques designed specifically for the purpose of exploring people's opinions, attitudes and beliefs.

Exploring opinions, attitudes and beliefs

The major difficulty in the use of a conventional questionnaire to collect information on the thoughts and feelings or attitudes of individuals stems from the complexity of the enterprise. If a researcher wishes to find out, for instance, how satisfied parents are with their child's school, they are immediately faced with a number of problems. They could ask 'how satisfied are you with your child's school?' They could provide a 1–5 scale on which parents are required to mark the degree of their satisfaction, from very unsatisfied to very satisfied. This would be difficult to respond to in a consistent manner as a parent is likely to be satisfied with some aspects of the school and not others. To address the question they have to decide what weighting they will place on each of these aspects in assessing their own overall satisfaction. With such a complex judgement, a slight rephrasing of the question might lead to a different response.

This makes it difficult to test the reliability of the item by asking the same thing in a different way and comparing the answers to the two questions. In addition, the notion of overall satisfaction might itself have little meaning for the respondent. A parent might, for instance, be very satisfied with respect to one of their children, but not at all satisfied with respect to another child. The complexity of the issue thus makes the use of just one question highly unreliable. The same question asked at another time may well get a different answer from the same person. In this case there are also doubts about the validity of the item. It is not clear precisely what a particular response to the item might indicate to the researcher.

The use of a set of questions, rather than a single item, would increase reliability. In assembling a number of items that relate to the same phenomenon, the effects of, say, an unintentional bias in one of the items or of an idiosyncratic response to one of the questions is reduced. Having a number of questions relating to the same topic also allows questions to be asked about different aspects of the topic. Satisfaction with schooling could thus be broken down into components and more focused questions constructed. The problem here is that, in order to reap the increased reliability benefits of having a set of questions rather than a single question, all the questions have to be considered together. Treating each of the questions individually reintroduces the difficulties that we are trying to overcome through the use of multiple questions. So, it is necessary to have a way of combining the responses to the individual questions in a set so that the set as a whole can be considered as one item. Our questions relating to parental satisfaction with schooling would together enable us to distinguish between those parents who are satisfied with schooling and those who are not, with a comparatively high degree of reliability. It is thus important for the set of questions as a whole to have *discriminative power*.

Various techniques for the construction of scales for the measurement of attitudes have been developed to overcome these problems. The most straightforward, and most widely used, form of scale is the *Likert scale* (see Likert, 1932). A Likert scale consists of a number of statements, some positive and some negative, relating to the attitude being measured. The respondent is asked to indicate the degree to which they agree or disagree with each statement. This is commonly done using a five-point scale from 'strongly disagree' at one end through 'disagree', 'neutral' and 'agree' to 'strongly agree' at the other end of the scale. Often these options are represented as a 1–5 numerical scale. Some researchers prefer a four-point scale as the lack of a neutral position – neither agree nor disagree – effectively forces the respondent to make a decision on whether they generally agree or disagree with each statement. Others argue that the neutral response is an entirely valid one and should be facilitated, especially as respondents may simply omit items or even check both 'agree' and 'disagree' if they are not allowed to respond in a neutral way.

In order to arrive at a score for each respondent, a numerical value is given to the response made to each statement, the values being reversed for positively and negatively worded statements. On a five-point scale, if the respondent 'strongly agrees' with a positive statement, a value of 5 is given, if they 'strongly agree' with a negative item a value of 1 is given, if they 'disagree' with a negative statement a value of 4 is given, and so on. These values are added together to give an overall score. Comparisons between respondents, or between groups of respondents, can now be made on the basis of these scores. Where a respondent has checked 'strongly agree' for all of the items, both positively and negatively worded, then it probably makes sense to exclude them on the basis that they probably have not read the questions very carefully!

Great care has to be taken in the construction and use of a Likert scale. It is vitally important to understand the logic of this form of instrument, even if you are using a scale constructed by another person. For this reason we will outline briefly the process of constructing a Likert scale (see Robson, 2002, and Oppenheim, 1992, for more detailed accounts).

Suppose you wish to draw up a Likert scale to explore parental satisfaction with schooling. You need, first, to create a pool of statements, both positively and negatively worded, that relate to this issue. You can do this by referring to relevant literature, by taking statements from existing instruments, or by setting up a panel of people with particular knowledge of the field and asking them to suggest statements. The statements must have *face validity*, that is, they must be seen to relate clearly to the topic being investigated. Your list might include statements such as 'The work my children do at school is worthwhile' (positively worded) and 'Teachers do not give us enough information about our children's progress' (negatively worded).

Having compiled a preliminary list you need to reject extreme statements to which you suspect all or most respondents will react in the same way. This is because, if you are to distinguish between those parents who are satisfied with schooling and those who are not, you must have statements that discriminate. To select the final statements for your scale you will need to compile a draft from the statements that you have collected, making sure to have approximately the same number of positive and negative statements. They should be arranged randomly (for example, by drawing the item numbers from a bag). In order to test the discriminative power of each item, and to reject those that are the weakest in this respect, the draft should be given to a large (as a rule of thumb, at least thirty) *pilot* sample of respondents. The profile of the pilot sample should, if at all possible, match that of the population you wish to investigate in the main study. On the basis of the scores obtained, the respondents should be placed in rank order and the power of each item to discriminate between the top 25 per cent and the bottom 25 per cent tested (see Robson, 2002, p. 295 for the procedure for this). The final scale should have around twenty-five statements (again with approximately equal numbers of positive and negative statements) selected from those with the greatest discriminative power and again arranged randomly.

The aim of this procedure is to produce an instrument for the measurement of opinions, attitudes, beliefs or orientations that has face validity, is internally consistent, has discriminative power and is reliable. We have presented this to illustrate the difficulty in gathering information and making comparisons that go beyond collection of reports of personal experience and accounts of ready-at-hand knowledge. In our experience, beginning researchers do not take sufficient care in the construction of these kinds of instruments. In particular there is a temptation to treat the responses to individual statements in Likert, and similar, scales as if they were discrete items in a questionnaire. Errors such as this are common, even amongst more experienced researchers.

Online resources

There are a number of online resources that may be useful in conducting surveys.

• University of Surrey's ESRC-funded Question Bank

The Question Bank is an information resource, in the field of social research, with a particular emphasis on quantitative survey methods. This website has been designed to help users locate examples of specific research questions and see them in the context within which they have been used for data collection. It is intended to assist with the design of new survey questionnaires, the search for data for secondary analysis, and the teaching of survey research methods.

(qb.soc.surrey.ac.uk)

• Online surveys – tools for carrying out online surveys

  • Bristol Online Surveys (£500 p.a. site licence)

A standard Bristol Online Surveys (BOS) account costs £500 plus VAT per annum. This allows you to create as many surveys and account users as you wish. You can upload a logo of your choice and then use this on a survey-by-survey basis. There is no limit on the number of people you survey or their location. We only ask that you notify us if you plan to survey 100,000's or millions of potential respondents!

(www.survey.bris.ac.uk)

  • Zoomerang

  Free 'basic' service – thirty questions and 100 replies – responses available only for ten days (info.zoomerang.com).

  • Survey Monkey

  Free basic service – ten questions and 100 replies (www.surveymonkey.com).

Interviewing

The advantages of the use of interviews to a large extent mirror the limitations of questionnaires discussed above. Interviews enable the researcher to explore complex issues in detail, they facilitate the personal engagement of the researcher in the collection of data, they allow the researcher to provide clarification, to probe and to prompt. Similarly the limitations mirror the advantages of questionnaires. Interviews are time-consuming and thus place practical restrictions on sample size. Freeform responses to open ended questions can be difficult to analyse and the direct interaction of the interviewer and the interviewee can give rise to forms of interviewer bias less evident in the setting of a self-completed questionnaire. As in our treatment of other ways of collecting information, we will not attempt to argue the superiority of one method over any other. The selection of one particular method or combination of methods has to be related to the problem being addressed, and thus to the general theoretical framework within which the researcher is working, and to the particularities of the empirical setting.

In its most operationally structured form, an interview can resemble a personally administered questionnaire, with the interviewer following a standard format and reading a list of predetermined questions in an attempt to make the realisation of the interview as consistent as possible across the sample. Each interviewee is offered a series of stimuli (the questions) in a standard form. That is, the same wording is used for the questions and the questions are always asked in the same order for each interview. The responses of the interviewee are recorded, usually in terms of precoded categories. The main advantage over the use of, say, a postal questionnaire is that the interviewer can provide clarification if the interviewee experiences difficulties or appears to misinterpret questions. It also enables the interviewer to collect contextual information not accessible using a respondent-administered questionnaire.

At the other extreme, the interview might be described as relatively unstructured. The term 'semi-structured interview' or 'loosely structured interview' is commonly employed. We do not wish to legislate on the use of these terms, but have avoided them, here, as they seem to leave open a space for an interview without any structure at all. We shall use the term 'unstructured interview' together with a caveat that it should not be taken too literally, because there can be no such thing as an interview without any structure. The interviewer will always bring some agenda or general purpose to bear on the activity and will generally impose some theoretical and/or methodological selection in terms of the location and conditions in which it takes place and so forth.

With these qualifications, the 'unstructured interview' might be described as more closely resembling a conversation, with the interviewer working from a relatively loose set of guidelines. Here the questions are open and the format flexible. The prime concern of the interviewer might be to explore the world from the perspective of the interviewee and to construct an understanding of how the interviewee makes sense of their experiences. In this case the use of standard questions and a fixed format would be unduly constraining. The intensity of the interaction between interviewer and interviewee will necessitate that the interview be recorded in some way, for example, using an MP3 audio recorder or perhaps a digital pen that also records audio, such as the one described in the previous chapter. The analysis will focus on making sense of what the interviewee says and how they say it.

These two forms of interview are often presented as the products of contrasting views of social knowledge. On the one hand, a positivist approach to social research is construed as a search for social facts, which, therefore, gives rise to a closed, survey-style interview. On the other hand, an interpretivist approach is understood as a search for meanings that generates a more open, ethnographic form of interview. More pragmatically the contrast is commonly drawn, first, between structured interviews and unstructured interviews. Between these two extremes is often constructed a more or less complex typology of interviews which variously combine structured components with opportunities for more open interaction.

Making sense of these forms of interview in terms of opposing epistemological positions (positivism versus interpretivism) is, in our opinion, not tenable and, in any event, is unlikely to advance your research in respect of your addressing of your specific problem. As with our earlier consideration of observational methods, we wish to look at this diversity neither in epistemological terms nor in terms of whether interviews are themselves structured, semi-structured or unstructured, but rather as a range of approaches that differ with respect to the point at which the researcher imposes structure on information to produce data. Rather than engage in an exposition of interview typology and the relative merits of each type, we will concentrate on those features of the design and conduct common to all forms of interview.

All interviews involve interaction. We shall consider both the form of the relation between interviewer and interviewee and the nature of the interview as an interactional context. The interviewer clearly has an agenda and has constructed what we might refer to as the interview-as-event as a setting for data collection. Each step in the construction of the interview-as-event warrants close attention. For instance, the location of the interview is important. In interviewing parents about their views on their child's school, for example, a strong identification of the interviewer with the school may have an inhibiting effect on the interviewee. The researcher thus has to consider whether the interviews should be held in the school, at the interviewee's home or elsewhere. If, in order to make the interviewee feel at ease, they are offered a choice of location, the researcher has to consider to what extent the data from interviews held in school and interviews held at home are comparable.

There is no 'correct' answer to this kind of question. There are no neutral locations, nor are there hard and fast rules for determining the effects of location, just as there is no way of determining what effect the presence of an observer has upon activity in a setting. It is incumbent upon the researcher to ensure that any obvious and unintended effects of the setting are minimised and taken into account when formulating the findings of the research. In particular, if comparisons are to be made, the researcher should ensure that, as far as possible, like is being compared with like.

Similar consideration has to be given to the manner in which interviewers present themselves to interviewees. Few interviews occur spontaneously. In most cases interviewers make a deliberate effort to introduce themselves to their interviewees, by letter, email, telephone or in person. Exactly who the interviewee thinks they are talking to, and why, will affect what they say. The researcher thus has to consider what they tell the interviewee prior to the interview, both with respect to their own position and the nature of the research being carried out. Should letters asking parents if they are willing to be interviewed be written on university letterheaded paper? Should interviewers present themselves to teachers as colleagues, or as outsiders? Sometimes the interviewer is already known to the interviewee, and no introduction is necessary. Even more care has to be taken in considering the effects that this may have on the interview. The authority relations that characterise the relationship between a headteacher and a member of their staff, for instance, might not be conducive to a frank discussion of teacher attitudes to appraisal. A trainee teacher will talk in a particular way to a lecturer associated with their training programme. The nature of the interaction will change further once the trainee becomes a qualified teacher.

Consideration needs to be given to other features of the relationship between interviewer and interviewee and the positioning strategies brought into play in the interview setting. In some cases there are fundamental interviewer characteristics that have an unavoidable effect on the interview. For instance, children become accustomed to certain forms of questioning in school. Often, questioning is used by teachers in order to test children's understanding or knowledge. The relationship between the child and the teacher is such that the child might make every effort to say what they think the teacher wants to hear. Any adults asking children questions can thus find themselves engaged in this kind of interaction.

Gender and social class relations will also affect the form an interview takes. An interview with a middle-class man about childrearing practices might be viewed somewhat differently by working-class as compared with middle-class young mothers. Sometimes social distance can be useful in a research setting (for instance, talking to an obvious outsider might encourage interviewees to be more explicit about their practices), in other cases it might prove inhibiting. In some circumstances, through deliberate control of the form of introduction, dress and manner, these effects can be manipulated or moderated; in others this is not possible and may not be desirable.

There are additional issues that arise with online or *e-interviews* that relate to the discussions on internet research in Chapter 5. Two key distinctions in modes of e-interview might be made: is the interview to be conducted synchronously or asynchronously; and what mode or modes of communication are to be used? In synchronous format, text chat and audio or video chat or a combination (e.g. by Skype) are available, as is high-quality video conferencing, if you have access to such facilities; email would be the principal asynchronmous format. It is also possible, using, for example, Yahoo Groups (groups.yahoo.com), to set up a discussion board that would allow the structuring of the interview by threads (i.e. interview topics); a similar result would be possible using the email 'subject' field to differentiate between topics. Group e-interviews are also facilitated by the discussion board format. Synchronous video conferencing is clearly quite close to the f2f interview, but we move progressively further away from this situation as video and audio are eliminated and, finally, as we shift into asynchronous communication. This last form is particularly useful when interviewer and interviewee are in different time zones and it may be difficult to arrange synchronous communication. Email also has the advantage of allowing for reflection during the interview by both interviewer and interviewee and does permit the diversification of modes of communication (image and voice, for example) by email attachments. In addition, email, of course, does not need transcription. On the other hand, some cues that may be important in synchronous interviews – delays or uncertainties in response, for example – are missing. Spoken and written language use generally take different forms; we tend, in informal conversations, not to speak in sentences, for example, and the fact that the interviewee has time to reflect on and edit their responses allows for *post hoc* rationalisation; these features of text-based asynchronous communication may not be in keeping with the kind of interview environment that the interviewer wants to establish. Ultimately, decisions have to made in relation to the research question as well as to what is practically possible and, if the demands of the former cannot be met by the exigencies of the latter, then this will have implications for the kinds of claim that can be made.

The brief discussion above illustrates the importance of thinking the interview through from the point of initial contact with the interviewee. The management of the interview itself requires equally close attention. Thought needs to be given to how the interview begins. What form of preamble do you need to place the interview in context? Do you need to provide reassurance that what is said will be treated as confidential and reported anonymously? Do you need to gain consent for the interview to be audio (or video) recorded? The initial stages of a live interview are particularly important in helping the interviewee to feel at ease, so the preamble should cover the necessary ground but not be too formal; a short 'warm-up' period is generally advisable. Similarly at the end of an interview there is a need for a 'cool-down' period and closing section in which the end of the interview is clearly marked. Here the interviewee can be thanked and clarification given regarding what will be done with the information gathered.

At the beginning of the main body of the interview it is essential to provide the interviewee with initial stimuli – questions or activities – with which they can easily engage. As a rule it helps to move from the particular to the general as interviewees often find abstract questions difficult to address, particularly if they concern issues to which they have given little or no prior thought. Brown (1999) showed parents examples of mathematical activities that they had previously carried out with their children. The initial questions asked for an account of what the interviewee had done with the activities. Later questions moved on to consider, in a more analytic fashion, what they thought the activities achieved and what they thought each activity was designed to teach. Following on from this, the interviewee's criteria for the evaluation of school mathematics tasks were explored. To move directly from the preamble to abstract questions concerning criteria would not have been fruitful. Questions drawing on the direct experience of the interviewees and calling for a narrative response acted as a way in to detailed discussion of more general concerns.

Questions of a personal or sensitive nature, which the interviewee might feel awkward about answering, are also best left until later in the interview. Just what constitutes a potentially sensitive question is itself not always easy to judge and will vary between interviewees. As a general rule, it is better to be safe rather than sorry and leave all questions soliciting personal information (other than identification details) until the latter part of the interview. At this point there will be greater rapport between interviewer and interviewee. Furthermore, if the interviewee is reluctant to address a particular question, all is not lost as the main part of the interview will have been completed.

The form that questions take will vary according the type of interview. The interviewer needs to be clear about the extent to which it is important to ask the same questions in the same order, that is, to standardise the interview process. They also need to consider what prompts they will give if interviewees have difficulty in answering questions and decide how far they are willing to probe and what form their probes will take. As with the design of questionnaires, interviews should avoid double-barrelled, long and complex questions, questions involving technical or esoteric language, leading questions and loaded questions. In the interview itself the interviewer needs to show that they are engaged and interested, deliver questions in a clear and straightforward fashion and avoid providing cues. No matter how many interviews you have carried out or how much the interview process has become routinised, it is important to be seen to enjoy and value the interview and to listen attentively to what the interviewee says.

The points raised above provide very basic advice on the design and conduct of interviews. The researcher should have a high degree of control over the interview and it is important that sufficient thought go into its design and realisation. As with other means of data collection it is vital to carry out a number of pilot interviews and to refine the interview on the basis of this work; this applies to e-interviews as well as to more conventional forms. It is also important to practice interviewing as there are distinct interviewing skills that do not come naturally to everyone. Recording yourself and listening back through the recordings will help you to develop your live interviewing technique. At the end of practice and pilot interviews you can ask the interviewee to reflect on the experience of being interviewed. This provides invaluable feedback and will help develop both the interview schedule you are working on and your own expertise as an interviewer.

The conduct of the interviews is, of course, just a start. Unless the responses are recorded using precoded categories or email is being used, it will be necessary to transcribe the interviews. We suggest that, unless the number of interviews is prohibitive or you are working in a language in which you are not fully fluent, you should transcribe the interviews yourself. This fosters greater familiarity with the interview text and enables you to note the subtler nuances of the interaction. You will need to adopt a set of transcription conventions (see, for instance, those used by Silverman, 2006, pp. 398–9). It is important to ensure that the level of detail of the transcription matches the use to be made of the transcripts. In some forms of analysis, such as *conversational analysis*, it is important to have a record of the duration of hesitations between utterances (usually measured in tenths of a second), but for most forms of analysis such detailed transcription is not necessary.

The production of accurate transcripts from audio recordings is, in any case, a lengthy process. It certainly helps if the source media are of a good quality. We recommend that you use good-quality microphones, preferably lapel microphones for one-to-one interviews or a stereo microphone for group interviews. If using a tape recorder, avoid the use of integral microphones that can pick up a lot of noise from the motor; this is not a problem with a digital recorder that is unlikely to have any moving parts. The use of a stereo rather than a mono recorder can also greatly enhance the clarity of your recording. Ideally, use an MP3 digital recording device and a good-quality stereo microphone or lapel microphones. With high-quality source media and good typing skills, each hour of tape will take at least three hours to transcribe. With poor-quality recordings and/or complex settings, such as a group interview, transcription can take a good deal longer.

Gathering information and asking questions: conclusion

In this chapter we have discussed a range of approaches to the use of accounts as a source of data. These accounts might be the product of a direct encounter between the researcher and the subject in a setting specifically designed for the purpose (e.g. the clinical interview). In contrast the accounts might be the incidental products of everyday activity (e.g. policy documents produced within a school). As with the approaches to observation discussed in the previous chapter, there might also be variation in the extent to which the method of data collection structures the data at a very early stage. The most marked contrast here is between the use of a self-completed postal questionnaire on one hand and the open-ended, apparently unstructured interview on the other.

In considering these contrasting forms of data collection we have attempted to evaluate the strengths and weaknesses of each and to make some practical suggestions regarding their use. We have taken care to avoid the promotion of one form of data collection over and above any other. This does not mean that we see the selection of methods of data collection in purely pragmatic terms. Although we have refrained from engaging in the form of epistemological positioning that would ultimately lead us to argue the essential superiority of a particular method, we have conducted our discussion within an overall approach that stresses the need to articulate the design of the empirical component of the research with the theoretical framework within which the research is conducted. To do this the researcher must be clear about the form of data they require and the logic of the various forms of data collection available to them.

The possibility of in-depth discussion and extensive probing that is offered by the clinical interview makes this approach particularly apposite for the exploration of types of human reasoning. The precise form of the interview and the manner in which the utterances and actions of the interviewee are interpreted are related to the theoretical perspective adopted by the researcher. There are, for instance, distinct differences between the form of clinical interviews carried out by Piaget and colleagues and those conducted by Luria (from a broadly Vygotskian perspective). There are even more marked differences between the ways in which the utterances and actions of the interviewees are interpreted.

A highly structured questionnaire would not be appropriate in these circumstances. A questionnaire simplifies the gathering of information from a large sample. Once the empirical data requirements pass beyond the informational, however, the limitations of questionnaires become clear. The questions by necessity have to be viewed as stimuli, held constant across the sample. The recipient of the questionnaire becomes a respondent, reading the question and marking their response. On collecting together the responses, the researcher can ascertain that when asked a given question a specific proportion of certain kinds of people responded in a particular way. For example, the statement might be made 'in our survey, 75 per cent of cat owners said that their cat preferred Tiddles cat food to any other brand'. Exactly what this might mean is, again, dependent upon the researcher's theoretical framework: what is it that enables cat owners to stand as key informants in respect of their pets' preferences, or is it, in fact, their own preferences that are actually being measured? If not, just what are the concept variables that are being addressed via the survey? Ultimately, the selection of a particular technique and its realisation in the empirical setting are the result of an interaction between the possibilities offered (and denied) by a particular form of data collection and the theoretical framework within which the research is conceived.

When dealing with accounts, the researcher has to be particularly clear about the status accorded to the accounts they are analysing. The survey of cat owners, for instance, does not tell us that Tiddles is the best-tasting cat food nor that cats particularly like it. The human respondents are not in a position to judge this. They are only able to respond to questions that lie within the scope of their knowledge and experience. In a clinical interview, the responses of the interviewee are probed and tested by the interviewer and their utterances are interpreted as indicators of the operation of underlying cognitive processes. In an unstructured interview conducted from an interpretivist viewpoint it is not the response of the interviewee to a given stimulus (e.g. a question) that is of interest but the manner in which this is interpreted by the interviewee. The interview is an investigation of the way in which the interviewee constructs meanings. In all these cases different status is accorded to what people say (and how they say it).

Whatever the status given to what is said and done by an interviewee or respondent, there must be a clear distinction between the interviewee/respondent as the source of data and the researcher as the analyst of the data. In conducting a study you are not asking your interviewees to provide explanations, unless, of course, you are studying their explanations – in which case it is these that you have to analyse. Nor are you asking them to validate your analysis. The analysis is the responsibility of the researcher and in many cases may be at odds with the way in which the interviewee/respondent views their own behaviour. It is to the process of analysis that we now turn in Chapters 7 and 8.

Chapter 7

Quality in analysis

Introduction: organisational language

Previous chapters have explored various approaches to the collection of data; this chapter and the next will consider what you do with the data once you've collected it. In our experience in working with masters students on their dissertations, we have very often encountered the belief that, once the data has been collected, then the job is pretty much done – no, no, no! In fact, as doctoral students, who have more time for their projects, very soon realise, it's only just begun. Data analysis – and in this chapter we are referring to qualitative data analysis – is difficult, messy, uncertain and highly demanding in respect of intellect and inspiration. Certainly, the availability of qualitative data analysis software has made easier certain of the tasks associated with this phase of research. Such software has allowed us to do away with the need to make multiple photocopies of transcripts of interview and fieldnote data to be colour-coded, cut up and arranged in sets on the floor, for example, and has greatly expedited search-and-retrieve actions. However, qualitative analysis software does not do the analysis itself and, indeed, actually does far less than the equivalent software used in quantitative analysis – more of that in the next chapter and more on the use of software in qualitative data analysis later in this chapter.

Qualitative analysis is very often undertaken by individuals working alone and the process itself is rarely spoken about. Supervisors will engage with their students' data to a limited extent, though often this is made difficult when, for example, the data is in a language that the supervisor does not speak. We have found collaborative research to be highly effective in generating dialogic inspiration for analysis. Inevitably, though, analysis is achieved by reading and by thinking, and these activities tend to be carried out in private.

This is not to say that nothing can be said that can assist this process; far from it. There are numerous approaches that provide some structure to the work of analysis. Very influential in educational and social research is the approach of 'grounded theory'. This was first introduced by Barney Glaser and Anselm Strauss (1967) and, since then these two authors have produced different versions that are somewhat in tension with each other (for example, Strauss, 1987; Glaser, 1992; Corbin and Strauss, 2008). The works cited here provide apparatuses that are intended to assist in the generation of theory out of data, though there is a widespread tendency for educational and social researchers to make selective use of them. We do not propose to provide a detailed account of grounded theory, here. However, it is worth mentioning one aspect that was a key feature of the earlier work and retains a high profile in the Glaser version of grounded theory; this is the method of constant comparison. As one might expect, this entails the constant comparison of emerging categories and their theoretical description with the data that has been collected. A very productive strategy here is the writing of memos. As a category emerges, the analyst attempts to outline the concept that they are developing in general terms, also including direct references to the data. Memos may be of any length and may be amended, rewritten, refined or even discarded as the analysis proceeds.

It is worth also adding that grounded theory very much sees data collection and data analysis in dialogic relation, the one informing and directing the other. It may not always be possible to maintain an ideal dialogue – the data collection phase may be tightly framed in terms of when, where, with whom, etc. – but we would nevertheless want to emphasise that qualitative data collection and analysis should never be seen as sequential phases; data analysis begins at the same time as data collection begins, even if the former may continue for some time after the latter ends.

So what is data analysis? Well, the data that you will have collected (whether or not the collection process is complete) will consist of interview transcripts, fieldnotes, images, documents and so forth. All of these data will be associated with particular contexts in the empirical setting and, in general, you will assume that their meanings will be given in relation to those contexts. The analysis of these data involves referring them to a more or less coherent theoretical framework, or what Dowling (2009) refers to as an *organisational language*. This language consists of the categories that, in general, have been developed during the process of the analysis itself. Let's take as an illustration the construction and deployment of a computer database for personal records.

Most of us will be in possession of diverse items of information about our family, friends, colleagues, various services that we use more or less frequently and so on. These will be in various forms, including, perhaps, entries in an address book, visiting cards, letters and postcards, scraps of paper and post-it notes, telephone directories and so on. Each of these items will have an individual form that is to a greater or lesser extent unique and specific to the particular context in which it was generated. However, suppose that we now decide to incorporate all of these items of information into a contacts list on a computer. The contacts list is a form of database that is designed to enable us to perform a number of tasks. For example, it may enable us to search our list under various headings, it may print address labels, allow us to make phone calls directly from the computer, or enable the automatic importing and exporting of entries. In order for these functions to work in respect of each entry in the list, the entries must comply to a common format. The names, addresses and phone numbers must be entered in specific forms, we will be required to specify categories and, perhaps, keywords for each entry, and so forth.

When we have completed the contacts list, each item of localised information will have been transformed into a datum within a general structure. We will have lost something of the context specificity of the entries – the little heart drawn next to the phone number carefully and invitingly written on the back of my hand – but we will have gained a powerful tool. Powerful because of the generalisability of the database in retrieving and organising its contents (and I can now wash my hands). Of course, in this illustration, it is likely that most of us would use generic software – 'Address Book' on the Apple Macintosh OS – but it is, of course, perfectly possible to design one's own database that develops in structure as we work through our raw data of personal records. In either case, at the completion of the exercise, we will be able to refer to our data in terms of different categories of record – family, friends, services, romantic potential – and refer to any given category in terms of a range of subcategories – name, address, phone, email, lost hearts. This is, minimally, what analysis does: it organises our data according to a common organisational language that now gives its meaning to each datum.

The power of our database will depend upon a number of things. First, it should be as internally explicit and coherent as possible, so that its various categories are clear in terms of the ways in which they relate to each other. What, for example, is the distinction between the first and second lines of the home address in terms of the ways in which the database will make use of them? Second, it should be as relationally complete as possible. The various functions of the database cannot make full use of its contents unless they cover all of the various fields. Third – and this is the central issue for the purposes of these two chapters – the information must have been entered in a way that is consistent with the operational intentions of the database. Clearly, there is a considerable amount of flexibility in terms of the entering of data. The database may not allow us to enter 'text' in a 'date' field and, sadly, the heart on my hand will probably have to go, but it will probably not prevent us from entering a telephone number as the 'city' or categorising our grandmother as a plumber.

Similar criteria can be established for the evaluation of the analytic stage of the research process. Some form of theory is absolutely essential. There must be some structure that generalises our local observations. The power of our analysis will then depend upon three criteria:

- the internal explicitness and coherence of the theory;
- the relational completeness of the theory;
- the integrity of the concept–indicator links.

The last criterion refers to the extent to which data is being read appropriately and consistently, that is, to the validity and the reliability of the data, respectively.

Qualitative and quantitative analysis

Analysis can be performed in many different ways. A distinction is often made in terms of whether or not the information is counted, that is, whether the analysis is made in quantitative or qualitative terms. For example, we could precode the addresses of our contact list database as London postal districts. The address for each record for a London address would be entered simply as a mark (say a '1') against the relevant district. This would enable us to plot out the distribution of our contacts in the London area as a chart and to investigate possible patterns in terms of the other precoded categories of our database (do the plumbers that we know tend to live in South London?). It would not, of course, enable us to print out the envelopes for our Christmas cards.

Unfortunately, in our view, a great deal of educational research has tended to be polarised as either quantitative or qualitative in approach. Indeed, many of the available books on research methods announce themselves, often in their titles, as being concerned exclusively with one or the other. As with so many of the distinctions that are made in this area, the basis for the qualitative/quantitative polarisation is frequently argued in terms of traditional epistemological divisions. Qualitative approaches are often associated with research that is carried out in an interpretative frame in which the concern is with the production of meaning. Quantitative methods are, correspondingly, associated with positivist forms of enquiry that are concerned with the search for facts. In turn, these forms have become polarised in politically motivated debate that has associated interpretivism with the so-called 'softer' social sciences and positivism with the 'hard' and more fundable natural sciences. This latter distinction was brought to the foreground by the insistence by the Conservative Party former Secretary of State for Education and Science, Sir Keith Joseph, on the Social Science Research Council (SSRC) changing its name so as to eliminate the word 'science'; it became, and still is, the Economic and Social Research Council (ESRC).

There are, in other words, traditional and political motives for maintaining the qualitative/quantitative distinction. There are also reasons that relate to the training of educational and social science researchers. Specifically, a high degree of mathematical competence is not universally required or provided by university courses. This being the case, we are unlikely to be able to subvert the division by our argument in this book. In any case, we do see some value in sustaining the distinction for analytic and for pedagogic purposes, provided that we can resist any temptation to allow it to harden into a binary choice: either qualitative or quantitative, but not both.

As we shall argue in Chapter 9, empirical research is fundamentally concerned with the *generalising* of local findings to wider ranges of empirical settings. The distinction between qualitative and quantitative approaches is, in our opinion, best described in terms of the different sets of resources that are deployed in establishing such generalisations. Quantitative approaches rely on probability theory. We cannot give an elaboration of this highly technical field in this book. Essentially, though, it construes the world as ultimately describable in terms of equally likely events. To take a simple example, the numbers one to six may be taken to represent, exhaustively, the six equally likely outcomes when you throw an ordinary die. Of course, the notion that these six outcomes are equally likely is built into the way in which we use dice in games or for gambling. The existence of such a close association between the elements of probability theory, on the one hand, and the structures of social practices more generally, or even those of natural phenomena, on the other, is far less obvious. In their recruitment of probability theory, then, quantitative research methods impose a particular theoretical framework, a particular *bias*, upon the world.

The considerable advantage of quantitative analysis, however, lies in the very high degree of coherence of this theoretical framework. This coherence enables issues of reliability and of generalisation to be addressed with a high degree of consistency and, for those who are prepared to become familiar with statistical language, with a high degree of transparency. Paradoxically, the disadvantages of quantitative methods lie in precisely the same place. The coherence and self-referentiality of statistical knowledge also entails that it is relatively immutable with respect to local empirical settings and educationally specialised, theoretical problems. In this respect, it might be argued with some justification that what quantitative methods gain in reliability, they lose in respect of validity. Statisticians, of course, will reply that they can measure validity. But, again, they can achieve this only by imposing the same probabilistic framework.

Qualitative approaches do not impose probability theory or even, necessarily, the natural number system on their settings. They thereby lose both the power and the rigidity of quantitative methods. The researcher employing qualitative techniques is relieved of the requirement to specify their coding principles sufficiently uniformly to enable their data to be counted. But if it cannot be counted, then it must be represented in some other way. In general, accounts must include extracts from texts or transcripts, summaries of fieldnotes and so on. The researcher is then able to present an argument that establishes the validity of their interpretations, that is, they present an *elaborated description*. This process both develops and makes visible the operationalisation of the theoretical problem, elaborating its validity. In our own experience, it is also an invaluable stage in the development of the theory itself and might be realised in the writing of the memos mentioned above in relation to grounded theory. This is, of course, immensely expensive in terms of both time and, in an account, space, especially if new description is to be produced for each element of the data that is to be represented. In the account of the research, an argument must be made – again in terms of elaborated description – about the representative value of each data element that is presented as an example.

Unfortunately, there is a tendency for some researchers employing quantitative and qualitative approaches to hide behind the method and ignore the crucial area of theoretical development. The naive use of quantitative methods imagines that statistical techniques themselves will guarantee the value of the work. Correspondingly naive qualitative research tends to substitute narrative for analysis.[1] On the other hand, the adoption of a dual approach involving both qualitative and quantitative techniques can help in overcoming such tendencies to what we might refer to as naive empiricism. The qualitative imagination will tend to demand that quantitative analysis explain itself in terms of the non-statistical concepts that it is claiming to measure. The quantitative imagination will demand a degree of precision in definition that qualitative work may slide away from. It is our position, then, that the best option will often be for a dialogical use of a combination of qualitative and quantitative methods.

For pedagogic reasons, however, we will continue to maintain a general distinction between the approaches. In the remainder of this chapter we will focus on qualitative methods of analysis. We will move on to quantitative techniques in Chapter 8.

We will add one caveat. There are, in our opinion, two very good reasons why research writing and, in particular, writing about research methods is comparatively silent on the process of data analysis. First, the process is always intimately bound up with the very specific nature of the research problem and the local characteristics of the empirical setting and the data that has been gathered. This means that an adequate description of the analytic process must involve a considerable amount of contextual information. Second, in describing analysis, one is, as we have pointed out above, attempting to get at one's own thought processes. This is a project that is itself worthy of research. Writing about analysis is, in other words, difficult. You should be warned, then, that this might not be an easy chapter to read. Our intention is that your coming to grips with some of the analyses that we present will, itself, contribute to your apprenticeship as a researcher.

Reading the signs: semiotic analysis and the location of the problem

We shall begin with an example of a qualitative analysis of a text – in this case an image. There has been an expanding interest in the analysis of texts in educational research over the past twenty years or so (see Dowling, 1998, 2009). In fact, however, we are using this example as an introduction to and illustration of approaches to qualitative analysis more generally. In particular, the analysis and the subsequent discussion illustrate the importance of defining adequately both the empirical setting to which the data relates and the theoretical problem that enables the researcher to think about the setting. Specifically, we shall indicate the importance of aligning the theoretical problem with the motivation for the research. The general methodological basis of the analysis in this section lies within the field of semiotics, which itself is associated with structural linguistics and with the very broad theoretical fields of structuralism (which includes Piaget and is more loosely associated with Vygotsky and Luria), post-structuralism and postmodernist writing. These fields have been immensely influential in educational research and are becoming more so. Our example, then, also provides something of an overture to this substantial body of work.

The analysis that follows was originally conducted by Dowling as a part of a conference workshop which he ran on the analysis of texts. Its object text is the photograph in Figure 7.1. This is the data that is to be analysed. The form of analysis that is being conducted here is, in general terms, referred to as semiotic analysis. We shall say a little more about this below.

Figure 7.1 'Gun Law'.

The text shows an American soldier suppressing a Haitian. The soldier is a very powerful man, rendered almost monumental by the camera angle. He is armed with a fearsome weapon, which he is prepared to fire – his finger clearly rests on the trigger. The soldier is vigilant, on the watch for further trouble. Yet this is a benevolent soldier. Although he holds a deadly weapon, it is pointed downwards and not at anyone. He holds the Haitian down with his knee – a minimum amount of force.

The Haitian contrasts starkly with the soldier. He appears physically small – a feature exaggerated by the foreshortening effect of the camera angle. He is weak and easily suppressed by the soldier, who does not need to use his gun. A stick lies on the ground. This might have been a weapon dropped by the Haitian as the soldier pinned him down; a primitive weapon for primitive people. There are two groups of Haitians in the background. One group, on the left, seems to be engaging in a brawl. The members of the other group, in the top right, appear indifferent to the action. Behind the soldier lies a pile of rubble. Behind him and to his left, a media sound recordist is recording the action for the news.

Clearly, some interpretation has already taken place in this description of the text. The stick might not, after all, be a weapon, for example. This interpretation has been guided by an orientation to another level of description that we want to make, that is, of what we shall term the 'mythical' figures constituted by the image. The USA – represented by the soldier – is constituted as a powerful but benevolent state. This state takes on an altruistic responsibility for other, less developed nations, protecting primitive societies from self-destruction. Haiti is represented as precisely such a society, characterised by criminality, apathy and low-level technology, and already lying in ruins. The press, represented by the sound recordist and by the photographer (in the place of the observer), is shown as a neutral organ, telling it like it is.

Now the question that must be asked is: does it matter where the photograph appears? If it appears on the cover of *Time* magazine, then we may well feel that the above reading is appropriate. Suppose, however, that it appears on the cover of *Living Marxism*. In this case we would probably reject the celebration of America and the disparaging of the Third World state. Rather, we would probably interpret the text as ironic: this is how America thinks of itself and of its neighbours and this is precisely the problem in contemporary global politics. After all, the gaze of the soldier resembles nothing so much as the optimistic gazes of the blond youths in so many Nazi images. In fact, the text was taken from the front page of *The Guardian*, a UK newspaper with a broadly centre-left editorial orientation. Here, perhaps, the text signifies the journal's own neutrality in the play between the literal and ironic readings of the photograph.

So now we have three readings of the text: a literal reading; an ironic reading; and, in the terms of the other two, a neutral reading. Which is the correct one, or is there another? Clearly, the choice depends upon the adequate definition of the empirical setting. In this case, this entails, minimally, naming the publication in which the image appears. However, the situation is more complex than that. In fact, each analysis violates the condition that the theoretical framework, or organisational language that enables it, should be explicit. One or more of the analyses may appear plausible, but this is because they implicitly address organisational languages that the reader already possesses. They make assumptions about the reader or, in other words, they construct an ideal or model reader. This being the case, they cannot tell us very much that we didn't already know, about this particular image, about global politics, or about the news media.

Another example may help. Roland Barthes's *Mythologies* (Barthes, 1972) has been very influential in semiotic forms of analysis. Semiotics is an expression introduced by the linguist Ferdinand de Saussure to refer to the study of *signs*. A *sign*, Saussure suggested, is constituted by a *signifier* and a *signified*. The former term refers to an acoustic or visual memory of a word, spoken or written; the latter refers to the concept to which the signifier attaches. Thus, the image of the word 'cat' attaches to a concept of a furry, domestic quadruped that catches mice. In *Mythologies* Barthes famously introduced another soldier. In this case, the text appeared as the front cover of an issue of the French popular journal, *Paris Match*. The illustration on the cover showed a young black soldier in the uniform of the French army. The soldier was saluting, his eyes raised, as if gazing on the tricolour. Barthes argued that this sign becomes the signifier, a higher order of signification, thus:

> France is a great Empire, that all her sons without any colour discrimination, faithfully serve under her flag, and [. . .] there is no better answer to the detractors of an alleged colonialism than the zeal shown by this negro in serving his so-called oppressors.
>
> (Barthes, 1972, p. 116)

The new, higher-order sign, Barthes referred to as *myth*. The cover illustration appeared around 1954, at the height of the Algerian uprising. Barthes approached the text from a politically left-of-centre position. His reading of the myth was clearly constituted within the context of his understanding of the political positioning of *Paris Match*, which is to say, of its construction of its ideal reader. In the absence of such knowledge, it is clearly possible to constitute alternative myths, for example:

> France is a major colonial power. This soldier, serving in the uniform of his oppressors, illustrates the extent of the domination of Algerian culture by the French hegemony.

Or, again:

> France has not been content with educating the savages of Africa, it has risked the contamination of its own culture by allowing them to participate in it. This soldier represents the extent of this contamination of a white race by black primitives.

The particular interpretation that is made depends upon the ideological position that is occupied by the interpreter. Because this is always implicit, it is no substitute for an explicit theoretical framework. Barthes's contribution, however, was less in the political specificity of his analyses – which, nevertheless, have considerable literary value – than in the general method that he was applying and which he summarised in a diagram, which is reproduced in Figure 7.2.

Essentially, Barthes is extending the schema of the linguistic sign, as proposed by Saussure, to enable analysis to refer to broader cultural schemes. Language constitutes signs, but myth attaches higher-order significations to these signs. The cover of *Paris*

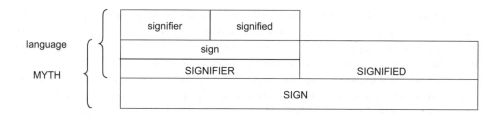

Figure 7.2 Barthes's analytic schema (from Barthes, 1972, p. 115).

Match incorporates a number of signs that we can recognise because we participate in a common visual language. Thus, the image of the black soldier is understood to signify, precisely, a black soldier. Once the text is read within language, it is available for the higher-order interpretation, which is constituted by the level of organisational languages that have facilitated the analyses of both of the soldiers referred to here. This higher, mythical level of interpretation is dependent upon the 'linguistic' interpretation of the sign; if we don't recognise the image, then we won't be able to constitute the myth.

Barthes's interest is in how the text works culturally as well as strictly linguistically. The theoretical scheme is comprised of semiotic concepts – signifiers, signifieds, signs, language and myth. It provides a common framework for the analysis of potentially any text. But each analysis that we conduct will serve only to confirm that the analysed text can, indeed, be understood to be working according to Barthes's semiotic scheme. Each text is thus constituted as data in respect of a semiotic claim. There is, however, no way of choosing between the different ideological or mythical systems to which we refer the text. Each of the above analyses is, in this respect, equivalent. This is because Barthes's theoretical problem lies within the field of semiotics and not sociology or, say, political science. You may be interested in producing a semiotic grammar of the text. This would certainly be of value to an educator wishing to develop an educational programme in reading such texts. However, if you want to produce a sociological or a political analysis of the text, then your theoretical problem must comprise concepts that relate to these fields. Your theory must be concerned with what you are interested in, otherwise it is, like statistical methods, not a theory so much as a technique.

Biasing the description

The discussion above enables us to write a fourth criterion for the evaluation of the analytic stage of educational research to add to those that we introduced earlier:

*   the organisational language must relate directly to the system about which claims are to be made.

If you intend to constitute your information as psychological data, then your organisational language must employ psychological concepts. This, of course, entails that any text is susceptible to any number of analyses, depending upon the nature and specificity of the organisational language that we are employing. This is not to say, of course, that any analysis will do. Our position is that they must, at least, measure up adequately in terms of the other three criteria. Nevertheless, the text very definitely does not tell its own story. Rather, its description must be *biased* according to an explicit and coherent organisational language. Here, we are using the term 'bias' in a positive sense provided that it refers to an intentional and explicit structuring of the description.

Luria's work, which we described in Chapter 2, clearly performs well according to this fourth criterion (and, indeed, to the other three). To reprise, briefly, Luria proposed that societies that were limited to individualised production did not develop language to the extent that it could constitute independent systems. Rather, language in such societies was always used in such a way as to refer to direct experience. Since – as he further proposed – language provides the structure for thought, the thinking of individuals in such societies would be context-dependent; they would be characterised by 'participation'. More advanced societies that engaged in collaborative production developed language to a far greater extent so as to facilitate the production of relational or self-referential systems. The thinking of individuals in such societies would be taxonomic, which is to say, it would be governed by such relational systems as conceptual structures rather than by practical experience. This theoretical structure enabled Luria to predict that individuals of the simpler society would, when presented with questions relating to familiar or novel situations, always try to relate the questions to their own lives. Failure to make such a relation will result in failure to comprehend the task. Individuals of the more developed society would recognise the systematic structure of the questions and would be able to respond without such experiential references. Thus:

> The following syllogism was presented: *White bears exist only where it is very cold and there is snow. Silk cocoons exist only where it is very hot. Are there places that have both white bears and cocoons?*
>
> Subject: Kul, age twenty-six, peasant, almost illiterate.
>
> 'There is a country where there are white bears and white snow. Can there be such a thing? Can white silk grow there?' . . .
> 'Where there is white snow, white bears live. Where it is hot, there are cocoons. Is this right?' . . .
> 'Where there is white snow, there are white bears. Where it is hot, there are white silkworms. Can there be such a thing on earth?' . . .
>
> (Luria, 1972, p. 105)

Luria's theoretical structure – his organisational language – and its operationalisation enables him, first, to analyse this text in terms of the nature of the society in which the subject participates. The subject is a peasant and 'almost illiterate', which indicates that he has very little if any contact with more developed (in Luria's terms) forms of society. Second, Luria is able to categorise the subject's responses to the question as indicative of participative thinking. Referring to the sequence of transcripts in which the above is included:

> These examples show that syllogisms are not perceived by these subjects as unified logical systems. The subjects repeat different parts of the syllogisms as isolated,

logically unrelated phrases. With some, the subjects grasp the interrogative form of the last sentence, which they then transfer to the formulation of both premises, which they have registered as two isolated questions. In other instances the question formulated in the syllogism is repeated regardless of the preceding premises; thus, the question is perceived as unrelated to the two interconnected premises. In all instances, when a subject repeated the premises he did not give them the character of universal assertions. Rather he converted each into a specific assertion logically unrelated to the other and unusable for drawing the appropriate logical conclusions.

(ibid., p. 106)

Because Luria's organisational language concerns the relationship between the social, linguistic and cognitive domains, he is able to make or confirm his assertions in respect of these domains. To return to the earlier analogy, the database of contacts can place telephone calls to individuals on the condition that its structure facilitates a direct relation between these domains and, further, that it relates the telephone data to a function that acts upon the telephone system.

Elaborating the description

In the above extract from Luria's book we can see that he is elaborating an argument; he is providing some justification for his classification of these examples as instances of the lower level of thinking. This is a characteristic of qualitative forms of analysis. This is because there are generally limitations to the level of generalisability with which the principles of the analysis can be given. Luria's definition of participative thinking is, of course, given in terms of the other elements of his organisational language. His theory is, in this sense, self-referential. In fact, to use his own terms, it facilitates a particular formalisation of taxonomic thinking. The practical problem of analysis involves the constitution and application of recognition principles whereby the theoretical concepts can be applied in the analysis of his data.

This is comparatively easy with some of Luria's concepts. Thus he presumably felt that there would be general agreement amongst his readership on a set of suitable indicators for the age and literacy status of his respondents. That is why these attributes are simply given and not elaborated. Also, the subjects have been selected on the basis of their participation in what Luria describes as comparatively simple or comparatively advanced societies. Having precoded his subjects in this way, he needs simply to record that Kul is a peasant.

Assigning Kul to a mode of cognition is a more complicated matter. This is because the originality of Luria's message lies precisely within this area of his organisational language. It is, of necessity, unfamiliar territory and so must be elaborated with worked examples of analysis. This process constitutes an apprenticing of the reader into the researcher's principles of recognition of his indicators. Ideally, it should enable the reader to reproduce Luria's own analysis with a high degree of reliability, which is to say that the reader's analysis should substantially coincide with the researcher's.

As is often the case, Luria presents his work in a form that suggests that his organisational language was substantially in place prior to his embarking on his field study.

Because this framework rests heavily on the prior work of Lev Vygotsky, we may suppose that this was, in fact, the case. As we have indicated in Chapter 2 and have suggested above, however, it is rarely the case that the beginning researcher can expect to begin their empirical work having already fully formulated their theoretical position. Indeed, to do so would be to minimise the impact of the empirical work on the study. As we have said, conceptual structure and data are, more commonly, generated together in a dialogue between the developing theoretical and empirical domains. An important strategy in this dialogue is to engage in precisely the kind of elaborated description that Luria offers.

Generating the description: network analysis

The semiotic analyses presented earlier in this chapter were substantially tacitly biased in so far as they made claims within an untheorised space. Luria's analysis is biased by his well-developed theoretical problem. The real problem of analysis, then, is how to move from the former to the latter situation. Decisions on the nature and specialisation of the theoretical field, on the nature and localisation of the empirical field and, crucially, on the articulation between them, are being made from the very start of the research process. These decisions begin to place a bias on the data long before you reach the stage of formal data analysis. In these and in subsequent analytic decisions your aim should be to make your principles as explicit as possible so that you can work towards the coherence that we are establishing as the fundamental criterion by which research is to be judged. We will try to illustrate this through a partial analysis of some diary data. The approach that we shall use in generating and refining analytic categories and structures is referred to as network analysis.

Before looking at the diary data we shall describe what we mean by a network by reference to another study by Mellar and colleagues (Mellar *et al.*, 1994). This research sets out to explore school pupils' reasoning with computational modelling tools. The data analysed include interview transcripts and observation notes. Part of the analysis involves trying to identify the kind of reasoning used by pupils in particular contexts. To achieve this, five aspects of reasoning are identified: using knowledge; comprehension; planning or deciding; analysis; and evaluation. Networks are drawn up for each to enable a more delicate level of analysis to be carried out. The network for the evaluation component of reasoning is given in Figure 7.3.

The use of 'braces' (in this case, the connector defining the relationship between 'evaluate' to the left and 'about' and 'mode', to the right) in this kind of network signifies complementary subsystems of choices. Thus, the network in Figure 7.3 entails that evaluative reasoning carried out by a pupil will be 'about' something *and* will be in a particular 'mode'. The other form of forked connective (e.g. connecting 'about' to the left and 'task', 'model', 'given data' and so on to the right) signifies a mutually exclusive set of options. Thus, the evaluation may be about a task, or a model, or given data, and so on, but not more than one of these. The 'mode' of the evaluative reasoning will be to criticise, doubt or judge. In 'judge' mode, the options are to accept or reject or to judge something as being possible or as being irrelevant. Both forms of connective may be used at any level of the network, although in this case, the braces occur only at the first level.

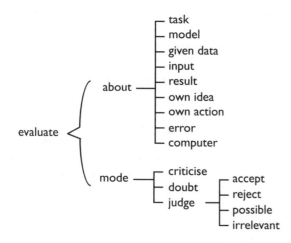

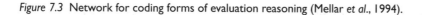

Figure 7.3 Network for coding forms of evaluation reasoning (Mellar *et al.*, 1994).

The categories that are in braces constitute a logical set in so far as they can be taken to refer to what is evaluated and how it is evaluated. The categories at the second level of the network – 'task', 'model', 'given data', etc. – seem to derive from the data, but it is not clear that they have been incorporated into the theoretical description of the problem. In other words, they represent untheorised aspects of the data. This is to be expected; your theory will never fully exhaust the description of your data. However, your intention should be to try to extend the theoretical description of the data in your development of the analysis. We shall try to illustrate what we mean by using some data from Brown's (1999) study.

Brown's data consists of written comments made by the parents of primary school children after they had worked at home with their children on some school mathematics tasks. These tasks, set by the school at either weekly or fortnightly intervals and carried out at home, were part of the IMPACT project, an initiative, now widespread, designed to foster greater involvement of parents in the mathematical education of their children. A key objective of IMPACT is to enable a dialogue to develop between parents and teachers by asking parents (and children) to comment on the tasks and to send these comments to the teacher. This is usually done in the form of an IMPACT diary, which provides, for each task, some boxes to be ticked and a space for a written comment. The IMPACT project provided Brown with 282 completed diaries (covering 1,657 tasks) from four primary schools. These diaries were part of the ongoing work of the schools and were not produced specifically for the purposes of research. Here is the entire text of two IMPACT diaries. They comprise the comments made by Charlene's and Jenny's parents to IMPACT tasks set by their teachers.

Charlene's diary:

1   Charlene finds it difficult to add with money.
2   Charlene found it difficult to understand but then she learn what was all about target.

3   Charlene had difficulty in counting over 100. Defining colours was easy.
4   It was just right.
5   Charlene found it interesting but easy.
6   Just right.
7   Charlene found it a bit difficult and needed help.

Jenny's diary:

1   Jenny was aware of selecting items that were too expensive and replaced them without any guidance. PS please help her to write better than her Dad.
2   Jenny was not at all clear about what she had learnt. She thought it was about counting – how many smarties in a box etc. Presumably though this is part of Data Handling and probability?
3   We were not sure what to do – it was badly explained on the sheet. Once we sorted it out the game was good. We will spend more time on this later – Jenny is still not sure of 10s and units.
4   To follow the instructions and make 3 figure numbers we took the 10s out as well. This IMPACT must have been well explained in class as Jenny knew exactly what to do.

(Brown, 1999, p. 217)

From initial inspection of these and the other diaries it was clear that some of the comments made by parents were lengthy and consisted of a range of observations about the child and the task, whereas others were very brief. Take the following example.

John enjoyed the activity. He coped well with the numbers under 20. The numbers over 20 we used Lego Bricks to help him work out the odds and the evens by making pairs. He needs a lot more practice at odds and evens.

(ibid., p. 207)

Here information is relayed about the child's enjoyment of the task, how well the child was able to do part of the task, how the parent organised the task and about the parent's judgement of the child's competence in a particular area of school mathematics. This contrasts sharply with a comment that states bluntly that 'it was fun'. The task of analysis at this point is to be able to clearly identify and describe these differences in a principled manner. In the absence of a well-defined theory, this involves working intensively through the diaries and developing descriptive categories. Producing a network is a useful way of organising these categories.

In Brown's original analysis an initial distinction was made between comments that focus on the acquirer and those that focus on the task. These kinds of comments are then subdivided again to distinguish between acquirer-focused comments that refer to the competence of the child (for instance, 'she was able to add the small numbers together') and those that refer to their dispositions (for example, 'John likes cutting and sticking activities'). The task-focused comments are divided into those that focus on the realisation of the task (for example, 'we made a ruler from card') and those that focus on evaluation of the task (for instance, 'this was a good activity'). This gives four

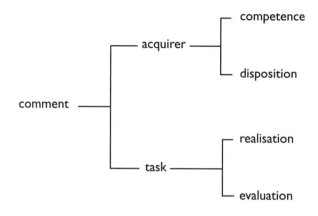

Figure 7.4 Analytic network from Brown's data, 1.

subsystems, differentiated in terms of the focus of the statement being described. This is illustrated in Figure 7.4.

In this case, subsequent levels of the network share the same structure. First, a distinction is made between comments that are task-dependent, that is, comments that refer directly to the activity of doing the task (for example, 'she did some good colouring' or 'it was fun') and task-independent comments, that is, those that pass beyond the context of the specific task and make more generalised statements (for instance, 'she knows her multiplication tables'). Task-dependent statements are then divided into those that are specific (i.e. make reference to a particular aspect of the task, its realisation, the child's performance and so on) and those that are unspecific. Specific comments are further divided into those that make reference to school mathematics and those that do not. Finally a distinction can be made between positive and negative comments. This generates the subordinate levels of the network, which are shown in Figure 7.5. This diagram shows the continuation of the network from the upper track of Figure 7.4, that is, following the acquirer/competence route. The complete network is constructed by appending the additional levels shown in Figure 7.5 to each of the terminal points of Figure 7.4.

At this point, you may notice that there is some resonance between some of the categories in the network and certain of the theoretical distinctions that we have been making in this book. In particular, the distinction between task-dependent and task-independent resonates with context-dependence/independence. Clearly, Brown's organisation of the empirical findings has been achieved with some sense of theoretical direction. However, it is quite apparent that the network is not fully theorised. It is not theoretically clear, for example, why a distinction should be made between acquirer and task or between competence and disposition. These categories are variables in respect of the data – they are indicator variables – but it is not clear, at this point, just what concept variables they are associated with. The development of this network is principally a process of *induction* from the information collected about the setting.

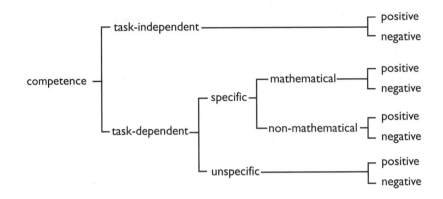

Figure 7.5 Analytic network from Brown's data, 2.

In order to develop the analysis further, we may move into the theoretical field. In this case, we can draw on an organisational language, social activity method, produced by Dowling (2009, see also 1995a, 1998). We cannot present the theory fully here. Briefly (and with some necessary simplification and changes in terminology), Dowling proposes that sociocultural action is directed towards the formation, maintenance or destabilising of alliances and oppositions. Texts, such as the diaries, can be construed as instances of sociocultural action and constitute alliances and oppositions between textual *positions* including authorial, reader and other positions or 'voices'. In particular, the author of the text (e.g. the writer of the diary entry) may address the reader directly or through another voice. In the diaries, the parent/author may describe the task that they and their child performed directly, or they may describe it in relation to, or through their child. These can be referred to as 'direct' and 'displaced' authors. In the latter case, the parent may make comments such as 'she is good at . . .' or 'she likes . . .'. In these examples, an attribute of the child is being 'identified' with the task.

Alternatively, the relationship between the child (or the parent) and the task may be described objectively, such as 'she/we put the numbers in rows . . .'. Note that 'we' is a first person pronoun and so serves as an indicator of a direct author. All of these categories have been or can be derived or deduced from Dowling's organisational language, although you will have to take this on trust, here (or refer to the source work, in terms of the displaced author, Dowling, 1998). This analysis generates the network in Figure 7.6.

In our discussion of Luria's work, we have already made reference to the theoretical distinction between context-dependence and context-independence. Dowling makes a related distinction between localising and generalising. This distinction is given some elaboration in Chapter 8. Finally, Dowling establishes a distinction between specialised and non-specialised forms of text. These are referred to as 'esoteric domain' and 'public domain' respectively. This completes the theoretically generated network that is shown in Figure 7.7.

It is now possible to read the comments from Brown's data directly into locations on the theoretically generated network. Thus, 'she knows her multiplication tables' will be located on the branch signified by displaced author/identification/generalising/

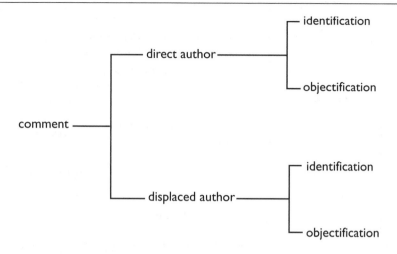

Figure 7.6 Analytic network from Dowling's theory, I.

esoteric domain. The new network, then, both describes the data and articulates it with a theoretically coherent problem. The data set as a whole can also be further analysed by mapping the distribution of comments of different categories of parents on the network.

There are two crucial points to be made. First, the theoretically derived network has not been, nor could it have been, derived from the theory without any reference to the empirical data that it is to analyse. Thus the empirically induced network in Figures 7.4 and 7.5 were necessary precursors to the further theoretical work.

Second, you may notice that the new network does not describe the data as completely as the empirically generated version. Specifically, it makes no distinction between comments relating to competence and to disposition of the acquirer or between comments focusing on the task realisation and on evaluation. Further, it does not distinguish between positive and negative comments. There is, in other words, what Bernstein (1996) refers to as a discursive gap between the theoretical and empirical fields. Further analysis would seek to reduce this gap.

One approach might be to map the distribution of these different responses in terms of the different categories of parent (e.g. in terms of social class). In fact, Brown found that working-class parents tended to make about the same number of dispositional comments about their children as they did competence comments, whereas middle-class parents tended to make twice as many competence comments as dispositional comments. Further movement between these empirical findings and the theoretical problem might enable social class to be more fully incorporated into the theory in order to enable the network to describe the data more completely. Once the theory describes the data adequately, then you will have generated an explanation.

Data analysis, then, is properly conceived as a dialogic process that involves moving between the empirical and theoretical fields. The intention is, first, to produce as tight and coherent a definition of the problem and as extensive a description of the findings as is possible. Second, the articulation between problem and findings – that is, between concept variables and indicator variables – should be made as explicit as possible. It

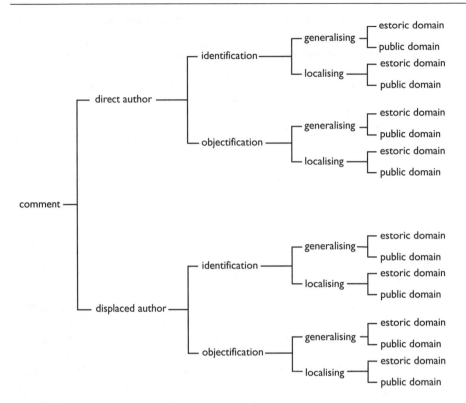

Figure 7.7 Analytic network from Dowling's theory, 2.

is only through this bringing together of the theoretical and empirical fields that the research is able to make more statements that extend in generality beyond its particular empirical setting. We shall return to the issue of generalisability in Chapter 9.

The theoretical and empirical dialogue in analysis

As we are emphasising throughout this book, and perhaps in this chapter in particular, research entails a dialogue between the theoretical and empirical fields. The theoretical sets up a bias in the way that the empirical is to be viewed; the empirical challenges, questions, asks more of the theory. In order to illustrate this, we shall take a brief look at a very limited empirical setting that concerns the authorising of academic identities. Consider the business card shown in Figure 7.8 (the home address and personal phone numbers have been obscured).

We can see that the card is divided into two triangular regions, upper left and lower right. This division is established by the clustering of the text in each region and also (though not visible in the reproduction here) by colour differentiation – the upper right text is in blue, the lower left text is in black. The name of the presenter of the card appears only in the lower left region and here it appears three times, at the head and in the email address and WWW URL. The upper right region does include a name, but it is the name of an institution, the Institute of Education. Reference to this name

Figure 7.8 Paul Dowling's business card.

appears four times: below the strapline – 'Leading education and social research', and abbreviated in the logo and in the email address and WWW URL. 'ioe' also appears twice in the lower left region.

Of course, the card is used to convey contact information; a cheaper, though less convenient alternative would be for Dowling simply to write down his details on any available surface (with or without romantic decoration). But the card is used to do more than this: it also establishes the specific authority of the presenter; but it does this in different ways. The upper right region of the card associates the cardholder with a specific institution that is introduced in respect of a particular practice; it's a university institution and not a tobacco company. This part of the card announces that the individual whose name appears on the lower left carries, in a yet-to-be-specified respect, the authority of this particular institution. We want to describe this as an *authority strategy* that closes the category of a *practice*: the authority is vested in the cardholder by virtue of their legitimate association with a particular, institutionalised practice, in this case concerning education and social research. At this point, it does not matter whose name appears on the lower left portion of the card; any name claims the same authority. In this sense, the category of *author* – that is, the author of the action of presenting the card – is open.

The lower left region, however, operates differently. The top line introduces in bold (the only other bold text on the card being the strapline on the upper right) the name of the cardholder and initials signifying that he is the holder of a doctorate; the second line indicates, also, that the holder is a Professor of Education. Now, whereas the authority established by the upper right region is available to anyone having a card that includes this text, neither a PhD nor the conferred title, Professor, is transferable; they attach, in this case, only to Paul Dowling. Of course, both 'PhD' and 'Professor of Education' close the category of practice – Dowling would not be able to use this card to establish his medical credentials – but they also close the category of author – only Dowling can use this card to claim the academic authority associated with a doctorate and a professorial title.

At this point, we have generated, empirically, two authority strategies. The first closes the category of practice, but leaves the category of author open. The second

Table 7.1 Authority strategies

	Field of practice	
Category of author	Open	Closed
Closed	Charismatic	Traditional
Open	Liberal	Bureaucratic

closes both categories. In fact, however, we have established the basis for a rather more complex strategic space. Essentially, we can regard closure of the category of author and closure of the category of practice as independent variables. If we then take the cross-product of these variables, we obtain the strategic space revealed in Table 7.1.

Only two categories emerged from our initial analysis of the business card. We might have left it at that. But, by considering the analytic categories, rather than their empirical instances, we now have four authority strategies. In fact, Table 7.1 was generated by Dowling in the analysis of a letter, carried out as part of a workshop. It has now been incorporated into his organisational language, Social Activity Method (see, for example, Dowling, 2009). The generation of strategy spaces by taking the cross-product of two variables is a characteristic (though not unique) feature of this approach. The names of three of these strategies were borrowed from Max Weber (1968), though they are being used in a different way. The two strategies that we have described in respect of the business card are *bureaucratic* – the strategy deployed in the upper right region of the card – and *traditional* – the strategy deployed in the top two lines of the lower left region. We might now add that the third and fourth lines of the lower left region of the card are also bureaucratic strategies, as is the use of 'ioe' in that region. A feature of this method is that it provides a kind of map that allows us to trace the different strategies that are deployed within and between texts and contexts. It is not intended to totalise the description of any given text or context.

Figure 7.9 (the title of which is Paul Dowling's business card written in Japanese) shows the reverse side of the business card (again, personal numbers have been obscured). The upper right portion of the card remains the same, but now the lower left region is written, mostly, in Japanese. Presenting this card in a non-Japanese context (Dowling has only one set of cards) might be taken to be a *charismatic* strategy; the category of practice is certainly being opened up, firmly locating the authority with the cardholder even though their name is probably not legible to a non-reader of Japanese. We might also describe the distinction between authority claims in terms of institutional and domestic identities on both sides of the card as traditional/bureaucratic, as described above, on the one hand, and charismatic, on the other.

Just to extend the illustration of charismatic strategies a little. On the doors of our offices at the Institute of Education, we have nameplates showing Professor Paul Dowling and Professor Andrew Brown, respectively; traditional authority strategies. One of our colleagues has GUNTHER KRESS – capitals, no title; who needs a title if you're Gunther Kress (we'd agree with that). This is clearly a charismatic strategy, though one probably not authored by Kress himself; such strategies do not have to be the deliberate actions of authors.

The *liberal* strategy is the one in which neither the category of author nor that of practice is closed. In this respect, it signals the absence of authority, or its handing

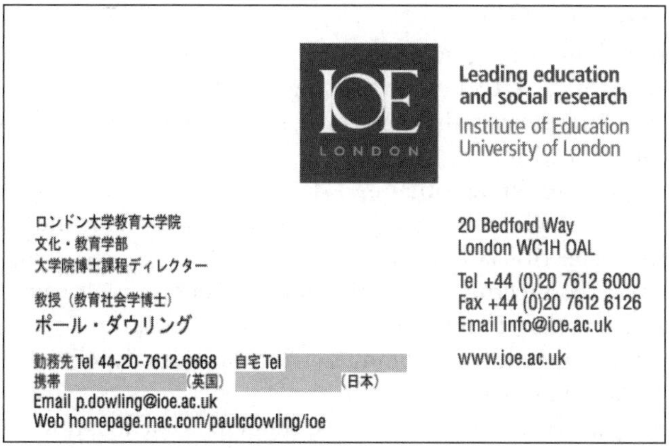

Figure 7.9 ポール・ダウリングの名刺.

over from author to audience. Dowling (2009) refers to a text deploying this kind of strategy as an *exchange* text contrasting this with a *pedagogic* text that deploys one or more of the positive authority strategies. The liberal strategy is deployed – though not exclusively – in all of those texts in which the university hands over authority to, say, its students (course evaluation forms, for example).

In this section we have carried out an analytic exercise that is intended to illustrate, as clearly as is possible in a short chapter, one way in which analysis might involve a theoretical–empirical dialogue. Before summing up, we shall provide some exposition on how this dialogue might be efficiently managed using qualitative data analysis software.

Managing the analysis: using information technology

Any form of detailed and systematic analysis of qualitative data will take a substantial amount of time. A significant proportion of this time can be spent organising, annotating, coding, relating and recalling data. This requires a high level of organisation and the development of effective systems for managing data and keeping track of one's analysis as it evolves. For the form of analysis described above, it is possible to mark codes for each segment of text on copies of the transcripts. Summary sheets of the results of the coding can be kept and a cross-referencing system developed. This enables one segment of data to be related to another. However, with a large amount of data this becomes cumbersome. Although there are no shortcuts in the process of data analysis, developments in information technology have produced a number of computer programs that can be of help. These range from familiar computer applications, such as word processors, databases and spreadsheets, through to programs specifically designed for the analysis of qualitative data. The following list, from Miles and Huberman (1994, p. 44), gives an indication of the wide range of ways in which computers can be of assistance in the process of conducting research and analysing qualitative data:

1   Making notes in the field.
2   Writing up or transcribing fieldnotes.
3   Editing: correcting, extending or revising fieldnotes.
4   Coding: attaching keywords or tags to segments of text and making them available for inspection.
5   Storage: keeping text in an organised database.
6   Search and retrieval: locating relevant segments of text and making them available for inspection.
7   Data 'linking': connecting relevant data segments and forming categories, clusters, or networks of information.
8   Memoing: writing reflective commentaries on some aspect of the data as a basis for deeper analysis.
9   Content analysis: counting frequencies, sequences, or locations of words and phrases.
10   Data display: placing selected or reduced data in a condensed, organised format, such as a matrix or network, for inspection.
11   Conclusion drawing and verification: aiding the analyst to interpret displayed data and to test or confirm findings.
12   Theory building: developing systematic, conceptually coherent explanations of findings; testing hypotheses.
13   Graphic mapping: creating diagrams that depict findings or theories.
14   Preparing interim and final reports.

(Miles and Huberman, 1994, p. 44)

It is clearly important for beginning researchers to consider carefully the ways in which a computer can be of help in their work. Certainly, the possibilities listed above will not all be relevant to every research project. Many of these tasks listed can be accomplished using readily available, non-specialist applications. A word processor, for example, can be used to make and edit notes and memos, for transcription, to store and search data, to produce tables, and so on. A database can be used to set up a structure for the recording and storage of data, to enable links to be made between data segments and to facilitate the quick retrieval of data. A spreadsheet can be used in the numerical analysis of data and the production of graphical representations. A graphics or presentations program can be used to produce diagrams, networks and data displays. We have used all of these types of program in the production of this book. As a beginning researcher, you should explore what these programs offer and make use of them as and when appropriate.

Specialised qualitative analysis programs (such as NVivo, Atlas.ti and HyperResearch) are usually modelled on a particular view of the process of qualitative analysis. They all offer means by which text can be segmented and coded, and tools for the manipulation of codes and the recall of text. Recent versions of these programmes make it possible to code, link and manipulate digital audio and video, as well as text. Used to manage information in this way, software like this can speed up the process of coding and analysis. The range of facilities offered by such software varies and it is important, if you are considering the use of a computer in your work, to be aware of the particular characteristics of each application (see the annotated bibliography for sources of information). In many cases the researcher will not use all of the facilities that are offered. This will often be because the form of qualitative analysis they are employing differs from the model of qualitative analysis on which the program is modelled.

Brown, for example, used HyperResearch in his inductive analysis of IMPACT diaries. Each diary was transcribed and a word-processed text file created. Using HyperResearch, he coded segments from each diary. The software was then used to count how many times a particular code was used, to list all the diaries in which a specific code, or combination of codes, appeared, to display all the segments of text that were given a particular code, and to produce summaries of the analysis at various points in the process. It was also used to add, change or delete codes as the analysis progressed. These facilities helped in the management of the process of analysis. The software also offers other facilities, such as hypothesis testing, that were not used because they had no part in the form of analysis being conducted.

Problems can arise when assumptions that have been built into the design of the software come into conflict with the research problem. For example, a doctoral student asked for assistance in using a text analysis program in her comparative study of linguistic structure in conventional (conversational and written) and computer-mediated interactive texts. She had made use of a computer tagging service that 'tagged' her data texts to identify in linguistic terms each word in the text. So, she received back a text in which each word was labelled according to, for example, whether it was a noun, a verb, an adverb, and so on. She intended to use the text analysis program to identify instances of certain linguistic categories. Clearly, many words may be interpreted, contextually, as more than one part of speech. 'Play', for example, may be a verb or a noun. The tagging program made decisions on the basis of probability distributions, which, themselves, had been derived from previous analyses of a large number of various kinds of text. It transpired, however, that no computer-mediated texts had been included in this earlier work. The student was, therefore, proposing to compare computer-mediated texts with other forms of texts using a device that had been constructed on the assumption that there was no such thing as a computer-mediated text.

It is vital, then, that computers are seen purely as tools that can help researchers in their work. It is, after all, the researcher who carries out the analysis, not the computer. Sometimes beginning researchers select a particular analysis program believing that, if they follow all the procedures listed in the manual, then the analysis will be done for them. It will not. The process of qualitative analysis cannot be codified, far less mechanised. As the case above suggests, much time and/or expense can be wasted putting data in the required form and working through it using a software application only to discover that the form of analysis towards which you are being led is not appropriate. In short, just because this software is available, and offers certain facilities, it does not mean that you have to use them.

Qualitative data analysis: conclusion

Quite clearly, there is a very limited extent to which it is possible to demonstrate the process of data analysis in a book such as this. Very often, the data that are to be analysed constitute a very substantial quantity of texts in a variety of forms. Ideally, perhaps, we might have incorporated such an extensive data set into the chapter and presented a narrative of our analytic activity. When we teach research methods courses, we try to proceed in this way by performing and getting our students to perform live analysis on visual and symbolic texts, video material and so forth, and even the seminar room itself often ends up as data. We have tried to approximate this by incorporating the deliberately incomplete network analysis of Brown's data and the exercise on Dowling's business card. In the end, however, you will have to learn through your own engagement with your own empirical setting. Be warned, it will be a drawn-out and frustrating task. Unfortunately, if you are conscientious and produce a well-developed qualitative analysis, your presentation of it will, in all likelihood, completely conceal all of the angst that has gone into its production. Good analysis has the irritating tendency to look as if it was obvious all along. It wasn't, of course, and the fact that your reader is delighted with the simplicity of your conclusions certainly does not mean that they could have generated them with any lesser effort.

In this chapter we have introduced four criteria by which your development of your theoretical problem and its relationship to your findings should be judged. Here they are again, collected together:

- the internal explicitness and coherence of the theory;
- the relational completeness of the theory;
- the integrity of the concept–indicator links.
- the direct relationship of the organisational language to the system about which claims are to be made.

What we hope to have achieved in this chapter is to emphasise that qualitative data analysis of necessity entails a janusian attitude. Janus was the two-faced Roman god who looks both ways at a portal. You must be prepared to look both to the theoretical and empirical fields in your research. Assuming, however, that you have only a single face, your approach must be dialogical. You must have a good sense of your theoretical problem before you begin your data collection, let alone its analysis. But you are unlikely to have developed it fully (even if you think you have).

With your problem in mind, you will engage with your information set inductively, generating categories and organising them, perhaps as a network of indicator variables, as we have illustrated. You will then cast your gaze into the theoretical field and do some developing of your concept variables, perhaps, again, generating a network or the kind of strategic spaces that Dowling uses in Social Activity Method. The analysis then proceeds as a dialogical movement between the problem and findings, tightening up their respective structures and closing the discursive gap between them to generate the highest level of explicitness and coherence that is possible given the conditions under which you are working.

At some point you will have to stop and present your report. We will consider this stage of the process in Chapter 10. In the next chapter, however, we will move to a consideration of how quantifying your data may be of value to your research.

Chapter 8

Dealing with quantity

This chapter is concerned with the production and presentation and analysis of data in quantitative form. It will include a discussion of the more common forms of data presentation as tables and charts. We will also be introducing the use of statistics in the analysis of quantitative data. We have included instructions for calculating several statistical measures. These may be helpful if your use of statistics is to be very limited and if your data is in a suitable form. In general, you would be better advised to make use of computer facilities, such as SPSS or a spreadsheet, for your statistical work. We have not introduced these facilities for two reasons. First, it would have involved us in introducing the use of at least one computer software package, which would have extended the length of the chapter considerably. Second, as former teachers of mathematics, we believe that there is considerable value in running through the simpler computations to get some sense of how the mathematics is working, of what is going on inside the computer's head.

However, of more importance than these computational instructions are the descriptions of what these techniques do and of when and how they can be used. These descriptions are also more easily understood when placed alongside the computations themselves. Often, in our experience, beginning researchers delegate their analysis to a sophisticated computer package or (perhaps even less appropriately) to a statistically competent colleague. The output is then presented without any discussion of the relevance or limitations of the tests that have been performed. The quantification and statistical analysis of data is potentially of immense value to all researchers. As with all methodological tools, however, they must be used with deliberation and reflection. Our intention is that this chapter will enable you to begin to make use of quantitative methods in this way in your own research and to ask appropriate questions of research produced by others. We also hope to provide you with an adequate basis to enable you to approach a statistical methods handbook with some confidence.

We have tried to present the instructions and descriptions so as to make them accessible to the non-mathematician. This has not, we have felt, ruled out the use of mathematical formulae where appropriate. However, we have given very little mathematical explanation of the formulae that appear in the text. If you wish to interrogate the mathematical rationales of the techniques, you will find suitable references in the annotated bibliography.

Quantifying qualities

The presentation of results where a qualitative mode of analysis has been adopted generally employs elaborated description of one or more exemplary texts. Such elaborated description is an important strategy both in the development of theory and in the apprenticing of the reader of the research into the relationship between theory and data. However, it is often helpful to present an overview of the sample as a whole, particularly where the sample size exceeds that which can reasonably be presented in the form of elaborated description. Table 8.1, for example, is Luria's summary of the distribution of his subjects in respect of the classification tasks (described in Chapter 3).

The table is a cross-tabulation of the *frequencies* of the occurrence of the two variables, group and method of classifications. These indicators are both ordinal scales, which means that their values are ordered. Thus, the three values for 'group' shown in the first column of the table are given in an order that represents social and cultural development in terms of relations of production (individualised/collective) and level of literacy. The three values of 'method of classification' shown in the first row of the table are ordered according to the cognitive level that they indicate. 'Graphic method of grouping' is the lowest level and employs participation. 'Categorical classification' is the most advanced level and is taxonomic. 'Graphic and categorical methods of grouping' is an intermediate level. The relationship between the two variables is clearly represented by the structure of the table. That is, the non-zero entries in the main data columns (columns 3, 4 and 5) form an echelon. The inclusion of percentages in the table is helpful because the sample sizes within each group are different. Representing the figures as percentages as well as frequencies allows direct comparison. It is worth noting, however, that presenting a table only in terms of percentages is generally not a good idea and that the comparison of percentages can be misleading where numbers are small.

In order to generate the table, Luria has had to quantify his data. However, although we now have numerical data – the figures in the table – there has really been no explicit change in the nature of the analysis. All that has happened is that the researcher has counted the number of subjects that he has already categorised in each way. The analysis itself remains qualitative in nature. The result of the counting, however, is a clearer picture of the overall distribution of the data. On the other hand, we have lost the

Table 8.1 Luria's summary for groups and method of classification

Group	Number of subjects	Graphic method of grouping	Graphic and categorical methods of grouping	Categorical classification
Illiterate peasants from remote villages	26	21 (80%)	4 (16%)	1 (4%)
Collective-farm activists (barely literate)	10	0	3 (30%)	7 (70%)
Young people with 1–2 years' schooling	12	0	0	12 (100%)

Source: Luria (1976, p. 78).

specificities of individual responses. Furthermore, had the data been presented only in this way, we would have been unable to assess the validity or the reliability of Luria's coding of his subjects. There would have been no possibility of our apprenticing into the principles of his analysis. Clearly, Luria gets the best of both worlds by doing precisely as he has done, which is to provide both elaborated description and quantitative summaries of his data.

The elaborated description of qualitative analysis has advantages in respect of both the formulation of theory and the representation of the research. However, it tends to be very expensive in terms of time and space. When the problem is sufficiently well defined, it is often possible to generate indicators for the concepts that can be described in simple terms and are operationalisable to a high degree of reliability. Such a simplification of the analytic process can enable the coding and representation of a far greater amount of information than would be possible using elaborated description. We shall use, as an example, the analysis of a school mathematics textbook scheme by Dowling (1996, 1998). In discussing this example, we shall include some description of the process whereby an indicator variable is constituted in respect of a specific concept variable. You will recall that a concept variable is a theoretical object. An indicator variable is the empirical object that enables the recognition of the concept.

Dowling's research had involved a semiotic analysis of the scheme[1] that had employed elaborated description, in the form of memos, in the development of an organisational language. The theory included the definition of various categories of 'textual strategy' whereby a pedagogic text constructs its ideal reader. *Generalising* and *localising* constituted an opposing pair of strategies. The distinction between them is redolent of and was, to a certain extent, influenced by the distinction that Luria makes between taxonomic and participative thinking. For the present purposes, we can describe them in a way that more closely resembles Luria's distinction. Thus, generalising strategies tend to constitute the text as relatively self-referential and so context-independent. Localising strategies, on the other hand, tend to constitute the text as referring to something specific and concrete. It is this referent context that gives the text meaning, so that the text becomes context-dependent.

Dowling proposed that texts directed at 'high ability' students would be dominated by generalising strategies, whereas those directed at 'low ability' students would be dominated by localising strategies.[2] The semiotic analysis of the texts seemed to bear this out. However, the elaborated description did not allow coverage of a very substantial quantity of information. It was therefore decided to operationalise the strategies to enable a quantitative analysis of the texts. This kind of quantitative analysis of texts is often referred to as a content analysis.

Indicators were needed for the concepts 'generalising strategy' and 'localising strategy'. These had to be described with sufficient precision to allow their occurrence in the books to be quantified. This was achieved by developing the additional concept variable 'signifying mode'. Essentially, this refers to the way in which the text signifies. A visual image or 'icon', such as a realistic photograph or drawing, signifies by physically identifying a viewpoint for the 'reader'. It constructs the page as a physical mapping of a specific physical location. Other forms of text, including symbolic, graphical and tabulated text, do not signify in this way. Written text may describe a concrete physical location. However, it does not achieve this by the physical reconstruction of the scene and by physically identifying the location of the viewpoint in relation to this reconstruction. It would seem, then, that icons more readily lend themselves to the purposes of localising strategies by facilitating the more direct signification of specific contexts. Other modes of text are, by virtue of the way in which they signify, more readily incorporated into generalising strategies.

This argument – which has been simplified for the present purpose – establishes a theoretical association between the two pairs of concept variables, that is, localising and generalising strategies, on the one hand, and iconic and non-iconic modes of signification, on the other. Iconic and non-iconic modes of signification, however, are comparatively easy to operationalise for the purposes of conducting a content analysis. We have to ask: 'does the text constitute the reader's physical position in relation to the page as a representation of the viewpoint in respect of the scene which it represents?' If the answer is 'yes', then the text or section of text is an icon; otherwise, it is not. 'Icon', defined in these terms, is an indicator for the concept 'iconic mode' and, by association, for 'localising strategy'.

There remains a further decision to be made. Whereas it may be a comparatively simple matter to distinguish between icons and other textual elements,[3] we have yet to determine how to quantify them. We may well be able to count the number of icons in a textbook. However, this would take no account of size. Furthermore, the study from which this example is taken required a comparative measure of a rather more complex structure of signifying modes than we shall be able to describe here. Clearly, alphanumeric text is rather more difficult to count in such a way as to enable a comparative measure to be made; is a picture worth a thousand words, or only one? It was decided, therefore, to quantify textual mode in terms of area. Operationally, a one-centimetre grid was laid over each sampled page. Each square was then coded according to the type of text that it contained and a distribution was constructed for each whole page. The average or mean page coverage by each type of text was calculated by dividing the total amount of each type by the number of pages sampled. These results, in terms of icons and other text are shown in Table 8.2 for each of four books in the scheme.

Of the four books represented in Table 8.2, G1 is the first and G8 is the final book in the series targeted at 'lower ability' students. Correspondingly, Y1 and Y5 are, respectively, the first and final books in the series targeted at the 'higher ability' students. G1 and Y1 are intended for students of the same age cohort, as are G8 and Y5. From the table, you can see that the incidence of iconic mode of signification, indicated by the mean page coverage by icons, decreases substantially in the sequence, G1, G8, Y1, Y5. By virtue of the association which has been theoretically established between iconic mode and localising strategies, it can be deduced that localising strategies are employed in the G series to a greater extent than in the Y series. Further, the use of localising strategies decreases between the first and final books in each series. Nevertheless, the incidence of icons in G8 is still approximately twice the level of that

Table 8.2 SMP 11–16: mean signifying mode page coverage

	Book G1 n = 40	Book G8 n = 40	Book Y1 n = 100	Book Y5 n = 100
Icon	116	77	39	13
Other	136	169	200	230

All figures given in cm²; total area of each page = 408 cm².

Table 8.3 SMP 11–16: number of photographs in the B series

Book	Number of photographs
B1	0
B2	5
B3	4
B4	21
B5	6

in Y1. The incidence of other types of text – indicating the level of use of generalising strategies – also increases within each series. Again, however, the level in G8 remains substantially below that in Y1. The content analysis thus provides some support for Dowling's proposition that generalising and localising strategies are targeted at 'high ability' and 'low ability' students, respectively.

This study, like Luria's, started with a qualitative form of analysis, but also made use of quantification. Luria's use of counting did not alter the fundamentally qualitative nature of the analysis; it merely summarised it. Dowling, on the other hand, has moved from a qualitative to a quantitative mode by the use of an indicator that can be described in terms that enable it to be recognised with a high degree of reliability. Thus, a very substantial amount of data was made available for the analysis represented by Table 8.2. Clearly, this kind of quantification entails a necessary loss of detail. However, as we suggested in Chapter 7, it is also quite likely to result in a certain loss in terms of the validity of the analysis. Another example from Dowling's study will illustrate this.

In the course of the content analysis, an additional measure that was employed involved the counting of photographic icons. Table 8.3 shows the number of photographs in each of the median, B series of books (targeted at 'average' students). 'Photograph' is a category of icon, which is, as we have said, an indicator for localising strategies. The data in Table 8.3 suggests that B4 employs localising strategies to a far greater extent than the other books in this series. Now it could be that the other B books incorporate more of the other categories of icon, 'drawing' and 'cartoon'. In fact, this is not the case. So why does B4 stand out in this way?

On studying the photographs in B4 it seems that 18 of the 21 are incorporated into material that uses photographic enlargement as a metaphor for mathematical enlargement. Here, it is the photograph as photograph that is foregrounded, rather than the content of the photograph as the physical reconstruction of a scene. In other words, these photographs do not signify in quite the same way as is intended in the definition of 'iconic mode of signification'. This explanation quite clearly weakens the validity of 'icon' as an indicator for localising strategies (although it does not invalidate it). However, because the specificity of the information text is lost in the quantification, this potential challenge is rendered invisible.

As we have represented it so far, quantification can enable the coverage of a larger amount of data than is generally possible using the elaborated description of qualitative analysis. It can also enable us to gain a clear overview of the data, whether or not qualitative analysis has also been employed. The quantification of data also constitutes it in a form that is accessible to mathematical manipulation. There are at least two reasons why you might want to manipulate the data mathematically:

- you may want to present your data in a mathematical table or chart;
- you may want to explore or interrogate your data statistically.

We will consider each of these forms of mathematical manipulation in turn.

Charting the data

We will start this section with a warning against extravagance in the use of charts in your research. Modern computer software in the form of spreadsheets and presentation packages makes it a simple matter to generate an impressive range of charts and diagrams. A number of the beginning researchers with whom we have worked have been eager to take advantage of these information technology resources and have presented, in their draft reports, pages of colourful histograms and pie charts and line graphs. The fact that these presentational forms are possible, however, does not mean that they are always a good idea. The question that must to be addressed is: how does the presentational form assist in making sense of the data? This question is relevant in the course of data analysis as well as in decisions relating to the final writing-up.

In our experience, a simple table is often the most expressive form for the written presentation of data. This is certainly the case with Luria's data in Table 8.1. This table provides access to the information in both absolute and percentage form and allows easy comparison between the cells. The structure of the results is clear because the two dimensions of the table show the scaling of the indicator variables. We could, of course, represent this data in a visually more imposing chart. However, it is likely that this would obfuscate rather than illuminate the results of the research. In our opinion, there need to be good reasons for representing data other than as a simple table. Where there are good reasons, then presenting information in diagrammatic form can be very useful. We will look at just two forms of bar chart.

When considering the data in Table 8.2, you will probably be making a number of comparisons. You will want to compare the two rows of data, also the G books and the Y books, and the first and last book in each series. It may be that a graphical representation of this data will make these comparisons easier. In this case, the iconic and other categories are exhaustive. If we discount the blank space, the page is made up of icons and other kinds of text. It may, then, be appropriate to use the kind of bar chart shown in Figure 8.1. The chart makes it very easy to obtain a fast visual comparison within each book and between books. Some of the precision of the numerical data is lost, although this could be retrieved by labelling the chart more fully.

An alternative to the bar chart in Figure 8.1 would have been to draw four *pie charts*, one for each book. However, we feel that a bar chart of the type that we have used always provides easier access to the data than pie charts. Our preference, then, is to avoid the use of pie charts.

Where the variable is of ordinal level of measurement, a different kind of bar chart may be often more appropriate, because this kind of diagram gives a sense of the shape of a distribution. Figure 8.2 shows the social class representation of home applicants accepted by UK universities through the Universities Central Council on Admissions (UCCA) in 1991.

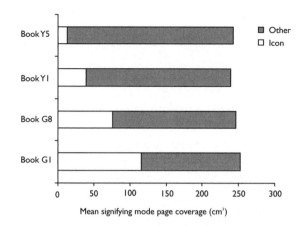

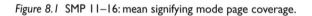

Figure 8.1 SMP 11–16: mean signifying mode page coverage.

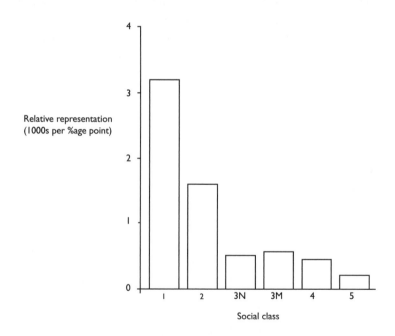

Figure 8.2 Representation of each social class by home applicants accepted by universities through UCCA in 1991 (source: Dowling, 1998).

The categories for social class are those used by the Office of Population Censuses and Surveys (OPCS) in the analysis of census data up to and including the 1981 census. They are:

1   professional, etc. occupations;
2   intermediate occupations;
3   skilled occupations
      (N) non-manual
      (M) manual
4   partly skilled occupations;
5   unskilled occupations (OPCS, 1980).

'Intermediate occupations' includes the 'junior' professions, teaching being an example. Of course, the assumption of ordinality in the variable 'social class' is open to challenge. After 1981, the OPCS abandoned the use of these categories in the analysis of census data.

The bar chart in Figure 8.2 shows the distribution of university acceptances in terms of social class in a very dramatic way. The particular choice of variable for the vertical axis is also important in this respect. It was obtained by dividing the number of acceptances in each social class by the percentage of the working population in that particular class. The picture is rather different if absolute numbers are used instead, as is the case in Figure 8.3. The radical difference in visual impact of the two bar charts illustrates the crucial importance of labelling the axes as clearly as possible.

The charts in Figures 8.1, 8.2 and 8.3 are of clear value in representing the data in a report or as a part of a presentation. Whether or not they are of equal value in the analysis stage of the research process depends upon whether you find it easier to read a table or a diagram.

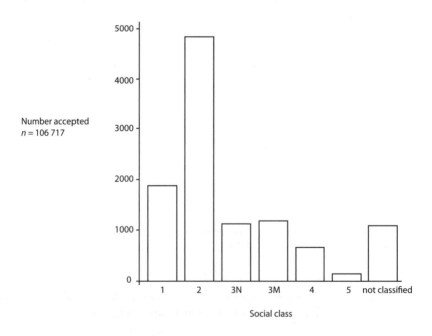

Figure 8.3   Social class profile of home candidates accepted by universities through UCCA in 1991 (source: Dowling, 1998).

These charts were drawn using a presentation software package.[4] They could just as easily have been drawn using a spreadsheet or a modern word processor. These applications offer a wide range of chart styles. In making a selection, you should not simply go for the one that you think looks the most impressive, but choose the one that most effectively displays the aspects of the data that you wish to highlight. In general, it is a good idea to try to keep your diagrams as simple as possible.

The second form of mathematical manipulation that may be applied to quantitative data is statistical analysis. In the next section, we shall give an introduction to some simple and commonly used statistical techniques and to the principles of their use.

Statistical analysis

This is not a statistics textbook and we are not able to cover the range of statistical techniques that might be applied to quantitative data (we clearly did not cover the range of qualitative analysis approaches either in Chapter 7). We can, however, give an introduction to some simple but widely used statistical measures and engage in some discussion of the circumstances under which they and related measures are appropriately used. We shall illustrate four statistics: the mean; the Mann–Whitney test; the chi-square test; and Spearman's rho; we also introduce the variance and standard deviation in the boxed text below.

Try not to be put off by the terminology and symbols in these sections. We are not going to set you a test at the end of it. If you are not (yet) mathematically inclined, just try to follow the general lines of the arguments and, perhaps, gain some familiarity with some of the terms. This will help you when reading research that involves a statistical element. You can always come back to the chapter later or, indeed, move on to one of the more complete statistical manuals that we have referred to in our annotated bibliography.

The mean and frequency distribution

Table 8.4 shows the number of alphanumeric symbols on each page of a random sample of twenty pages from each of two of the mathematics textbooks that were analysed by Dowling in the work cited earlier. Book G1 is the first book in the series targeted at 'lower ability' students; Book Y5 is the last book in the series targeted at the 'most able' students.

From an inspection of the table it looks very much as if the pages in the G1 sample generally contain fewer symbols than those in the Y5 sample. Nevertheless, there is a certain amount of overlap. A measure for the average number of symbols per page in each sample can be obtained by finding the total number of symbols in each sample of twenty pages and sharing them out equally, that is, by dividing each total by twenty. This kind of average is called the *mean* (or arithmetic mean or common average). The mean of a set of measurements is calculated by dividing the total or sum of the measurements by the number of measurements. For the twenty pages in Book G1, the sum of the numbers of symbols is 9,696, so the mean is calculated as follows:

$$\text{mean} = \frac{\text{sum of measurements}}{\text{number of measurements}} = \frac{9696}{20} = 484.8$$

Table 8.4   Number of alphanumeric symbols on each of a random sample of 20 pages of SMP 11–16 Book G1 and Book Y5

Book G1	Book Y5
194	1121
306	941
744	562
531	1114
420	1129
377	1921
161	1037
424	958
503	1162
286	0
901	974
487	1336
557	850
498	586
486	513
574	985
586	701
658	792
285	585
718	390

Source: Dowling (1998).

Statisticians generally use the symbol $\bar{x}$ to represent the mean of the measurements (each called x), n to represent the number of measurements, and Σx to represent the sum of the measurements (Σ is the Greek character sigma and represents 'sum of'). Symbolically, then, the mean of a set of measurements is represented by the following formula:

$$\bar{x} = \frac{\Sigma x}{n}$$

If you perform this calculation on the data in Table 8.4, you will obtain 484.8 for the mean number of symbols per page in the G1 sample (as indicated above) and 887.85 for the Y5 sample. These figures seem to confirm the conclusion drawn from inspection that the G1 sample pages contain fewer symbols than those in the Y5 sample.

Although these means look very different, it is not absolutely certain that they indicate substantive differences between the two books. You would, in fact, be surprised if the means of two samples were identical, even if the samples were drawn from very similar books or, indeed, even if the samples were drawn from the same book. You would expect the two sample means to be different purely on the basis of chance. The degree of difference will depend upon the mean number of symbols per page for each population from which a sample is drawn – in this case, for each book as a whole. It also depends upon the variation in the number of symbols per page within each population. Do most of the pages tend to have values close to the mean, or is there a wide spread of values? See the boxed text below for further discussion of the difference in the spread of a distribution.

It is clearer to see this in a diagram. We have grouped the data in Table 8.4, counting, for each sample, the number of pages having between 0 and 199 symbols, the number having between 200 and 399 symbols, and so on. The results are illustrated in Figures 8.4 and 8.5. The height of the first bar in each chart shows the number of pages in the sample having between 0 and 199 symbols, the second bar shows the number having between 200 and 399 symbols, and so on. The number of occurrences in each group is called the frequency. Figures 8.4 and 8.5 show the frequency distribution of symbols per page for each of the two samples. This kind of bar chart, which represents a frequency distribution, is called a *histogram*.

Looking at the two histograms, it is clear that almost the whole of the distribution of the G1 sample is below the mean value for the Y5 sample. However, the G1 sample mean lies within the spread of values of the Y5 sample. How confident can you be, then, that the two samples come from populations that are substantively different? In order to measure this confidence, you may wish to conduct a statistical test of *significance*.

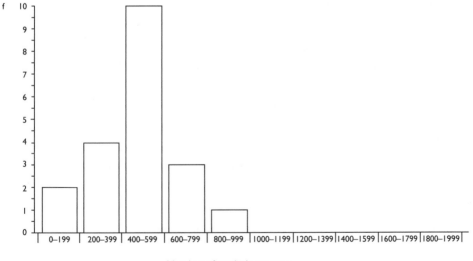

Number of symbols per page

Figure 8.4 Distribution of the number of alphanumeric symbols on each of a random sample of 20 pages from SMP 11–16 Book G1.

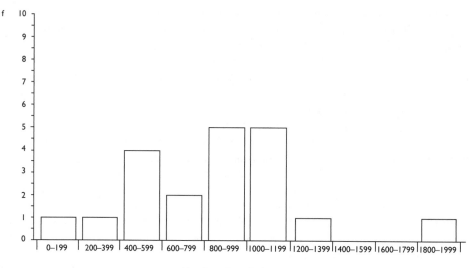

Number of symbols per page

Figure 8.5 Distribution of the number of alphanumeric symbols on each of a random sample of 20 pages from SMP 11–16 Book Y5.

The Mann–Whitney test

The argument that justifies the proposition about the two books runs as follows. For each book, a random sample was taken from the population that comprised all of the pages in the book. This means that every page in each book had an equal chance of being included in the sample for that book. The samples, then, are unbiased, and so can be claimed to represent the books. A difference was found in the mean number of symbols per page for each sample. Since the samples represent their respective populations, an *inference* is drawn to the effect that the difference in sample means is the result of a difference in population means. That is:

(i)   Book Y5, as a whole, contains more symbols per page than Book G1 as a whole.

This is the *research hypothesis*. In this case, the hypothesis is *directional*. That is, it specifies which book has the greater number of symbols per page. This kind of hypothesis is called a *one-tailed hypothesis*. Had the hypothesis merely predicted that the number of symbols per page was greater in one book than in the other, but without specifying which was which, it would have been a *non-directional* or *two-tailed hypothesis*.

We indicated, above, that we are interested in using statistics to measure the degree of confidence with which we can propose this hypothesis. This is equivalent to a measure of the degree of confidence with which we can reject the opposite or *null hypothesis*. The null hypothesis states that:

(ii)   There is no difference between Book Y5 and Book G1 in terms of the number of symbols per page.

Proposing a null hypothesis – the opposite to the hypothesis that we wish to test – may seem a strange thing to do, but there are sound statistical reasons for doing so. Suppose, for the moment, that the null hypothesis is, in fact, true and that there is no difference between the books in terms of the number of symbols per page. The question that you now need to ask is: just how likely is it that you would draw two samples that are as different as the ones that you have? Or, to use the technical term, what is the *probability* of drawing the samples that you have if the null hypothesis is true? If it turns out that the probability is very low – say 0.05 (or one in twenty) or less – then you might feel justified in rejecting the null hypothesis in favour of the research hypothesis. Fortunately, a measure of this probability can be obtained using a *test of significance*. We will conduct the *Mann–Whitney U test* for the figures in Table 8.4 and then discuss its interpretation.

First, all forty measures from Table 8.4 must be written down in order, smallest first and assigned *ranks*. The smallest measure is assigned rank 1, the second smallest rank 2, and so on. This has been done in Table 8.5.

Table 8.5 Mann–Whitney I: assigning ranks

Symbols	Rank (R)
0	1
161	2
194	3
285	4
286	5
306	6
377	7
390	8
420	9
424	10
486	11
487	12
498	13
503	14
513	15
531	16
557	17
562	18
574	19
585	20
586	21.5
586	21.5
658	23
701	24

continued overleaf

Table 8.5 Mann–Whitney I: assigning ranks (continued)

Symbols	Rank (R)
718	25
744	26
792	27
850	28
901	29
941	30
958	31
974	32
985	33
1037	34
1114	35
1121	36
1129	37
1162	38
1336	39
1921	40

Notice that the twenty-first and twenty-second figures are the same, 586. They are each assigned the mean of these two ranks, that is:

$$\frac{21+22}{2} = 21.5$$

The ranks are then entered next to their respective measures in the original table (Table 8.4) and the two columns of ranks summed. This has been done in Table 8.6.

The Mann–Whitney statistic is called U. Two values are computed for U using each sum of ranks respectively. The following formulae are used:

$$U_1 = N_{G1}N_{Y5} + \frac{N_{G1}(N_{G1}+1)}{2} - \Sigma R_{G1}$$

$$U_2 = N_{G1}N_{Y5} + \frac{N_{Y5}(N_{Y5}+1)}{2} - \Sigma R_{Y5}$$

N_{G1} and N_{Y5} are the sizes of the G1 and Y5 samples, respectively. In this case, they are both 20, although the Mann–Whitney test works even where the two samples are of different sizes. ΣR_{G1} and ΣR_{Y5} are the sums of the ranks assigned to the G1 and Y5 lists and are shown in Table 8.6; they are 272.5 and 547.5 respectively. Substituting these values into the formulae you will obtain:

$$U_1 = 20 \times 20 + \frac{20 \times (20+1)}{2} - 272.5 = 337.5$$

$$U_2 = 20 \times 20 + \frac{20 \times (20+1)}{2} - 547.5 = 62.5$$

Table 8.6 Mann–Whitney II: ranks assigned to each sample

GI	RGI	Y5	RY5
194	3	1121	36
306	6	941	30
744	26	562	18
531	16	1114	35
420	9	1129	37
377	7	1921	40
161	2	1037	34
424	10	958	31
503	14	1162	38
286	5	0	1
901	29	974	32
487	12	1336	39
557	17	850	28
498	13	586	21.5
486	11	513	15
574	19	985	33
586	21.5	701	24
658	23	792	27
285	4	585	20
718	25	390	8
ΣR_{GI}	272.5	ΣR_{YS}	547.5

The value that is used for U is always the lesser of the two values that are calculated; in this case, the value is 62.5. You will now need to consult a table of critical values for U. To do this, you will need to know the values of U and of N_A and N_B (in this case, both 20) and whether your research hypothesis is a one-tailed or two-tailed test. We used the tables provided in Clegg's (1983) introductory statistics book. Using these tables, we found that there is no more than a 1 in 200 (or 0.5 per cent or 0.005) probability of drawing these samples if the null hypothesis is true. This is a very small probability, so we can be confident in rejecting the null hypothesis, in this case.

Conventionally, you can reject the null hypothesis for probability values of 0.05 (or one in twenty or 5 per cent). A smaller probability increases the confidence with which you can reject the null hypothesis. If the probability value produced by the test allows you to reject the null hypothesis, then you can claim that your results are *significant*. In the above case, we can conclude that the results are *significant at the 0.005 level*.

'Significance', here, refers to *statistical significance*. A statistically significant difference between two samples is unlikely to have arisen purely by chance. Statistical significance does not reflect on the importance or absolute magnitude of the differences between the samples. Where sample sizes are very large, statistical tests will often show statistical significance even where the absolute differences between samples are really quite insignificant. Walden and Walkerdine (1985), for example, warn against placing undue emphasis on tests of significance in the comparison of girls' and boys' performances in school mathematics. The very large sample sizes of some of these comparisons result in quite trivial differences being declared 'significant'.

The Mann–Whitney test is appropriate where the two lists of data are independent of each other. In the textbook case, the two samples were drawn separately; the number of symbols on any G page is independent of the number of symbols on any Y page. The test can be applied where the size of each sample is different (if, say, Dowling had taken twenty pages from Book G1 and thirty pages from Book Y1).

Where the data is in the form of *matched pairs*, we need to apply a different test. For example, suppose that ten inspectors rate two teachers' performances. There will be ten pairs of ratings. However, these sets of ratings will not be independent, because the ratings in each pair will have arisen from the same inspector. One appropriate statistical test for such a set of data is the *Wilcoxon matched pairs signed ranks test*, which yields a statistic referred to as T. The Wilcoxon test also involves ranking the measures. You should refer to the bibliography, which includes a number of statistical textbooks that provide further details and calculation schedules for this and other statistical tests.

Normal and skewed distributions

You may have noticed that the calculation for the Mann–Whitney statistic did not involve the actual measurements themselves, only their ranks. This is also true of the Wilcoxon test. This means that the only requirement that the test has of the data is that it must be in ordinal form, so that it can be ordered and ranks can be assigned. No assumptions are made about the shape of the distribution – the shape of the histogram – of the scores. These tests are referred to as *non-parametric tests*. There are other tests that, although more powerful, in the sense that they provide better estimates for the probabilities, are rather more picky in terms of the kind of data that is required. Commonly used examples are the matched and independent *t* tests, which correspond to the Wilcoxon and Mann–Whitney tests, respectively.

The *t* tests are *parametric tests*. They make assumptions about the population distribution, which must be in the form illustrated in Figure 8.6. Figure 8.6 includes a curve drawn through the tops of the bars of the histogram. Figure 8.7 shows the same curve, but without the bars. This bell-shaped curve is symmetrical about the group having the highest frequency. This group is called the *modal* group. A distribution that conforms to this shape is called a *normal frequency distribution*.

Commonly, the data do not conform to this specification and their distribution is a different shape. Figures 8.8 and 8.9 illustrate distributions which are *skewed*, so that the shape is not symmetrical. The shape of the distribution illustrated in Figure 8.8 is referred to as *positively skewed*, because the long tail of the graph is on the positive (right) side of the mode. Figure 8.9 illustrates a *negatively skewed distribution*.

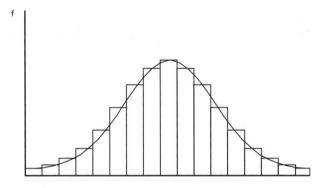

Figure 8.6 The normal distribution.

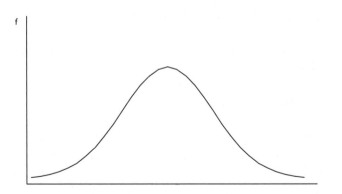

Figure 8.7 The normal frequency distribution curve.

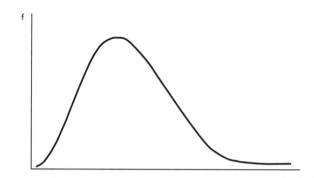

Figure 8.8 Positively skewed distribution.

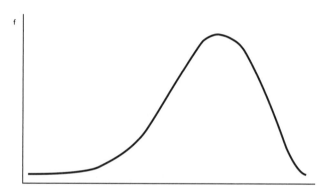

Figure 8.9 Negatively skewed distribution.

The standard deviation and p values

The frequency distributions that we have referred to in this chapter differ in terms of their *mean* values: a higher mean value will shift the distribution to the right, a lower mean value will shift it to the left. The distributions also differ in respect of the spread of values that they represent. The spread of a distribution is measured by a statistic referred to as the *variance*, or by its square root, the *standard deviation*. The variance is the mean of the squares of the difference of each datum from the distribution mean. A distribution that is bunched around the mean, such as that shown in Figure 8.10, has a small standard deviation; one that is more spread out, such as that shown in Figure 8.11, has a larger standard deviation.

Now, if the distribution is *normal*, then the mean value will coincide with the mode at the central, high point, marked in Figures 8.10 and 8.11. The

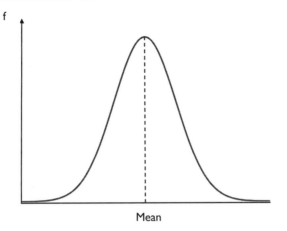

Mean

Figure 8.10 Normal distribution: smaller standard deviation.

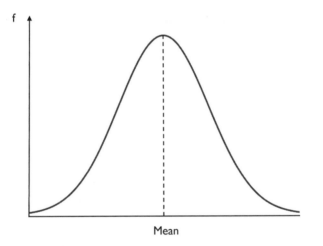

Mean

Figure 8.11 Normal distribution: larger standard deviation.

normal distribution is symmetrical about the mean, so half of the distribution is to the left of the mean and half to the right. Mathematically, it is possible to demonstrate that, if we divide the distribution into two parts, where the left hand portion extends to one standard deviation above the mean (Figure 8.12), then about two-thirds of the distribution will be included in this left hand part and one-third in the right hand part. If we extend the left hand portion to two or to three standard deviations above the mean, as in Figures 8.13 and 8.14, then the left hand part will contain approximately 95 per cent or 99 per cent of the distribution, respectively. This fact about the normal distribution forms the (still arbitrary) basis for setting the conventionally used confidence levels at 5 per cent and 1 per cent (i.e. 100–95 and 100–99).

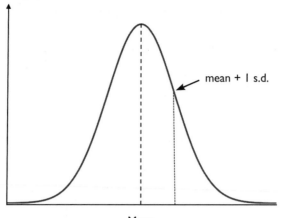

Figure 8.12 Normal distribution: mean and mean + 1 standard deviation.

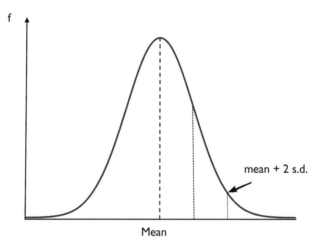

Figure 8.13 Normal distribution: mean and mean + 2 standard deviations.

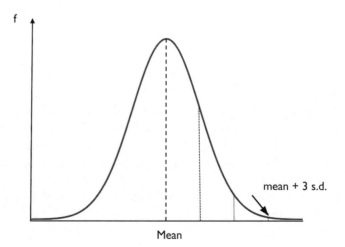

Figure 8.14 Normal distribution: mean and mean + 3 standard deviations.

As in the main text, these confidence levels are generally expressed as probability or p values. A p value of less than 0.05 (5 per cent) means that, if the null hypothesis is true, then there is less than a 0.05 probability, or 5 in 100, or 1 in 20 chance, of obtaining the result that has in fact been obtained; a p value of 0.01 represents a 1 in 100 chance. Essentially, this means that, if the data collection were to repeated a large number of times, then only in one case in every twenty (or one case in every hundred) would we expect to obtain the same level of association or correlation etc. that we actually did obtain, *if the null hypothesis is true*. Clearly, in both cases, this is a small chance and we have to make a decision in respect of how small is small enough. Conventionally, we can claim that our results are *statistically significant*, which is to say, we can reject the null hypothesis, if the p value is no more than 0.05. In the days before the use of computer software packages for statistical analysis, researchers would state that their results were significant at the 0.05 or 0.01 levels. Nowadays, the software will generate a specific value for p and this value will generally be published along with the results, rather than making specific reference to the conventional confidence levels. Nevertheless, the conventional levels are still relevant; a researcher would (conventionally) be justified in claiming that their result is statistically significant given a p value of, say, 0.03, but not if the value was 0.07. Clearly, the smaller the p value, the more significant the result *in statistical terms*; as we have noted in the main text, a result may be statistically significant, but this does not necessarily entail that it is educationally or socially significant.

The chi-square test

The next test that we shall consider operates by a comparison of the shapes of the distributions of two samples. It is called the *chi-square measure of association*, often written χ^2 (χ is the Greek letter which is rendered as chi, in English, and pronounced kie – with the ie as in pie). The chi-square test measures the probability that two (or more) samples could have been drawn from the same population. Again, if this probability is found to be sufficiently small (less than 0.05) then you can have a degree of confidence that the samples were, in fact, drawn from different populations. In other words, you can reject the null hypothesis.

We shall illustrate the calculation and application of the chi-square test on a set of results from the research by Brown that we have referred to in Chapters 6 and 7. Table 8.7 shows the distribution of two samples of parents according to whether they are classified in Brown's work as 'generalisers' or 'localisers'. The samples are drawn, respectively, from parents whose children attend East Wood and Chambers Schools. This kind of table is called a *contingency table*. It is important for the chi-square test that the figures in the cells are frequencies and not percentages or scores of some other kind. The chi-square test also imposes two other requirements on the data. First, the items in each cell of the table must be independent of each other. In the case of Brown's data this condition holds, because the unit of analysis is the individual parent and each

Table 8.7 Distribution of generalisers and localisers amongst parents at East Wood and Chambers Schools

	East Wood	Chambers	totals
Generalisers	28	6	34
Localisers	28	48	76
Totals	56	54	110

parent is classified as either a generaliser or a localiser and as either an East Wood or a Chambers parent. Each parent, then, is classified in only one cell of the table. The final condition is that the expected frequency should not be less than five for any cell; we will explain what is meant by the *expected frequency* below.

Inspecting the table, you will notice that the East Wood sample is divided equally between generalisers and localisers, whereas the Chambers sample is heavily dominated by localisers, who outnumber the generalisers by a ratio of eight to one. It is hardly necessary to draw the histograms of the two sample distributions to see that they are very different in shape. Nevertheless, the histograms are drawn in Figure 8.15.

Now, it looks very much as if the two samples of parents are drawn from populations that differ in terms of the distribution of generalisers and localisers. Nevertheless, there is, as with the textbook data, a finite probability that even such obviously different samples could have been drawn from the same population or from two populations with the same characteristics. Chi-square will enable us to estimate this probability.

The null hypothesis states that there is no difference between the populations from which the two samples are drawn and so no association between school and generalizing/localising. If this were to be the case, then the expected ratio of generalisers and localisers would be the same in each sample of parents. Altogether, 34 of the 110 parents are generalisers and 76 of them are localisers. If the 56 East Wood parents were divided between generalisers and localisers in this proportion, then:

$$\text{the number of East Wood generalisers} = \frac{34}{110} \times 56 = 17.309$$

$$\text{the number of East Wood localisers} = \frac{76}{110} \times 56 = 38.691$$

Similarly:

$$\text{the number of Chambers generalisers} = \frac{34}{110} \times 54 = 16.691$$

$$\text{the number of Chambers localisers} = \frac{76}{110} \times 54 = 37.309$$

Obviously, the East Wood sample could not actually have been divided between 17.309 generalisers and 38.691 localisers, since the categories are mutually exclusive. Each

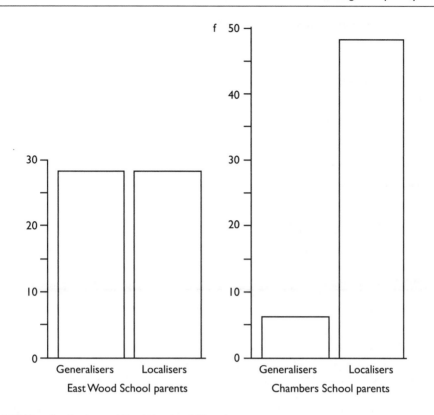

Figure 8.15 The distributions of East Wood and Chambers parents.

parent has been classified as either generaliser or localiser and not a bit of each. Nevertheless, these figures are those that a proportional distribution of generalisers and localisers would give. They are called the *expected frequencies*. As we have mentioned, the use of the chi-square test requires that these values should not be less than five for any cell. As you can see, this condition is met by Brown's data. The original, observed frequencies and the expected frequencies are shown in Table 8.8. The final column in Table 8.8 includes the calculation of chi-square.

The formula for chi-square is:

$$\chi^2 = \Sigma \frac{(|O - E| - 0.5)^2}{E}$$

This needs a little explanation. $|O - E|$ means the positive difference between O and E. That is, you should subtract the lesser value from the greater so that the result is always a positive number.

Before referring to tabulated values of chi-square, there is one more consideration. In a 2×2 contingency table, such as the one used here (that is, it is 2×2 without the totals), then provided that the totals are known, only one other figure needs to be known in order to enable you to fill in all the rest. Try it on Table 8.9.

Table 8.8 Calculation of chi-square

School	Category	Observed frequency (O)	Expected frequency (E)	$\dfrac{(|O-E|-0.5)^2}{E}$
East Wood	Generalisers	28	17.309	6.000
	Localisers	28	38.691	2.684
Chambers	Generalisers	6	16.691	6.222
	Localisers	48	37.309	3.064
			χ^2 = total =	17.970

Table 8.9 An incomplete 2×2 contingency table

	a	b	Totals
A	?	25	60
B	?	?	50
Totals	40	70	110

The table is described as having one *degree of freedom*. The chi-square test can also be used (calculated in exactly the same way) where the contingency table has more cells. More cells means more degrees of freedom. A 3×4 table, for example, has six degrees of freedom, because you need to know the values of at least six cells, in addition to the totals, in order to fill in the rest. The number of degrees of freedom of a table is calculated by multiplying one less than the number of rows by one less than the number of columns. So, an 8×5 table has 7 × 4 = 28 degrees of freedom.

You need to calculate the number of degrees of freedom, because the critical value of chi-square depends upon it. In the case under consideration, here and in all 2×2 tables, the number of degrees of freedom, or *df*, is one. Referring to the tabulated values for chi-square in Wright (1997), we found that Brown's results are significant at at least the 0.01 level for a one-tailed test. The null hypothesis can confidently be rejected. We can infer that the populations of East Wood and Chambers parents are significantly differently distributed in terms of generalisers and localisers.

Correlation

The last kind of statistical technique that we shall consider provides an estimate of the strength of association between two variables, or the extent to which one variable is *correlated* with another. Such a statistic is called a *coefficient of correlation*. Two variables are said to be correlated when an increase in one variable is regularly accompanied by an increase or by a decrease in the other. For example, the cost of filling up your car with petrol is correlated with the quantity of petrol that you have to put in, because the more petrol you buy the more it will cost.

There is a range of ways in which two variables can be correlated. The petrol example is an instance of *positive correlation*. If you draw a *scatter graph* of the cost of petrol against the quantity, you will get something like Figure 8.16 (at 2008 prices).

Figure 8.16 Positive correlation.

The term *scatter graph* or *scattergram*, which denotes this kind of diagram, is rather a misnomer, in this instance. You will notice that the points in the graph lie in a straight line. The correlation is *positive* because both of the variables are increasing together, so that the graph goes upwards from left to right. Negative correlation is also possible. Figure 8.17 graphs the distance remaining of a (fictitious) 300-mile journey against the time that a motorist has been driving at a steady fifty miles per hour. The correlation is *negative*, because an increase in one variable is accompanied by a decrease in the other, so that the graph goes downwards from left to right.

Both of these examples are artificial. They have been produced using mathematical relationships rather than empirical observations. Empirical observations, even of physical phenomena observed under laboratory conditions, rarely produce such simple relationships. You could, of course reproduce the first graph empirically by purchasing the various quantities of petrol and recording the cost. But you had better make sure that you use the same filling station and that the price doesn't change during your 'research'. Producing the second graph empirically might prove an interesting, if dangerous challenge.

Empirical observations, then, are likely to produce rather more messy arrays of points. For example, Figure 8.18 shows examination performances and authorised absences for the secondary schools in a local education authority. This time, the data are 'real'. From an inspection of the scattergram, it looks as if there is some degree of negative correlation between these variables. It is clearly not a perfect negative correlation. Indeed it would be astonishing if it were to be so. Moving from one point to another from left to right sometimes involves a downward movement, sometimes an upward movement, and sometimes a horizontal movement. In other words, an increase in authorised absence between two particular schools might be associated with either an increase or a decrease in examination performance, or their examination performances might be the same. Nevertheless, there are clearly more downward moves than upward moves.

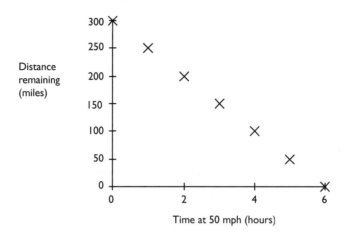

Figure 8.17 Negative correlation.

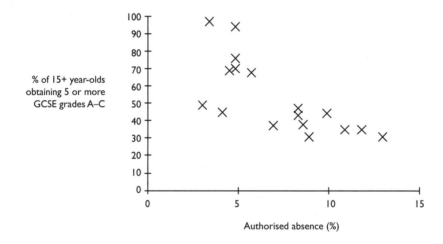

Figure 8.18 Negative correlation: GCSE passes and authorised absences at schools in one LEA in 1994–5.

Unlike the previous examples, there is no straight line that will pass through all of the points in Figure 8.18. However, there are statistical techniques that enable the calculation of the position of the line that is closest to most of the points. This line is called a *line of best fit*, or a *regression line*.

If you were to take a sample of secondary school students and graph the distances of their homes from the school against their reading ages, you would probably be surprised to find any pattern of association at all. In fact, you might expect the variables, reading age and distance from school, to be *normally distributed*, that is, clustering around the central values with few extreme points, as in Figure 8.7. When two

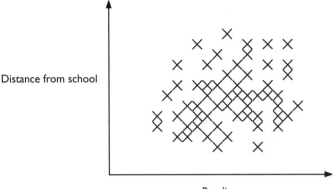

Distance from school

Reading age

Figure 8.19 Zero correlation.

normally distributed variables are graphed against each other, the result is a roughly elliptical cluster of points as shown in the artificially produced Figure 8.19. For this scattergram there is no single line of best fit. A rectangular pattern of points would also have no line of best fit. In these cases, the level of correlation is zero.

The strength of correlation between two variables ranges from perfect positive, through zero, to perfect negative. The coefficients of correlation that correspond to these are +1, 0 and –1, respectively. In virtually all cases, the coefficient that you calculate will lie between 0 and +1 or between 0 and –1. As with the other tests that we have discussed, you can use tables giving critical values of coefficients of correlation to determine the significance level of the association between your variables.

We are going to illustrate the calculation of a particular coefficient of correlation called *Spearman's rho*. Rho is another Greek letter, written ρ. The data that we shall use are those that are illustrated in the scattergram in Figure 8.18. It is part of the published information on schools in a particular local education authority in England for the year 1994–5. The data are shown in Table 8.10 and show the rate of authorised absence and the percentage of students obtaining five or more General Certificate of Secondary Education (GCSE) subject passes at grade C or above.

As we indicated above, the shape of the scattergram suggests a negative correlation between absences and examination performance. This is interpreted to mean that schools having lower absence rates tend to have higher rates of examination passes and vice versa. The coefficient of correlation is therefore expected to lie somewhere between 0 and –1. In order to calculate the coefficient, we have completed the values in Table 8.11.

The values in the fourth and fifth columns of Table 8.11 are the ranks, R_A and R_P, assigned to absences A, and percentage of students obtaining five or more GCSEs at grade C or above, labelled P. The ranks were assigned in the same way as for the Mann–Whitney test, described earlier in this chapter, except that each column (A and P) was ranked separately. The values in the final column of Table 8.11 are obtained by squaring the difference between the ranks for each school. For example, the ranks

Table 8.10 GCSE passes and authorised absences at schools in one LEA in 1994–5

School	Authorised absence (%)	Students obtaining 5 or more GCSE passes at grade C or above as a percentage of students aged 15 or above
A	3.1	95
B	8.3	47
C	6.9	37
D	8.6	38
E	4.1	45
F	4.8	70
G	11.8	35
H	3.4	97
I	4.5	69
J	8.9	31
K	13.0	31
L	4.8	76
M	3.0	49
N	5.7	68
O	9.9	44
P	8.3	43
Q	10.9	35
R	4.8	94

for School A are 2 and 17; the difference between the ranks is 15; the square of 15 is $15 \times 15 = 225$. This final column is totalled to give the sum, 1754.5. Rho is calculated according to the following formula:

$$\rho = 1 - \frac{6 \Sigma D^2}{(N^3 - N)}$$

where ΣD^2 is the sum of the squares of the differences between the ranks, 1596.25, and N is the number of schools. Thus, in this case:

$$\rho = 1 - \frac{6 \times 1754.5}{(18^3 - 18)} = 1 - \frac{10527}{5832 - 18} = 1 - 1.811 = -0.811$$

You will immediately notice that the prediction that the coefficient would be negative is confirmed. It remains to determine the level of significance of the negative association. Referring to Clegg's (1983) table of critical values for Spearman's rho, we found that the results are significant at at least the 0.005 level for a one-tailed

Table 8.11 Calculation of Spearman's rho

School	Absence (%) A	GCSE passes P	R_A	R_p	$D^2 = (R_A - R_p)^2$
A	3.1	95	2	17	225
B	8.3	47	11.5	10	2.25
C	6.9	37	10	5	25
D	8.6	38	13	6	49
E	4.1	45	4	9	25
F	4.8	70	7	14	49
G	11.8	35	17	3.5	182.25
H	3.4	97	3	18	225
I	4.5	69	5	13	64
J	8.9	31	14	1.5	156.25
K	13.0	31	18	1.5	272.25
L	4.8	76	7	15	64
M	3.0	49	1	11	100
N	5.7	68	9	12	9
O	9.9	44	15	8	49
P	8.3	43	11.5	7	20.25
Q	10.9	35	16	3.5	156.25
R	4.8	94	7	16	81
		$\Sigma D^2 =$			1754.5

test. Therefore, the null hypothesis, which states that there is no association between authorised absences and GCSE passes, can be rejected. You can conclude that there is a negative association between authorised absences and GCSE passes that is significant at the 0.005 level.

There are other coefficients of correlation that can be used. *Pearson's product–moment coefficient*, r, is one that is commonly used. However, as is the case with the t tests, Pearson's test is parametric. This places additional demands on the data including that the two lists of scores should be normally distributed. In the case of the schools data, both lists are heavily weighted towards the lower values – they are positively skewed. The data is represented in the histograms in Figures 8.20 and 8.21. On visual inspection, they are clearly not normal distributions.

Another requirement of the Pearson product moment technique is that the association between the two variables must be *linear*. That is, the scattergram must approximate to a straight line. This is, in fact, the case with the schools data, as can be seen from Figure 8.18. However, it is possible that two variables may be related in a way that is *non-linear* and that the scattergram may cluster around different shaped curves, such as the one illustrated in Figure 8.22. Pearson's statistic is not appropriate here. The Spearman technique, on the other hand can be applied in a wider range of cases, including the one illustrated in Figure 8.22.

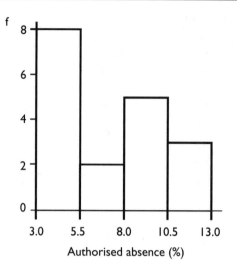

Figure 8.20 Histogram: authorised absences in schools in one LEA.

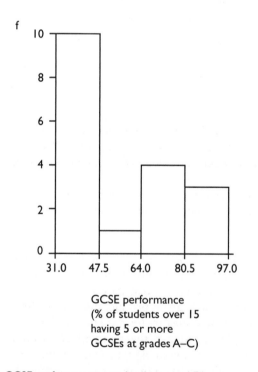

GCSE performance
(% of students over 15
having 5 or more
GCSEs at grades A–C)

Figure 8.21 Histogram: GCSE performances in schools in one LEA.

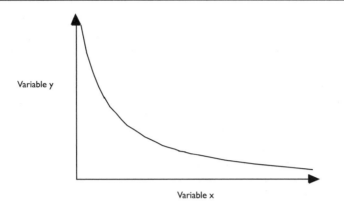

Figure 8.22 A non-linear association.

In general terms, the parametric techniques, some of which we have mentioned, but have not described in detail, provide better estimates for the significance level or for the coefficient of correlation. However, they will do this only if the data conforms to much more stringent requirements. If you are considering using these tests, or if you are assessing other work that uses them, you should consult a statistics textbook, such as one of those that we have included in the bibliography.

Some caveats

Our own research has tended to be dominated by qualitative methods. Unlike some authors of books on research methods, however, we do not perceive a rigid divide between qualitative and quantitative approaches. Few would regard the Luria research as quantitative, yet he has counted and tabulated his findings in support of his conclusions. We have both, in our own work, made use of the kind of quantitative representation and statistical analysis of data that we have introduced in this chapter. Our feeling is that this has significantly added to the quality of our work. Furthermore, few researchers in education can avoid engaging with research that is more extensively statistical in nature. In part, the intention behind this chapter is that it should enable you to engage with such work with at least some degree of understanding of how the claims that are being made are justified. We also hope that you will be encouraged to make use yourself of some of the quantitative strategies that have been introduced, where their use will extend and develop your work, either in conception or in presentation. We should, however, emphasise a number of caveats, some of which we have already made in the course of this chapter.

First, and rather counter to the general thrust of this chapter, presenting essentially qualitative data in quantitative form can have negative results. For example, a colleague of ours – a very experienced and widely published researcher – submitted what we certainly felt to be an interesting paper on educational assessment to a journal in the field of educational assessment. The paper reported on a small-scale piece of research that had involved clinical interviews with a couple of dozen school children using

National Assessment Standard Assessment Tasks as the focus of the interviews. The paper made a number of important points about the students' interpretation of these tasks and about the validity of the tasks for the purposes of assessing the UK National Curriculum. Our colleague had collated some of the results in much the same kind of tables as Luria's in Table 8.1. The editor of the journal rejected the paper on the grounds that the sample was too small.

Now this certainly suggests a fundamental lack of understanding of the relevance of sample size on the part of the editor. Presumably, they would also have rejected Luria's work on the same grounds. Whereas the tabulation of the data had been intended to provide a clear overview of the sample, it had allowed the research, in the editor's mind, to be interrogated as if it were of a quantitative nature. Where resources are finite, there is bound to be a trade-off between the richness of the data and the number of subjects in the sample. This precisely corresponds to the comparison between the elaborated description of qualitative presentation and the more extensive but summary potential of quantification.

Second, there is commonly a certain tendency amongst those offering advice on research to a doctrinaire attitude to statistical testing. This attitude insists that, if data are in quantitative form, they should always be subjected to statistical analysis. In our opinion, such a position is misguided. As we have indicated, statistical *significance* should not be confused with significance per se. When sample sizes are sufficiently large, almost any difference is likely to prove statistically significant. Furthermore, the availability of statistical packages as computer software has enabled and even encouraged the unprincipled application of highly sophisticated statistical tools in lieu of serious analysis. As Tony Halil, a statistician and former colleague of ours, used to say, if you torture data sufficiently, they're bound to confess to something. The danger is that, if you are not really clear on what the techniques do or how they work or what assumptions they are making about your data, it is difficult to see how you can have any confidence in the conclusions you build on these 'confessions'. This having been said, if your data are or can be organised into an appropriate form and if you have a specific question to put to them, then statistical techniques may be of considerable use and should be considered. All instruments of analysis, however, should be used deliberately, correctly and with an explicit purpose in mind.

We will give an example of an inappropriate use of a statistical technique from a case that we have already mentioned in an earlier chapter. A student on one of our courses wanted to see whether there was any difference between the use of gender-specific and gender-neutral pronouns by primary age girls and boys. The students presented a number of primary school students with a series of sentences that they were to complete. The sentences had been designed to encourage the use of a pronoun in their completion (although some of the students used alternative parts of speech). Each sentence ending was recorded as masculine (he, him, his, etc.), feminine (her, she, hers, etc.), or neutral (it, its, etc.). The results were tabulated according to whether the response was made by a girl or a boy, giving a table similar to Table 8.12.

The table is a 2×3 contingency table. It looks ripe for a chi-square test. So the test was run, the value for χ^2 being calculated as 24.101. With two degrees of freedom, significance for a one-tailed test was claimed at at least the 0.005 level. Where's the problem?

The problem is that the items in the cells are not independent. The unit of analysis,

Table 8.12 Pronoun use by primary school children

	Masculine	Feminine	Neutral	Totals
Boy	26	12	112	150
Girl	59	0	91	150
Totals	85	12	203	300

here, is the individual sentence completion. But there were several different sentences and a classful of girls and boys. Endings provided for the same sentence are not independent of each other in so far as the form of the sentence influences the choice of ending. Endings provided by each individual girl or boy are not independent of each other in so far as each may be expected to respond with a degree of consistency.

In fact, given that the interest was in responses made by individuals, the research should more properly have been designed to make the individual the unit of analysis, as is the case, for example, in Luria's table (Table 8.1). This could have been done by rating each individual in terms of, say, the following score:

$$\frac{\text{masculine endings} - \text{feminine endings}}{\text{all endings}}$$

This would have face validity as a measure of the tendency to masculine-dominated pronoun use. It is not an ideal measure. It would not, for example, distinguish between those making equal use of masculine and feminine endings, on the one hand, and those making exclusive use of neutral endings; in both cases, the rating would be zero. Nevertheless, it would enable the ranking of the two groups (girls and boys) and, if necessary, the application of the Mann–Whitney test.

This example emphasises the need to be clear about the assumptions that you are implicitly making about your data by using a statistical test. Just because, as here, the numbers will fit into the formula or the computer package, doesn't mean that the test is appropriate.

The next point concerns the distinction that must be made between association and cause. Take, for example, the regression analysis that we conducted on the schools data. We found that there was a negative correlation between absences and GCSE performance that was significant at the 0.005 level. Now a politician may wish to infer that a high level of absence is directly responsible for poor examination performance. A politician of a different persuasion may want to argue that the students of a school which has a low examination performance rate might reasonably feel that there is not much point in going to school, so that the absences are, in a sense, caused by the examination performances. The prevalence of this kind of inappropriate inference is quite possibly exactly what Disraeli meant when he pronounced that there were lies, damned lies and statistics.

The fact of the matter is that the data that we have provided and the analysis that we have conducted do not entitle you to make either inference. It is not appropriate for us to speculate, here, on the causes of such differences between schools. However, they are, we feel, likely to be the outcome of a highly complex set of factors that will, in all likelihood, operate somewhat differently even between schools exhibiting similar statistical profiles. The finding that there is an association between two or more factors does not, then, provide an answer, so much as raise a question for further research.

In addition, the manner in which we have obtained the data – from the published lists available on the internet – does not allow us access to the way in which they are produced. The list of schools, for example, contains both independent and state schools. These two sectors do not have the same requirements when it comes to the publishing of their results. 'Absences' are recorded as 'authorised' absences. It is unlikely that all schools have the same procedures for registering authorisation. These and other questions can and should be asked about the validity and reliability of these figures as measures of school culture and performance.

Finally, unless your own use of quantitative techniques is very limited, we strongly suggest that you go on from this text to one of the more sophisticated handbooks that we have listed in our annotated bibliography. If you are registered on a course at an academic institution, you may well have access to specialist advice from professional statisticians. If this is the case, then it is generally a good idea to seek their advice very early on. A final word of warning is appropriate here, as well. Do not go to the statistical adviser or, indeed, the book, with the expectation that they will tell you what to do with your data; far less that they will do it for you. What they will want to know from you is precisely what you want to know of the data. Only then will they be in a position to advise on the selection of the appropriate statistical techniques. Statistical tools are no different from any other methodological techniques in that they are resources to be recruited in a deliberate and reflective research endeavour, whether it be your own research or reading someone else's. It is the integrity and enthusiasm of such deliberation and reflection that measures the quality of your research, not the sophistication of your statistics.

Chapter 9

Specialising, localising and generalising

A mode of interrogation

In this book we are taking a particular stance on educational research. Essentially, we are presenting a description of educational research activity as the production of a coherent set of statements. These are established and located within explicitly stated theoretical and empirical contexts. The research process, conceived in this way, begins with vagueness and hesitation and plurality and moves towards precision and coherence. You can think of this as the imposition of order, which we refer to as a *constructive* view. Alternatively, you may consider yourself to be engaging in the discovery of order – a *realist* view.[1] For the record, we are inclined towards the former and, in this chapter, we have for the most part chosen our language accordingly. We feel that this is appropriate, especially as the language chosen throughout the earlier chapters is probably more consistent with a realist position. However, constructivism and realism are *metatheoretical* positions. Essentially, they are concerned with the nature of research (and other cognitive acts) rather than the doing of it. They are concerned with *epistemological* concerns – relating to the nature of knowledge – and *ontological* concerns – relating to the nature of being. They are concerned with the origins of structure rather than its practical description or production. From our perspective, then, it is no more necessary to resolve your epistemology or ontology in your empirical research than it is to incorporate a declaration of your religious affiliation, though some would consider one or more of these essential. Unfortunately, however, the tendency to make a pass at metatheoretical discussion is commonly presented in lieu of adequate theoretical development.

We have tried to give an introduction to a range of methodological resources that you may draw on in your research activity. In many instances, our exposition of these resources has been the explicit message of our text. At a more implicit level, we have also attempted to provide some guidance on how to move towards coherence. It is coherence that we are claiming to be the fundamental criterion by which educational research is to be judged. Now this is not to claim that perfect coherence is attainable; quite apart from anything else, the language that we use to present our research is not capable of the level of precision that such perfection would demand. Furthermore, as Dowling (2009) argues, it is possible to generate too much coherence in an organisational language or theory to the extent that it can see only itself; it becomes unable to learn. This kind of theoretical overdevelopment, however, is something that is not likely to be possible in the context of a single piece of empirical research; rather, such necrosis of theory is a possible product of considerable ageing. For most practical purposes, then, coherence is an appropriate aim for research and an appropriate criterion by which to evaluate its products.

Research must be generalised and generalisable in relation to its local empirical contexts. In this respect, it must, at least to some degree, be more like theoretical knowledge than situational knowledge, to borrow Luria's terms. Even if, somewhat naively, we regard ethnographic work as bringing back the story of the other, this story must be rendered intelligible within the academic culture in which it is to be presented. As Clifford Geertz (1988) elegantly argues, it's not so much the fact of having been *there*, in the field, that validates the anthropologist's account as their having been *here*, in the university, acquiring the principles of realisation of anthropological discourse. In this chapter we want to be more explicit about the process whereby the coherence of such 'theoretical knowledge' is to be produced. This will involve bringing together and organising elements of the discussions of the earlier chapters and particularly the contents of Chapters 2 and 3.

We must first re-emphasise another feature of the approach that we are taking. Essentially, if structural coherence is the intention of your research activity, then the search for structural coherence must inform your interpretation of research that has been carried out by others. The process that we are proposing for *doing* research is, to this extent, precisely the same as that to be adopted in the *reading* of research. You don't have to interview the author. But you do have to ask precisely the same kinds of questions of someone else's interviewing procedures as you do of your own.

The act of asking questions is crucial. We want to maintain that it is the process of asking questions that drives the development of structural coherence. The kind of questions to be asked and the way in which they are put make up a *mode of interrogation*. Our intention, in this chapter, is to make as explicit as we can the nature of this mode of interrogation. We shall argue that there is a sense in which it is the mode of interrogation that defines the activity – in this case, research. The activities of educational practitioners other than researchers generate alternative modes of interrogation. In this conception, educational research and other educational practices must be regarded as separate spheres. This position has implications for the practitioner-researcher and, in particular, for the approach to educational research that is often referred to as *action research*. We shall illustrate, briefly, an action research project in Chapter 10. We shall discuss the issue of the practitioner-researcher more generally in Chapter 11. We shall also make some reference to it in the discussion in this chapter, in which we concentrate on the presentation of the research mode of interrogation.

The research mode of interrogation: specialising the theoretical context

Since we are introducing a mode of interrogation, we felt that it would be appropriate to organise the discussion under headings that are the principal questions to be addressed in either conducting or reading research. We have collected these questions together into a schema for the mode of interrogation at the end of the chapter. The first set of questions concerns the development of the theoretical context of the research. We have referred to this process as *specialisation*.

What is the general theoretical field within which the work is located?

In Chapter 3 we referred to the *theoretical field* as a nebula of debates, theories and empirical findings. But the theoretical field more appropriately refers to a notional community of researchers and/or practitioners as well as to their output. Your work, or the work that you are reading, is entering into discursive relations with this community. In other words, the theoretical field comprises, first, the authors of whom the researcher is a reader. These are *authorities* within the theoretical field. Authors' names and journal titles in the bibliography should provide some sort of an indication of the relevant authorities. But it may also be important to consider the relevance of *disciplinary knowledge* to the research. An academic discipline, such as sociology, for example, incorporates a range of journals and practitioners, but it also entails a canon of knowledge and texts that are its foundations. This canon – not, of course, rigidly defined – will, in general terms, constitute the content of undergraduate work in the discipline and therefore may be generally assumed by more advanced writing in the discipline.

The theoretical fields within which educational research is developed are not confined to the academic disciplines and certainly not to the traditional, academic disciplines. There are also what might appropriately be referred to as *professional disciplines* related to the curriculum and to assessment and also to educational management and administration. These will also be associated with journals and practitioners and will also generate what might be referred to as canonical knowledge. The latter might include current and historical details of the development of a particular educational system. UK authors addressing UK audiences will probably assume some knowledge of (at least) the 1944, 1988, 1996 and 2002 Education Acts, the structure of the public assessment and examination systems, and school inspection, for example. Writing within professional disciplines will include academic educational research, but it will also include non-academic writing directed at practitioner and lay audiences. The professional journals of school subject associations and governmental publications, for example, fall into this latter category.

The second component of the theoretical field includes the readers or potential readers of the researcher's own writing. The researcher cannot anticipate all possible members of the second category. They can and should, however, have a clear sense of their ideal reader and make this explicit. This is the *readership* of the theoretical field.

The relationship between authorities and readership is an important one in defining the nature of the work and informing the way in which it is presented. Where the work is research, its readership may be understood as a subset of the authorities of the field. Research adopts a position and presents findings for peer evaluation and its texts might be described as what Dowling refers to as *exchange texts*, that is, there is a degree to which authority over the principles of their evaluation is handed over to the audience or readership (see Chapter 7 and Dowling, 2009, for discussion of pedagogic and exchange texts) and so the authority of the text itself is weakened by, for example, the use of hedging: 'on the basis of our findings, we suggest that, or it may be that, or it seems likely that some interpretation of social class is implicated in the evaluation of student ability', rather than simply, 'social class informs the evaluation of student ability'. If you are constituting yourself as a reader of research in these terms, then your responsibility to the field is to participate in its evaluation or, as we are presenting it here, its interrogation.

On the other hand, a work that is primarily pedagogic stands as an authority in relation to its ideal readership; naturally, this does not preclude the possibility that the actual reader might reject this authority, but the text will be formulated, more authoritatively, as a *pedagogic text*. You may give some consideration to the way in which this book is presented, linguistically; is it primarily a pedagogic text or an exchange text?

Further, the extent to which the authorities and readership of research coincide determines the extent to which the researcher can assume knowledge of the former. We can read this the other way. An important indicator of the coincidence of the authority and readership components of the theoretical field is the amount of field knowledge assumed by the text. Field knowledge is assumed by a text that indexes but does not elaborate upon its authorities.

What is the problematic?

The notional community that constitutes the theoretical field is inevitably very broad. In conducting and reading research, you must specialise. This entails the denoting of key work, positions and debates that define what we might call the *problematic* within which the research is situated. The problematic may be one that is already established. For example, the research may be concerned with factors effecting school effectiveness. In this case, there is an established body of work that is concerned with this area. This body of work may be conceived as a specialisation within a more general field comprising educational researchers, administrators and practitioners as well as, perhaps, politicians and public commentators. This field clearly incorporates a diverse range of motives and *genres*. In defining the school effectiveness problematic, it would be important to mark out the research as distinct from, for example, journalism and inspectors' reports. This is not because research is being constituted as superior, in any absolute sense, to these other genres. Rather, the mode of interrogation that is applied to any genre of work should be specific to that genre. In a sense, it is the mode of interrogation that defines the specificity of a genre.

On the other hand, the problematic may not be one that is established as an area of interest. Under these circumstances, the researcher must organise a space for themselves. A range of work is to be cited in such a way as to make clear how each item relates to the specialised area that is the problematic under construction. Again, however, the problematic is to be constructed with reference to work in the research genre.

What is the specific problem?

At this point, the level of theoretical development is at its sharpest and most specialised. The researcher is making one or more specific propositions or hypotheses and/or asking one or more specific questions. We shall refer to this highly specialised region as the *problem* of the research. At the end of a research write-up, the *propositions*, *hypotheses* or *questions* may be recast as *conclusions*. The problem is given in theoretical terms. It stands as an abstraction in relation to any local *empirical setting*. That it is an abstraction, however, does not entail that it may be vague. On the contrary, the interrogation of the propositions, hypotheses, questions or conclusions should aim to establish them to a high degree of precision whereby their terms are defined by the problematic.

For example, the articulation of a problem concerned with school effectiveness entails the shaping and/or selection of a definition (which may be multidimensional) of 'school effectiveness' in relation to or drawn from the school effectiveness problematic. When the problem is fully stated, its concepts will also be defined in relation to each other. That is, the problem recruits as much of the problematic as is necessary in order to establish itself as internally complete and consistent. Essentially, the *concepts* involved in the problem should be developed to a degree that enables their empirical measurement or *operationalisation*.

Operationalisation involves the movement between the theoretical and empirical contexts of the research. We shall now move on to the empirical sphere, starting at the level of the empirical field.

The research mode of interrogation: localising the empirical

What is the general empirical field within which the work is located?

The *empirical field* may be glossed as the broad range of practices and experiences to which the research relates. Examples might be the management of schools or children learning mathematics or attitudes to alcohol. Like the theoretical field, the empirical field also constitutes a community or communities. Again, these may be more notional than substantive. The field is being constituted by the research as an object of study that is to be described in terms of the theoretical problematic. It is this relationship of *objectification* that distinguishes between the theoretical and empirical fields. The theoretical field objectifies the empirical field and not the other way around. The community or communities comprising the theoretical field engage in the production and interrogation of research and of other modes of commentary on the empirical field.

This does not mean that there is a necessary division between those who are observers and those who are observed. Indeed, all educational practice properly entails both activity and reflection upon that activity (see Schon, 1983). Our position, however, is that the theoretical field consists of genres of reflection that are distinguished from the practices and experiences upon which they reflect. Preparing and evaluating a lesson both involve reflection upon teaching, but they are genres of reflection that are incorporated within the practice of teaching. It would be inappropriate to apply the mode of interrogation that defines the research genre to a lesson plan. On the other hand, it would be an interesting and possibly useful task to construct a mode of interrogation for lesson planning and to mark out the sources of its distinction from the research mode. Teachers as educational researchers are participating in a theoretical field; teachers as teachers are participating in what might be an empirical field for an educational researcher. The researcher might quite appropriately be the teacher themself. The division, then, is between the practices in which the human subjects are involved rather than between human subjects themselves.

What is the local empirical setting?

We have referred to the development of the theoretical context from theoretical field through problematic to problem as a process of specialisation. This follows Dowling's (1998, 2009) use of the term in his own organisational language, referred to as Social Activity Method. The corresponding process relating to empirical development is referred to as *localising*. The distinction is important. Specialised propositions or questions remain at a level of abstraction with respect to any particular empirical context. You can think of them as being measurable in a whole range of possible empirical settings. The task of empirical development in research is to localise this empirical space. This is essentially a process of selection in terms of research design, sampling strategies and data collection techniques. These categories are to be understood as reservoirs of methodological resources. They have been illustrated and discussed in Chapters 3, 5 and 6. Localising the empirical setting entails a selection from these reservoirs of resources and the deployment of the selected resources within the empirical field.

There will inevitably be contingent opportunities and difficulties in conducting empirical research. For example, the researcher may decide to enlarge the sample when offered unforeseen access to contexts or subjects. On the other hand, sample sizes may be reduced by circumstances beyond the control of the researcher. Any project that is carried out over an extended period of time is likely to be faced with a degree of *mortality* of its subjects. That is, participants who are selected in the sample and participate in the early stages of the research become unavailable subsequently. The use of questionnaires rarely achieves anything like a 100 per cent *response rate*; the researcher may anticipate this and inflate the planned sample size. This does not, of course, account for any possible *bias* that is introduced because of disparities between the characteristics of those responding and those not responding.

So you can expect inconsistencies within the empirical domain between what might be referred to as the planned setting and the achieved setting. We have emphasised consistency as the fundamental criterion for the evaluation of research. It is, therefore, important that attempts be made to reconcile these inconsistencies at least to the point of exploring their possible implications for the research.

What are the empirical findings?

The terminal point of empirical localisation is the production of the *empirical findings*. These are descriptions or summaries of the relations between *indicator variables*. They constitute the empirical correlates of the theoretical propositions and/or questions that make up the problem. These propositions and/or questions are in the form of relations between concept variables. Findings may be presented in the form of tables, charts, protocols, transcripts, narratives and so forth.

A central question in relation to the findings concerns the issue of *reliability*. In Chapter 3, reliability was defined as the repeatability of the process. For example, to what extent will the data be coded in the same way by different researchers employing the same coding instructions? The most direct way to address this issue is to incorporate a test of reliability that involves the comparison of the coding results of two or more coders. This is most easily achieved when the data are in quantitative form.

When data are presented in qualitative form, there will commonly be a need for selection. It is rarely possible to present all of the data that have been gathered. Neither is it necessarily desirable to do so. Nevertheless, it is important that the research justify its particular selection. The term 'reliability' can be expanded to include the measure of the extent to which the data presented are representative of the data generally. This may be addressed by presenting data in different forms, possibly employing a degree of quantification. This was the strategy employed by Luria that was discussed in Chapter 8.

Terminology: quantitative and qualitative approaches

Throughout this book, we have been using terms such as 'concept', 'indicator', 'validity', 'reliability' and so forth. It has been put to us that these are terms that are very commonly used in quantitative research, but less commonly in qualitative approaches, and that their use in the context of the latter tends to present a view of research that is fundamentally positivist. We disagree with this position. It is certainly the case that this series of terms is more commonly associated with quantitative than with qualitative research. However, our intention is precisely to challenge the widespread tendency to assume a strong differentiation between the two. Our proposition is that empirical research should be defined as an activity that justifies its general claims on the basis of the relationship between these claims, on the one hand, and specific empirical instances, on the other.

We therefore need a language to talk about this relationship and the language that we have, ready to hand, is the language of concepts and indicators etc. A concept is always going to be a theoretical category that is defined in terms of other concepts. An empirical category, by contrast, is one that is constituted in the language of the empirical setting – that is, in the language of the participants in the research – and should never be simply lifted out of the empirical setting and used as a theoretical term. The participants in Brown's work reported in Chapter 6, for example, would almost certainly not have used terms such as 'task-dependent' and 'task-independent' to describe their comments in the IMPACT diaries and the terms that they would have used would not have been usable as theoretical categories precisely because they would clearly have been more localised in the context of their use than the empirical setting as a whole. Once Brown had constituted these categories from his analytic engagement with his data, he had to devise a procedure for recognising them, for recognising task-dependent and task-independent diary entries; in other words, he had to generate indicators for his concepts. In quantitative research, this has to be done sufficiently explicitly to enable coding to be performed in a routine way. As we have suggested, qualitative research involves more active interpretation in the process of analysis and so its results are more likely to be presented in terms of elaborated description rather than in summary tables (though, as with Luria's work, this is also possible). Nevertheless, there must always be an argument regarding why and how a particular empirical observation stands as an instance of a particular theoretical category; there must always, in effect, be a discussion of the concept–indicator links and their validity and reliability and so forth.

None of this is to say that empirical categories should be avoided in all senses. In ethnographic work, for example, some of the key terms used by participants may be deployed in a more or less consistent way and may certainly be worthy of elaboration; the term 'earoles' famously applied to the academically earnest students in Paul Willis's *Learning to Labour* (1977), for example, might almost be emblematic of that work and its inclusion in the account is clearly vital. But it is not a theoretical category. Rather, we might say that its use constitutes an indicator in relation to what we might now want to refer to as the discourse of the 'lads' using the term in establishing a particular mode of masculinity.

We recognise that quantitative and qualitative approaches often tend to polarise the kinds of language that are used in formulating research reports and that this may be important in addressing respective ideal audiences. However, in conceptualising and prosecuting the research process itself – the process of reading as well as the process of doing – we are asserting the value of adopting a language that will assist us in moving towards coherence. That this language is associated by some with positivism (or whatever) is of no significance; we are not making that association.

The research mode of interrogation: from specialising and localising to validity and generalisation

The mode of interrogation describes the problem and findings as having been generated by the specialisation of the theoretical domain and the localisation of the empirical domain, respectively. This does not mean that either the chronological 'story' of the research process or its 'plot' as realised in its write-up necessarily takes this path. Applying the mode of interrogation – as it has thus far been introduced – in reading or in doing research affects or, at least, moves towards a coherent organising of the research in terms of theoretical specialisation and empirical localisation. This has been described as a dual movement that focuses in on the central concerns of the research from the theoretical and empirical directions separately, as is illustrated in Figure 9.1. The dual process has brought the theoretical domains and empirical domains into contact in a very specialised and highly localised region that relates the problem to the findings. At this point, we now have to consider the validity and reliability of this articulation and the nature of the implications of the research beyond this specialised and localised region.

How is the link between the problem and the findings established?

The link between the theoretical problem and the empirical findings is concerned with question of validity. In Chapter 3, we glossed validity as a measure of the extent to which you are measuring what you think you are measuring. It is concerned with the plausibility of the relationship between, on the one hand, the indicator variables that constitute the findings and, on the other, the concept variables that constitute the problem. As we have emphasised throughout this book, all research should incorporate an argument that attempts to establish this relationship. This argument may or may not include statistical measures of validity. In any case, the question that is to be put, here, is precisely how does the research establish the empirical basis of its theoretical propositions? Alternatively, put the other way round, how does the research justify its theoretical interpretation of its empirical findings?

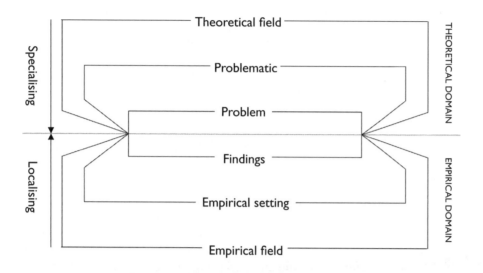

Figure 9.1 Theoretical and empirical domains.

How is the research generalised?

We have stated that what distinguishes the theoretical from the empirical domains is that statements within the former are abstractions with respect to situations within the latter. In particular, the problem stands in a relation of abstraction or context independence with respect to the findings. This entails that it can be construed as *preconceptualising* the findings of research conducted in alternative empirical settings. Thought of in this way, the problem imposes a *bias* upon future research; this is consistent with what we described earlier as a *constructive* approach. Alternatively, a *realist* approach might interpret the problem as *predicting* the findings of future research. Again, we do not believe that the choice of metatheoretical position itself imposes any particular bias upon the research. Nevertheless, whether you think in terms of preconceptualisation or prediction, the relationship between the problem and future research is an important one. It defines the *theoretical generalisability* of the research. Essentially, no piece of research is of any value as research at all unless it does impose upon the way in which you interpret the world on subsequent occasions; one might make the same claim for any work that intends to do more than simply entertain for a delimited period of time.

Central to the issue of generalisability is the concept of *implication*. We shall elaborate this concept by reference to an example. In Chapter 8 we conducted a chi-square test of Brown's data on the incidence of generalisers and localisers at two primary schools. Generaliser and localiser are the two values of the *variable* 'semantic selection'. The other variable is social class, Woods and Merttens (1994) having characterised East Wood as mixed middle class and working class and Chambers as predominantly working class. We should note that these two variables are operating on different *units of analysis*. Semantic selection refers to individual parents; social class refers, in this instance, to the school, which is to say, it classifies the school in terms of the social class of its intake. Brown is transferring the school variable ascription to the parents. He is claiming that if the school is, for example, predominantly working class, then there is a relatively high probability that any given parent sending their child to that school will be working class.

The group of parents who are represented by this data constituted a *sample*. The *population* from which this sample was drawn might be described at a range of levels. Minimally, the sample could have been a 100 per cent sample of this particular group of parents. On the other hand, it could have been a very small sample of the population of all parents having children currently attending primary schools in the UK. Or the population might be defined to lie anywhere between these extreme values. However the population is defined, the assumption is being made that it varies in terms of the two variables, semantic selection and social class.

The *null hypothesis*, in this case, states that there is no *association* between these variables in the population from which the sample was drawn. From the results of the chi-square test, we know that the probability of drawing this particular sample from a population having no association between these variables is very small – less than 0.0005. We can, therefore, be confident in rejecting the null hypothesis. In doing so, we are making an *inference* that there is an association between social class and semantic selection for the population as a whole. In other words, we are making a *generalisation* of the findings as they relate to the particular sample analysed by Brown to a larger population and therefore to a greater or smaller range of potential empirical settings. The theoretical structure that has enabled this generalisation is statistical knowledge. Generalisations of this form are referred to as *statistical inference*.

Statistical tests can tell you that you are justified in inferring an association between two variables. They cannot provide an explanation for this association. In order to address this issue, you will need to move into the theoretical domain. Nevertheless, the research may be designed in such a way as to enable certain explanations to be ruled out – again, in probabilistic terms – in the same way that the null hypothesis is rejected.

For example, you may suspect that the gender of Brown's subjects has implications for their mode of semantic selection, that is, that gender is a *confounding variable*. If this were the case, then the findings might be explainable simply in terms of the different gender composition of each group of parents. The researcher might have attempted to *control* the variable, gender, by testing for an association between gender and semantic selection. In fact, information on the gender of the parents was not consistently available to Brown. Thus, gender is an *uncontrolled variable* in this part of his work.

Control techniques are important strategies in eliminating confounding variables and in moving towards the explanation and so generalisation of one's findings. Of particular importance is the control of the Hawthorne effect, which may be glossed as the proposition that knowledge of their involvement as subjects of research may itself change people's behaviour (the Hawthorne effect is discussed in Chapter 5). Control strategies cannot, ultimately, provide *explanations*. Explanations are available only within the theoretical domain. Indeed, a degree of theoretical development is needed in order to establish which variables might need to be controlled. The move has to be made from indicator variables to concept variables.

In Brown's research, semantic selection and social class are both *indicator variables*. They refer directly to the organisation of the data. Semantic selection indicates the state of the *concept variable* 'cultural orientation'. The indicator variable 'social class' indicates the state of its theoretical equivalent, which is a concept variable, also referred to as social class. The inferred association between social class and semantic selection may be attributed to one of three theoretical possibilities for the relationship between the concepts of social class and cultural orientation. First, you may argue that the value of social class has an implication for the value of cultural orientation. Alternatively, you may try to establish that the value of cultural orientation has some implication for the value of social class. Third, it may be that there is a third variable that has some implication for both of them.

The identification of implication is explored in terms of the ways in which the concept variables are defined. We shall not consider Brown's work further in this respect, as this would entail considerable additional theoretical discussion. We can, however, refer again, briefly, to Luria's study. Essentially, the association that Luria established between the concept variables 'social relations' and 'cultural practices' was interpreted as the product of social evolution. Taking the society as the unit of analysis, Luria proposed that the development of collective relations of production demanded corresponding linguistic developments. The latter were not, on the other hand, a feature of societies exhibiting individualised relations of production. Luria further proposed that the terminal level of individual human cognition would correspond to the level of linguistic development exhibited by the society. Thus, individuals participating in the more advanced society should display higher forms of cognition than those participating only in the more primitive society. This constitutes, in simplified form, Luria's problem. Its concepts are defined in relation to each other. The definitions of social relations and linguistic development are implicated in the argument that establishes their association, as are the definitions of societal linguistic development and individual cognitive development.

The *problem*, in other words, is constituted as a coherent and *self-referential system*. The ways in which the concepts 'social relations', 'linguistic development' and 'cognitive development' are defined entails that the value of one has implications for the value of the others. Thus, if a society exhibits collective social relations, then it will have developed literacy. If an individual participates in a literate society, then they will have developed taxonomic thinking. Thus the theoretically developed problem imposes a bias on findings relating to other potential empirical settings. Alternatively, you may say that the problem predicts the outcomes of research that may be carried out in additional empirical settings. That is, it comprises one or more testable propositions. If you were to adopt this alternative formulation, you may also be inclined to speak in terms of causality rather than implication.

Whereas experimental and survey research tends to seek to generalise to the population that it has sampled, this is less likely to be the case with interpretive forms of research. Barney Glaser (1992) puts it like this:

> The real distinction is to contrast methods that generalize to a large population (unit sociology) to [sic] methods that generalize to a basic social process of scope and depth, one of which is grounded theory. For example, redesigning of life styles because of chronic illness can be further generalized to redesigning of life styles to a chronic condition in everyday life, e.g. occupational mobility.
>
> (Glaser, 1992, p. 107)

But generalisation may be even less specific than this. As we have noted, Clifford Geertz (1988) argues that what validates the anthropologist's work is, ultimately, their prior acquisition of the discourse of anthropology in the university. Anthropology, interpreted in this way, develops as the accumulation of transactions between its own discourses – the theoretical field – and the cultural locations that its practitioners visit.[2]

The mode of interrogation

The *research mode of interrogation* consists of three moves: respectively, *specialising*, *localising* and *generalising*. The first move establishes the theoretical specificity of the research *problem* in relation to a wider *problematic* and general *theoretical field*. The second move makes explicit the local *findings* of the research in the context of the particular *empirical setting*, the latter being a selection from a general *empirical field*. The third move challenges the research to move beyond its local findings through processes of empirical and theoretical generalisation.

The mode of interrogation may be thought of as a frame or a jig, perhaps: the kind of tool that holds in place the components of an object while it is under construction. This metaphor highlights two crucial features of the mode. First, it is equally appropriate for use in reading and doing research. In either case, the finished product emerges from an extended process of organisation and clarification. Second, there is no necessarily optimum sequence of application of the mode of interrogation. In effect, you can start anywhere and move along any of the three dimensions of the mode of interrogation.

The notion of a jig is a useful metaphor, but it should not be taken too literally. A jig is a rigid tool and, as such, it is prescriptive. The mode of interrogation is, by definition, interrogative. It asks particular kinds of questions of the research; it does not provide the answers. Furthermore, a response to one question may have an impact on a response to another that has already been made. Thus the mode of interrogation is an inherently dynamic kind of jig. There is, ultimately, no necessary termination point to its application. The situation is similar to that of sculpture, in which the decision on when a piece is finished must rest with the artist. Having made the decision, the sculptor may care to ponder on the nature of the object of their labour. Is it that their skill and imagination has enabled them to engage with the marble in constructing a statue, or have they simply revealed to the world a figure that was there in the stone all the time?

We shall terminate our presentation of the mode of interrogation with the schematic summary of its three dimensions in Figure 9.2.

Dimension 1: Specialising

1. What is the general theoretical field within which the work is located?

AUTHORITIES

    Academic disciplines
    Professional disciplines
    Readership

2. What is the problematic?

KEY ANTECEDENT WORK

    Research
    Other commentaries

3. What is the specific problem?

SYSTEM OF CONCEPT VARIABLES

    Propositions
    Hypotheses
    Questions
    Conclusions

Dimension 2: Localising

4. What is the general empirical field within which the work is located?

    Practices
    Experiences

5. What is the local empirical setting?

    Research design issues
    Data collection techniques
    Sampling techniques
    Practical issues

6. What are the empirical findings?
    System of concept variables
    Indicator variables
    Reliability

Dimension 3: Generalising

7. How is the link between the problem and the findings established?

CONCEPT VARIABLES AND INDICATOR VARIABLES

    Validity

8. How is the research generalised?

RELATIONSHIPS BETWEEN INDICATOR VARIABLES

    Units of analysis
    Statistical inference
    Control of variables

RELATIONSHIPS BETWEEN CONCEPT VARIABLES

    Implication/causality

Figure 9.2 The research mode of interrogation.

Chapter 10

Opening and closing the account

In this penultimate chapter we want to focus on the end points of the research process. We have already given some consideration to the early stages of doing research in Chapter 2. Here, we shall revisit this phase by looking at the first steps in developing some initial ideas for small-scale research projects. We also want to give some attention to the terminal point in the research process, which is the construction of an account of your work. These two phases are of necessity separated in time. But they logically go together as the portals into and out from your research activity.

Entering the mode of interrogation

Here are four of the initial ideas for research questions proposed by a group of education lecturers, working at masters level, at a workshop that we held in Fortaleza, Brazil:

- What is the influence of computer use on children's intellectual development?
- Can nutrition education improve health?
- Can the use of educational television improve schooling?
- How are gender relations formed and maintained in schooling and how do they influence career choice?

The questions reflect, perhaps, anxieties about the effectiveness and/or equity of the professional practices with which the lecturers were associated. They may also be tied to political motives concerning the transformation of these practices. As they stand, the questions are very open. It is not immediately clear how you might move forward with them in either the empirical or the theoretical field. In order to initialise the operation of the research mode of interrogation, it is necessary to give them sharper focus and begin to think about possibilities for data collection. In the following discussion, we shall outline and explain our preliminary reformulations of the questions. We should emphasise that our reformulations reflect a combination of our own interests and our interpretation of the interests of the original proposers. To this extent, they are arbitrary. Our purpose is to illustrate some possible moves from an initial expression of interest to something that will enable to research process to begin.

The first question signals, perhaps, a professional interest in the use of information technology in schools, but seems to want to treat computer use as a unitary activity. Children use computers for local and online video games, for communicating with friends and others through email and blogs, as well as standard tool packages (word processing and so on) and a whole variety of educational uses, ranging from computer-assisted learning programs to aid spelling and basic arithmetic, to simulations of historical events and scientific processes to programming languages, such as Logo. It is unlikely that the effects of such a diversity of computer use will be undifferentiated.

The question is also pretty vague on the nature of the effects that might be expected and does not specify an age range. Does 'intellectual development' refer to cognitive level or to the acquisition of specific skills or knowledge? Are we talking about pre-school, or primary- or secondary-age children? This is an important issue if we think that there are theoretical differences between children of different ages. We decided to interpret the question as expressing an interest in cognitive development focusing on the early years of elementary schooling, that is, at ages five to six years. This drew us to think of cognitive development in terms of Piagetian conservation (see, for example, Piaget, 1952; Donaldson, 1978). This is a long-standing and contentious area in educational research, and one with which most elementary school teachers will have some familiarity through their initial training. Approaching it from the direction of *new* technology looks interesting (although we are not claiming that it is completely original).

We are aware of work that has been done looking at the potential of interaction between children in the development of conservation (for example, Perret-Clermont, 1980). We therefore decided that the research should consider the possible effects of an interactive, computer, conservation training application. The research question thus became:

- Can an interactive computer conservation application contribute to children's cognitive development?

We decided upon an *experimental design* using the program as a *treatment*. There remained a decision to be made concerning which aspects of the treatment should be *controlled*. We decided to control the conservation training element, using an interactive drawing program for the treatment to be administered to the *control group*. We produced the following as a potential scheme of action:

(a) Design (or select) an interactive conservation-of-number training application (using number conservation tasks of various forms (rearrangement, addition, subtraction), voice-simulator instructions, three choices (more, same, less) and demonstration of correct solutions).
(b) Select or design interactive drawing application.
(c) Pre-test opportunity sample of five- to six-year-olds, using clinical interviews to select samples of non-conservers and intermediates on conservation of number (experimental task) and other conservation tasks (e.g. conservation of volume).
(d) Allocate subjects to experimental and control groups by stratified random sampling (stratified by cognitive level) (or quota sample if the sample size is small).
(e) Administer treatment: conservation application to experimental group, drawing application to control group.
(f) Administer post-test and delayed post-test (using clinical interviews) to both groups.

The second and third of the four original questions exhibit similar problems. They are, again, inexplicit regarding the particular educational programme and do not suggest how improvement or effectiveness might be measured. The question on nutrition education introduces a particularly contested concept, that of 'health'. Because of this, we felt that the question lent itself particularly well to an *action research* project. Action research is a term that is applied to projects in which *practitioners* seek to effect transformations in their own practices. In general, the processes of determining the objectives of such a project and of evaluating their effectiveness are themselves incorporated into the project. Some advocates of action research suggest an approach whereby objectives are redefined after each cycle of a rolling project. In this sense, there is no obvious natural termination to the programme. We decided to impose an arbitrary terminal point by the need to produce an account, in this case, after two cycles of the research.

In action research as we have interpreted it, it might be inappropriate to impose an academic or medical definition of 'health' on the community within which the project is to be located. We have, therefore, adopted an approach that seeks to identify local understandings or constructions of 'health'. Our revised research question is:

- Can we design and implement a nutrition education programme that transforms health-related nutritional practices?

The use of the 'can we' mode enabled us to interpret a project aiming at action as also embodying a question and, therefore, as legitimate empirical research, in our terms. Our initial proposals are, briefly, as follows:

(a) Identify a range of health problems that are believed to be mitigated through changes in nutritional practices by reference to *key informants* in the community in which the project is to be located.
(b) Design nutrition education programme targeting forms of information relating to problems and related changes identified in (a).
(c) Implement programme.
(d) Conduct immediate and delayed evaluation of changes in practices.
(e) Reflect on and, where appropriate, reconfigure of the problems identified in (a).
(f) Adapt programme and re-implement.
(g) Conduct immediate and delayed evaluation of changes in practices.
(h) Produce account.

This plan begs a large number of questions concerning, in particular, data collection under phases (a), (d), (e) and (g). This is entirely appropriate. The ethos of action research, in particular, discourages the taking of important decisions other than by direct reference to the participating community (however that may be defined). The *mode of interrogation* that we have introduced in this book is, as we have indicated, to be applied continually throughout the research process. It thus takes the place of the individual to whom Bridget Somekh (1995) – an exponent of action research – refers as a 'critical friend'. It is, in other words, analogous to the academic supervisor or 'outsider' of practitioner research. We do, however, claim, that the difference between our position on action research and that of some of its major voices is that we advocate the full apprenticing of the practitioner-researcher into the research mode of interrogation, rather than establishing a division of labour between participating individuals as practitioners, on the one hand, and academics, on the other. We shall return to this point in Chapter 11.

Clearly, the third question might also be interpreted as an action research project. However, the lecturer who proposed this question was particularly concerned with a scheme that is already in place in the State of Ceará, Brazil, where we were running the workshop. In effect, the scheme involved the use of video television programmes and non-specialist 'learning orientators' as substitutes for subject specialist teachers. The scheme was managed by the Secretariat for Education at the State Ministry of Education. It incorporated subject curricula, which were represented by the content of the videos, and instructional procedures, which were overseen by a 'learning orientator supervisor', an official at the Ministry. We can refer to these as the official principles of the scheme. The lecturer's interest was in the extent to which the realisation of the scheme accorded with the official programme; her own subject specialism was in science education. Her expectations were that the exigencies of the classroom would effect a transformation of the official principles of the scheme and generate one or more sets of local principles. We reformulated the question as:

- What is the nature of the recontextualisation of science discourse and pedagogic theory in the operationalisation of an educational television programme? How is the recontextualisation related to the structure of social relationships in the classroom (position of learning orientator with respect to official knowledge and students, relations between students, etc.)?

Our preliminary ideas on a plan of action were as follows:

(a) Select *case study* classroom and one thirty-minute biology TV programme.
(b) Access the official principles of the discourse and pedagogy through interview with learning orientator supervisor and analysis of programme.
(c) Interview learning orientator regarding local principles of discourse and pedagogy.
(d) Observe and video lesson having *habituated* the students and the learning orientator to the researcher and the video-camera over a period of two weeks.
(e) Re-interview learning orientator.
(f) Interviews with four students (two girls and two boys) at top and bottom of class performance (as indicated by learning orientator), plus group interview with some or all of the other students in groups of five or six.

The final research question, on gender relations, is immense in scope, covering, it would seem, the entire school age-range. It reflected a general concern, on the part of the proposer, with the issue of gender inequality in society. This is a concern that we share. However, a great deal of work has been done in this field and we felt that it was important to try to get a particular (which is not to say necessarily original) angle if the research was to generate something that would be likely to extend beyond the completely predictable. The question also needed to focus on a tighter age-range. We proposed the following question:

• How do school leavers negotiate counter gender-stereotypical career choices?

Our proposed scheme of action was as follows:

(a) Generate large opportunity sample of imminent school leavers. Administer four-question *questionnaire* (name, contact address, sex, intended career).
(b) Identify likely *critical case* studies.
(c) Administer sequences of loosely structured interviews over a period of two years: prior to leaving school; during job-seeking process, if applicable; on taking-up career; after one year; after two years.

These revised questions and associated plans of action took an average of twenty minutes' discussion to generate. We are not claiming that any of them would remain unmodified either in the initial phases of literature review and planning or in the longer term of the research. Indeed, it would run counter to our description of research as a continuous application of the mode of interrogation if we were to make such a claim. We do claim that they enable the researcher to begin to identify some of the elements of their theoretical and empirical fields. In other words, they constitute entries into the research process. They are sufficiently precise to enable the application of the research mode of interrogation.

As we have suggested, the original questions may have been associated to a greater or lesser degree with professional and political motivations. Initial thoughts regarding research questions may also be coloured by methodological or locational interests: it may be that what you really want to do is some participant observation or spend some time in a rural school in Brazil. It may even be that you feel that your career or social position would be enhanced by being able to put 'Dr' before your name on your debit card. Beginning researchers enter the research process with a variety of motivational baggage. In our experience, however, the more of this baggage that can be left at the door, the more effectively the research mode of interrogation can be applied, and the more likely we are to be surprised by what we find, to have our commonsense and theoretically informed views of the world challenged. Even in our initial revisions of the research questions that we have introduced in this section, there has been a substantial cooling out of the anxieties and political interests that shaped the original versions. Motives are not, however, to be lost and educational researchers quite rightly have political and professional interests that will shape the dissemination and application of their research. The baggage can be collected at the other end of the research process. It is to this phase that we shall move in the next section.

Exiting the mode of interrogation

We have described the research mode of interrogation as a continuous, complex process involving specialising, localising and generalising. In this interpretation, there is no unambiguous point of completion of the research, although particular research activities – such as data collection and library searches – may have planned beginnings and endings. You can, however, establish a point of exit from the process by addressing a readership, that is, by producing an account of or reporting your research.

In Chapter 9 we defined the potential readership of your research as a component of the theoretical field. Therefore, the process of clarifying the nature of the audience of your account is itself a specialising of this field. There are, of course, many possibilities for the readership. In particular, we have distinguished between practitioner or professional readerships and academic readerships. Your choice of readership is important, because it defines the genre in which you will be writing. In this chapter, we shall concentrate on the genre of academic writing. We noted, in Chapter 9, that the readership of academic writing should be thought of as a subset of its authorities. In writing an account of their research, then, the beginning researcher is making a claim to academic authorship. There is a sense, then, in which the account is a submission for evaluation by the field. We are of course asserting that the nature of the evaluation is precisely the mode of interrogation that we have introduced in this book. This clearly has implications for the content, emphasis and, as we mentioned in Chapter 9, style of your account. We shall describe a possible structure for the account, but must emphasise that this is not the only way to produce an account.

For example, your account must enable the reader to situate your work within a region of the general theoretical field. That is, it must construct its problematic. This involves an organised discussion of your key authorities, which is often referred to as a 'literature review'. The principal purpose of a 'literature review', however, is less to inform your readership of what work has been done in your area of interest, than to position your own research in relation to this body. Of course, an annotated summary of related research can provide a useful resource, not least for other beginning researchers whose own literature searches may benefit from your groundwork. However, you should avoid adopting a pedagogic attitude in constructing your review; you are locating yourself within the field, not enlightening its members.

A useful approach is to organise the contents of your library search into categories that relate to your own work. You can then discuss the categories in terms of the ways and extent to which your work coincides with or deviates from them. Individual items may be used in the form of examples of the work in each category. Where your work is very close to research in a particular category, you will need to enter into more detailed discussion in order to clarify the particular specialisation that you have adopted. Categories that are more obviously distinct from your approach may be dealt with more briefly. An initial, coarse classification may be made in terms of research that focuses on related empirical settings, on the one hand, and work that adopts related methodological or theoretical approaches, on the other. Work that falls into both of these categories is clearly that which is most closely related to your own.

Now we want to add a caveat here. Fairly recently – during the intervening period between the publishing of the first and second editions of this book – we have tended to avoid the use of the term 'literature review'. This is because we have found that it encourages our students to think of the part or parts of their research account that discuss the literature simply to be reviews of what has gone before. As we have attempted to make clear, here, this is not the function of the 'literature review', which we now tend to refer to as the *engagement with the literature*. By and large, a research report answers a small number of questions in a limited way and, if it's good research, raises a whole lot of others, including questions relating to the limitations on the way that it has answered the questions that it has answered – if you see what we mean! In engaging with a research report, your task is to open up some of these questions especially in respect of the way that they bear on your own research project. Now it's one thing to do this with a single research report; not necessarily easy to do, but a task that is at least fairly easy to conceptualise. It is something quite different to do this with a whole bunch of research reports and to organise the account of your engagement with this body of work in such a way as to formulate an argument that establishes the position of your own research in relation to this body of work. Essentially, producing an account of an engagement with the research literature – what used to be called the 'literature review' section of your dissertation or thesis – is a task that is pretty much the same kind of activity as the analysis of qualitative data; you may recall that, in Chapter 7, we stressed that qualitative analysis is very difficult and very time-consuming. In fact, in advising students regarding the analysis of research literature, we suggest that they adopt the same kind of strategies are appropriate in the analysis of data. In particular, we encourage the development of theoretical categories and the writing of memos that seek to define the categories and provide illustrations from their literature base. The account of the engagement with the literature should be structured in terms of these categories; the idea is to impose your own analysis – not, of course, your own unjustified opinions – on the literature and not to allow the literature to dictate the structure of your text; the latter would leave you without an argument. It is also important to point out that, although an account of your engagement with the research literature may be something that occurs quite early in the research process, the first version of this is likely to be very different from the final one; in general, and particularly with qualitative research, you can't adequately set up the basis for your own research until you know what that research is; in other words, make sure that you rewrite your account of your engagement with the literature after you have completed the first draft of your discussion of your findings.

Of course, not all literature will necessarily be treated in the same way in your research report. In particular, it is generally appropriate to include in a research report some discussion of the general theoretical approach that you are adopting. Now research introducing or discussing theoretical issues and approaches is just as susceptible to limitations as are accounts of empirical research. However, it is not necessarily the case that you will want to focus on these limitations in respect of theoretical writing. Rather, you may be aiming to set out how, in general terms, you are conceiving of, for example, human cognition or identity, or social class, or school effectiveness, and so forth, and it is important that you do this by reference to theoretical antecedents: Vygotsky on cognition, Judith Butler on identity and so forth. Again, coherence is an important ambition, but don't feel that you have to 'correct' Lev Vygotsky or Judith Butler; you may legitimately be simply recruiting their organisational languages in establishing your own.

In organising your account, you may choose to present the full statement of your research problem and the details of your empirical setting as emerging from your engagement with the literature. In this case, the initial statement of the problem and description of the empirical site will be made in general terms. The account of the engagement with the literature will then provide entry into a full theoretical elaboration of the conceptual space that constitutes your problem,, which, in turn, will provide an entry into the description of decisions relating to your empirical setting.

The problem having been established, you will be in a position to mark out the empirical setting in terms of research design issues, sampling, data collection techniques, etc. Now, clearly, the empirical work will have been shaped by deliberate decisions, on the one hand, and by contingencies, on the other. The latter will relate to opportunities that were or were not available, response rates of less than 100 per cent, mortality rates of more than 0 per cent, your own errors in respect of interviewing technique and practicalities, and so forth. Deliberate decisions can, to a greater extent than contingencies, be justified in relation to your problem. However, this does not entail that you should present an apology for the unintended features of your empirical work; on the contrary, try to make them work to your advantage.

Both the intentional and unintentional circumstances that have shaped your empirical setting and findings have implications for your conclusions, including the generalisability of your research. However, the conclusions are not constructed until the empirical work has been completed. They should, therefore, be formulated with reference to both the intended and the actual context of your empirical setting. This being the case, you should describe contingencies in terms of the qualifications and limitations that they impose upon your conclusions and, of course, unintentional circumstances may well have led to unexpected but productive opportunities. You will also want to include some reflexive discussion on alternative decisions or approaches that might have been adopted with hindsight. This discussion would commonly (but not necessarily) be incorporated into a concluding chapter or section. It is appropriate for this section or chapter also to look beyond your particular project to implications and suggestions for further research and, indeed for professional practice. What you should not do is produce a list of excuses for not doing the job properly in the first place; all research should involve a learning process and this is to be celebrated, not apologised for.

The termination of the localising process is the construction of the empirical findings. Here, you will need to make decisions relating to the form in which these are to be presented. We have suggested that research can often benefit from a combination of qualitative and quantitative approaches. If your approach is predominantly qualitative, then you will be presenting your findings by way of elaborated description. This clearly raises questions regarding the representativeness of the examples that you select from your data set. As we have pointed out in Chapter 8, the use of quantitative summaries can be of value here. Again, the fact that you have quantified your work does not entail that you have to carry out statistical analysis. Nor does it require you to present the results as anything more than simple tables. More sophisticated quantitative analysis and charts should be used only where they add to the force or clarity of the argument that you are making.

So far, in our description of a possible account, we have made reference to the following contents:

(i) general statement of the problem and outline of the empirical setting;
(ii) establishing of the problematic in terms of key antecedent work categorised by empirical setting and by theoretical and methodological approach;
(iii) detailed theoretical exposition of the problem;
(iv) description of decisions made and contingent circumstances relating to the empirical setting;
(v) findings;
(vi) conclusion.

These items could quite clearly be interpreted as sections of a 6000-word article, or chapters of a 20,000-word masters dissertation or parts (some of which may contain more than one chapter) of an 80,000-word doctoral thesis or book. In our experience, a great many successful accounts do indeed adopt such a format. However, it is not intended as a prescription and another form of structural organisation may be more appropriate in your particular case. Nevertheless, each of these elements should be included. They must be addressed with clarity and with a clear indication of their role in the general line of argument that you are seeking to establish. If one or more of these elements is distributed, in your account, then it's probably a good idea to indicate at the outset where and in what form they appear; you do need to address the expectations of your likely audience.

You will notice that our original description of these items has not been given in precisely the same order in which they appear in the summary list. Furthermore, it is unlikely that either order will coincide with the sequence of events and decisions that actually constituted the research process itself. After all, we have defined this process as the continuous application of the mode of interrogation and not as a sequence of neatly delineated phases. Nor will the order of the above list necessarily coincide with the order in which the account is written.

In describing literature, the Russian formalist school of literary scholars made a distinction between the story, or *fabula*, and the plot, or *suzhet*. Shklovsky described the technique of art as:

> to make objects unfamiliar, to make forms difficult, to increase the difficulty and length of perception because the process of perception is an esthetic end in itself and must be prolonged. Art is a way of experiencing the artfulness of an object; the object itself is not important.
>
> (Shklovsky, quoted by Kozulin, 1990, pp. 29–30)

This would certainly be an exaggeration were it to be applied to the relationship between the research story and its plot as realised in its account. Even so, the distinction provides a useful metaphor. As we have said, the account is always addressed to an audience. Its author will also wish to incorporate at least some of the motivational 'baggage' that they left at the door of the research process on the way in (of course, some of it may have been repacked somewhat in their absence). Furthermore, the structure of the argument that you are making will also impose itself upon your account. These considerations must have implications for decisions relating to the order, emphasis and style of the account. Nevertheless, if you are writing within the academic genre, you must not lose sight of the mode of interrogation that, we are claiming, will constitute the basis of the evaluation of your work.

There is a corollary. The fact that the structure and ordering of a written account is likely to deviate from the structure and ordering of the research process that it represents has an additional implication. Essentially, it means that you should not take research reports as simple guides to the doing (or even the reading) of research.

We shall conclude this section with some brief practical advice for beginning authors. We shall focus on four issues that have sometimes caused problems for students whose work we have been required to assess. First, the question of language. The first issue that we must mention here concerns the need to avoid the use of sexist language or terms which are or which may be interpreted as derogatory with respect to ethnic or other cultural categories. We will not provide detailed guidelines here, but guidelines on avoiding sexism and racism in sociology, for example, are available on the British Sociological Association website at www.britsoc.co.uk/equality/ (last accessed 18 December 2008).

Second in relation to language, it is not entirely inappropriate to include figurative and other literary devices in a research account. However, your principal concern should be to be understood as you intend to be understood. Essentially, this means writing clearly and explicitly. All educational researchers are dealing with ideas that are new, at least to themselves. Getting these ideas down into a word processor file is often a tortuous business. It is, then, very likely that your first write-through of a section or chapter or of the whole account will consist of excessively long and complex sentences making up excessively long and complex paragraphs which are woven into a confusing and incoherent structure; confusing to others, if not to you.[1] Go through it again. Lay out the central structure of what you want to say. Then rearrange your paragraphs. Remember that if you are starting a sentence with an expression such as 'although', or 'whilst', or 'in order to', and so on, you are going to need at least two clauses (see the beginning of the next paragraph). Often better to make two sentences.

Because putting difficult ideas into coherent English is a challenging task, there is sometimes a temptation to make use of someone else's words. This is quite acceptable where it takes the form of a quotation. All quotations should be indexed as such. Where the quotation is no more than a few words, you may use quotation marks and run it into your own text. If you want to use a quotation of more than one or two lines, then you really should indent it as we have done with the Shklovsky quotation above. It is also a good idea to use a smaller font size for emphasis. All quotations should be followed by a reference, including the number of the page or pages on which the original appears.

There are three caveats regarding the use of quotations. First, they should not be too long. For most purposes, you should consider 200 words to be an absolute maximum and generally aim to use shorter quotations. Second, you should not overuse quotations. Use them when an author has put something in a particularly apposite or elegant way, or when you want to discuss a particular phrase or definition that they have used. Too many quotations in a research account make the text hard to read and inhibit your imposition of your own authorship on your work. Third, and most importantly, all quotations must be signalled as such, either by the use of quotation marks or by indenting, and with an adequate reference. Do not represent other people's words as if they are your own, even in slightly modified form. Minimally, this weakens the authority of your text. In serious cases, it constitutes plagiarism. If your account is being submitted as part of the requirements for a higher degree, this could result in failure and the possibility of being banned from re-entering.

One method of uncluttering an account is to make use of footnotes (notes at the bottom of the page) or endnotes (notes at the end of the chapter or volume). We have generally avoided them in this book, although both of us make extensive use of footnotes or endnotes (depending upon the publisher's house style) in our research writing. In our opinion, a footnote or endnote should be introduced for much the same reasons as an appendix. That is, it should contain details or information that is useful or relevant or interesting, but which is not central to the line of argument that is being developed. Essentially, it must be possible to read the work without references to footnotes, endnotes or appendices.

If you have any choice, we would suggest that you do not use footnotes or endnotes simply to list references. We say this for two reasons. First, we feel that references are vital to the interpretation of an academic account and should be run in with the main text; more about this in a moment. Second, if you want your readers to read even some of your footnotes or endnotes, then you should make all or most of them interesting. This is unlikely to be achieved if most of your footnotes or endnotes contain no more than publication details. On the other hand, you may want to make a statement about a particular reference, like this:

> see, for example, Dowling and Brown (2009), which includes a brief discussion of the use of footnotes and endnotes in academic writing.

An annotated reference of this form would be an appropriate candidate for a footnote or endnote.

In our opinion, the identification of references is a crucial feature of the academic genre of writing. This is because an academic account is participating in a field of discourse that is populated and constituted by its authors. Your declaring of references assists your reader in positioning your work within this field and may help them to interpret any technical terms that you are using. Although house styles vary, our preference is for the reference in the text to consist simply of the author's name and date of publication – the so-called Harvard style. This should enable the reader to locate unambiguously the relevant item in your bibliography. Thus, if there are two items by Dowling and Brown that are both published in 2009, refer to them in the text and in the bibliography as Dowling and Brown, 2009a and 2009b.

We are firmly of the opinion that references should be used to assist the reader both to follow up on the cited work and ideas and to interpret and position your work. They should not, in our opinion, be used to bolster support for an assertion or a decision that you are not otherwise going to defend. Thus:

> I decided upon a non-directive interview approach (Cohen, Manion and Morrison, 2007).

Cohen *et al.* provide a very useful summary of a wide range of research methods and their book (the one referenced is the sixth edition) has possibly been the most widely used research methods handbook in the field of education in recent years. The mere mention of their names, however, cannot provide authority for your research decisions. Minimally, you would need to include some discussion of the nature and advantages and disadvantages of the approach that you adopt. You will then need to defend its selection in your particular case by reference to the questions that constitute the research mode of interrogation. Unfortunately, you will find many instances of the use of references to lend spurious support to assertions and decisions, even amongst experienced authors of research accounts. Indeed, we are all guilty of it at times. Nevertheless, try to avoid it.

This concludes our brief discussion of the writing-up phase of the research process. It also concludes this practical chapter on entering and quitting the research process. In the final chapter we shall present our 'Manifesto' for educational research, which, of course, derives from the position that we have been introducing throughout the book.

Chapter 11

The practitioner and educational research

A manifesto

We have claimed, in this book, that the fundamental criterion for the evaluation of empirical educational research is that it should aim at coherent closure. There are at least three directions from which we may be challenged on this claim. First, a number of authors within what may (very) loosely be referred to as the postmodern school self-consciously seek to avoid closure in producing their own texts. These are intended to reveal the deconstruction of what are only apparently closed texts produced by others. Well, we see value in such writing, too, just as we see value in modernist epistemological debates between, say, constructivists and realists. We occasionally engage in it ourselves. Such work is important in the generation of critical dialogue on and within the research activity. Suffice it to say, perhaps, that, if there were no texts that aspired to closure, the postmoderns would have very little to do.

The second line – surprisingly, perhaps – is represented by some of the work by one of the authors of this book. Dowling (2009) puts the situation like this in his introduction:

> Chapter 5, more than any other, calls into question the value of an all-out drive for coherence in an organisational language [. . .]. Equilibration – internally and externally – is an important theoretical strategy, but total coherence (and let's pretend such a state is achievable) terminates both as the sclerotic language necrotises the world. This, of course, is called bigotry.
>
> (Dowling, 2009)

And, opening the chapter that is mentioned:

> Every self-conscious act or utterance imagines itself the kiss of creator and created, structure and event, *langue* and *parole*, competence and performance (but which is which?). And there is anxiety: is this the kiss of my lover, or of Judas; does it wake me, or am I forever dream(t/ing)/betray(ing/ed)? All too often I sense that it's the kiss of Midas the necrophiliac.
>
> (ibid.)

Dowling is speaking here of an imagined total closure of an organisational language – the theoretical field: a closed theory cannot learn. Outside the formal systems of mathematics, no theory can ever be totally closed; the fluidity of natural language ensures this.[1] But then we do sometimes find a tendency to regard theory as complete, definitive, and we regard this as inhibitive of good research. So, perhaps this 'challenge' to our advocacy of coherence as the principal aim of research is more appropriately described as a caveat: work towards coherence, but don't expect or desire fully to achieve it.

The third line of challenge to our coherence criterion comes from the pragmatic professionals. Here, the criticism is that undue emphasis on internal consistency is onanistic. Although trumpeting the potential value of research as the basis of professional practice, this position claims that what is really important is that the research should help practitioners in their work (for example, see Barber, 1996). We also think that educational research should help practitioners in their work. However, our position, in a nutshell, is that educational practitioners need to move outside of their professional practice and into the distinct activity of educational research. This is essential if they are to generate the dialogue between research and practice that is a necessary condition for their mutual development. It is this position that we shall argue in this final chapter.

The mode of interrogation that we presented in Chapter 9 is intended and designed for application in the reading as well as in the doing of research. Research, then, is to be interrogated. This is not, however, the only way of utilising research. Here, for example, is an extract from a policy document, which is arguing for a particular approach to the choice of medium of instruction in schools:

> The gradual introduction of the language of wider communication as a language of learning is based on the *research evidence* which strongly suggests that the conceptual development of children is facilitated by initial learning in their home language.
>
> (ANC, 1994, p. 64; our emphasis)

The African National Congress – the authorial voice of this text – is laying claim to a reading of research. However, the form that the reading takes completely subordinates the research to the principles of the quite different activity in which the ANC is involved. This is a political activity. 'Language of wider communication' means English, but this cannot be stated, as to do so would rule out Afrikaans. English, as the symbolic language of the struggle, is acceptable in the new South Africa, but must not be allowed to dominate the African languages that are spoken by most of its population. A clear space must be established for each. The ANC document recruits 'research' in achieving precisely this. The 'research' itself is not identified or elaborated or criticised in any way. Nor should it be, because to do so might encourage a shift from the political activity of governance to the academic activity of enquiry. This is not an interrogation, but a consumption of research that entails its recruitment as a resource by political strategies (see Dowling, 1998).

Here is another extract, this time from the field of academic educational research:

> The results [of this study] support the thesis proposed by Luria (1976) and by Donaldson (1978) that thinking sustained by daily human sense can be at a higher level than thinking out of context in the same subject.
>
> (Nunes *et al.*, 1993, pp. 23–5)

Surprisingly, perhaps, the research cited in this piece is also being recruited for what might metaphorically be described as political purposes. It is being used to lend additional support to the authors' claims in what Dowling (1995b, 1998) describes as a 'positioning strategy'. Luria and Donaldson do no 'work' in this text. Their omission would not alter the sense of the claim that is being made. Furthermore, the citation elides the quite fundamental differences between the three pieces of research. Luria, as we have stated earlier in this book, was working with adult subjects in a remote area of the Soviet Union in the 1930s. Donaldson was drawing on work with the very young children of university staff in Edinburgh in the 1970s. Nunes and her colleagues were working in the early 1980s in Recife, Brazil, with 9- to 15-year-old children from 'very poor backgrounds'. Further, and more importantly, there are very substantial theoretical differences between the studies. It will be apparent from our description of Luria's work that his position was quite incompatible with that attributed to him in the extract.

In each of the two extracts the author attributes a degree of authority to the research, but denies it its own voice. The cited work is almost arbitrarily chosen in respect of its specific content. The ANC text would probably have worked as well by using an appeal to commonsense. The excision of Luria and Donaldson from the second extract would weaken its authority, but not significantly alter its sense. The specificity of the language of research and of the work of Luria and Donaldson are not allowed to speak. In each case, then, the consumption of research entails the transformative recontextualising of its principles in subordination to another project.

In his presentation of his Social Activity Method,[2] discussed and illustrated in Chapter 7, Dowling has argued that a more or less radical transformation in the principles of a practice occurs whenever it is recontextualised between distinct activities. The practices of the recontextualising activity include *strategies* that recruit those of the recontextualised activity as *resources*. Precisely what is recruited as a resource has a degree of arbitrariness. The manner in which resources are recruited, however, entails a subordination of the resources to the principles of the recontextualising activity. For example, Dowling (1996, 1998, 2009) has illustrated this recontextualising with respect to the recruitment and transformation of domestic and other practices by school mathematics. Elsewhere, we have illustrated the recruitment and transformation of domestic practices by a professionally motivated parental involvement scheme in the primary phase (Brown, 1999, Brown and Dowling, 1993) and we (Dowling and Brown, 2007) and Ensor (1995) have also problematised the relationship between teacher education and classroom practice.

We want to maintain that the general field of professional educational practice and academic research constitutes a range of distinct activities. Dowling has defined *activity* as the contextualising basis for all social practice. Any particular activity – say, teaching – establishes a range of positions that can be occupied by human individuals. The activity also constitutes a range of practices that are distributed to these positions. Thus, teachers are specialised according to their discipline and/or phase and also according to their post. Students are differentiated according to age, 'ability', 'needs', and other attributes such as gender, ethnicity and social class. Parents may be attributed differential levels of cooperativeness, and so on. What it means to be a teacher, a student or a parent is contingent upon the activity. For example, Brown (1999) has found that teachers who are also parents maintain a high degree of differentiation between these positions. Teachers, when speaking as teachers, can describe what parents are like, without appearing to accept these descriptions as applying to themselves.

Academic educational research, as an activity, defines a different set of positions and practices. In particular, the output of academic research is subject to peer review through the procedures of publication in journals and books and through conference arrangements. Furthermore, the nature of this output is always an abstraction from the immediate empirical context of the research. Local contingencies are more or less effectively eliminated through definition and/or control, so that the empirical setting is constituted as a laboratory. Research output is, in other words, relatively context-independent, indeed, this is a condition of its generalisability. The empirical site of educational research is, in this sense, consumed by research and this consumption entails the transformative recontextualisation of the site.

Professional educational practice and academic educational research, then, are distinct fields of activity. They are not, however, restricted to specific institutional sites. Teachers and other educational professionals can and do become involved in the production as well as the reading of research and universities are teaching as well as research institutions. In general terms, we might say that educational activities consti-tute the empirical basis of educational research, which is constituted as an arena for the interrogation of educational activities. The two fields stand in dialogic relation to each other. We want to maintain that this is potentially a productive relationship, but only to the extent that the dialogic potential is maintained. In other words, failure to recognise the distinctive natures of the two fields will result in the one being unduly subordinated to the principles of the other.

Thus, psychological research that defines out the social and political structuring of the classroom may well be good psychology, but it is perhaps an abstraction too far in respect of educational research. Some approaches to action research (though not all and not, we would claim, ours) aim at the direct development of professional practices, but perhaps give too little scope to the research to organise its own theoretical space. In these cases, educational research and professional educational practice respectively recruit the other as a reservoir of resources for the elaboration of their own strategies.

One of the outcomes of the failure to regard research as a distinctive activity is the plundering of research for the techniques that will facilitate the genesis of the all-singing/all-dancing practitioner-researcher. This accords with the view that all the teacher needs is some interviewing skills and a methodological lexicon in order to turn them into a research-based professional. Thus we find, within higher education, the curricularising of the practices of research in the construction of research methods courses and books on research methods for educational practitioners. A curriculum is an educational programme, which of necessity constitutes a content as a sequence of topics (whether or not they are spirally revisited). So, there are research methods books and courses that comprise a chapter or seminar on surveys, one on case stud-ies, another on interviews, another on participant observation, yet another on the use of secondary data, and so on. We do not in any way wish to deny the potential usefulness of such courses and books and have, indeed, appended to this volume an annotated bibliography that includes such items. Furthermore, we are clear that there is a degree of inevitability about this or some equivalent form of organisation and have not avoided it in our own presentation. Nevertheless, there are a number of potential dangers to the extent that the specificities of the research activity are subordinated to the exigencies of the educational activity.

One of these dangers is that an unprincipled organisation of the diversity of methodological approaches to research may lead to the fetishising of methods. Case study – which we referred to in Chapters 3 and 10 – is, indeed, a case in point. Some time ago, one of us attended a professorial presentation (not in our own institution) on 'Case study research in education' given to a group of about fifty masters students. After the presentation, a number of the students asked the professor to rule on whether the approaches that they had adopted in their respective studies were or were not appropriately described as case studies. The professor appeared to find it very difficult to rule one way or the other in most of the cases that were introduced. Just what is and what is not a case? One of the quotations that the professor had cited on the first page of his handout was from Robert Stake; it presents a widely held image of case study research:

> Case studies are special because they have a different focus. The case study focus is on a single actor, a single institution, a single enterprise, maybe a classroom, usually under natural conditions so as to understand it – that bounded system – in its natural habitat.
>
> (Stake, 1988, p. 256)

This is a mythologising of research and a romanticising of the world in general. The 'natural' world is presented as thinkable in terms of a collection of mutually independent (bounded) systems that are nevertheless transparently knowable to us. We, as the observers, are able to dispense with our preconceptions and motivations. It recalls, perhaps, an image of a whispering David Attenborough tiptoeing around a tropical forest followed by an equally silent production crew using night-sights on their cameras and telling it like it is – or, rather, like it would be, even if they weren't there. But of course Attenborough and his production and editorial teams are highly skilled producers within a hugely costly media enterprise. They can and must act selectively and productively, that is to say transformatively, on their object environment in constructing their programmes, irrespective of the relationship that they or their viewers believe might exist between the programme and the pristine environment (whatever that might be).

Stake's description is also mythologising in its reference to the singularity of the object of the case study. The expression 'single actor' may seem clear enough. But what is to be the context in which the actor is involved? Will educational research consider the behaviour of the subject in their domestic and leisure activities as well as in the classroom? Will it address the entire life cycle and, indeed, family history of the subject? Will it be concerned with physical aspects such as the subject's cardiovascular system? The fact of the matter is that even a single actor participates in a multiplicity of research sites upon which research acts selectively, which is to say, it samples. To assert that each of the potential research sites is independent of the others is to constitute a radically schizoid subject. The situation becomes even more complicated when the unit of analysis becomes institutional.

There is, in other words, no such thing as 'the case study approach' other than as constituted by the curricularising of research methods. Within the context of a specific research study, the use of the term 'case' is probably best interpreted as simply a way of describing one's sampling procedures, which is to say, 'this is a case of an object that is defined in the following terms . . .'

Our position, then, is that research must constitute its object just as educational practices have constituted 'the case study approach'. That is to say, research must impose selective and organisational principles upon its object site in establishing the empirical basis for its data. The rationality of these principles is precisely realised in the principles of the research activity that we have presented in Chapter 10 as the research mode of interrogation. The motivational source for research may, as in the action research tradition, be a question or a problem that arises within professional educational practice. However, if the dialogic relationship between professional and research practice is to be maintained, the nature of the imposition of research upon its site must be constituted as a gaze from another position and employing the practices of another activity. A dialogue, by definition, involves more than one voice. The professional practitioner intending to engage in educational research in the interrogation of their own practices will need to acquire the principles and not merely the trappings of these research practices. This entails a kind of apprenticeship into the practices of research. This book is intended to stand as a contribution to such an apprenticeship.

Evaluation

Whenever we have presented the courses out of which this book has developed, we have included a session for participant evaluation. This is a little difficult when writing a book. We would, however, like to invite you to contact us with your response to the book. We are keen to receive critical comments (regarding both what works and what doesn't), suggestions and anecdotes about your research experiences. Most of all, we would like to see the opening up of the vast amount of authoritative writing on and practice in education to the rigorous scrutiny of the research mode of interrogation which we have introduced.

Paul Dowling and Andrew Brown
Department of Language, Curriculum & Communication
Institute of Education
University of London
20 Bedford Way
London WC1H 0AL
email: p.dowling@ioe.ac.uk and a.brown@ioe.ac.uk

Notes

1 Introduction

1 In the earlier works cited the expression *social activity theory* was used; this has been changed to *social activity method* in Dowling (2009).
2 The Cyprus government actually denies foreigners the right to teach Higher Education courses on Cypriot soil. It was therefore necessary to fly the Cyprus cohort of students to London for the face-to-face element of their course.

2 Declaring an interest

1 See, for example, Bourdieu (1977, 1990).
2 The advanced search facility is at http://www.datastarweb.com, though you will need to log on, for example, via an Athens account supplied by your institution.

3 Articulating the theoretical and empirical fields

1 The researcher would need to develop a way of precoding responses to these questions. This would involve making advance decisions on, for example, how to count part-time teaching experience and how to distinguish between middle and senior management.
2 In the first edition of this book, we used the expression 'theoretical sampling'. We have modified this term here to avoid confusion with 'theoretical sampling' in the context of grounded theory, which is a more particular use.
3 The electoral register is only an approximation to the adult population of a constituency because not every adult resident in the constituency will be on the register (they may have failed to complete the relevant form or may have moved into the constituency between the annual circulation of the forms) and some entries in the register may not refer to adult residents (for example, when people move or die between the circulation of electoral register forms).

4 An ethical dimension to research

1 See Whiteman (2006) for an informed discussion of the ethics of conducting internet research.

5 Experience and observation

1 Multi-User Dungeon (or Domain or Dimension) combining gaming and chat facilities in text environments.
2 Massively Multiplayer Online Game.
3 It is worth mentioning that our interests, in this study, changed very soon after we began our data collection. It quickly became clear to us that the pedagogic practices in the three schools were very different and this difference seemed to resonate with differences in the

community structures and with the place of the schools within these structures. Furthermore, in one school, in particular, we were able to take advantage of an interview with a particular informant who was both a school student and a senior figure in the local community. Fortunately, we were able to redirect our research questions in response.

7 Quality in analysis

1 This is not to deny the value of narrative analysis itself, which is a well-theorised approach. We are not able to deal with this approach in this work and we suggest that you refer to specialist works, such as Riessman (1993).

8 Dealing with quantity

1 School Mathematics Project, 1983–5, *SMP 11–16*, Cambridge: CUP.
2 In Dowling's analysis, 'low ability' and 'high ability' refer to the constructions of the ideal reader of the texts. They do not, in other words, constitute necessary attributes of the students or teachers who actually make use of these books. It is for this reason that these expressions are enclosed in quotes.
3 Although there remain some operational problems, which are discussed in Dowling (1995).
4 The program used was Claris Impact on a Macintosh computer.
5 The formula presented here includes Yates's correction. This involves the subtraction of a value of 0.5 as shown. This is omitted in some expressions of the formula and there is some disagreement amongst statisticians as to its value. However, we suggest that you include it for 2×2 tables or where the sum of the frequencies (the figure in the bottom right hand cell of the contingency table) is less than 25. Its effect is to make the test more demanding.
6 In fact, the data have been modified slightly. Two categories have been combined in order to simplify the explanation offered here. This modification does not impact on the argument being made and is probably an improvement on the original organisation.

9 Specialising, localising and generalising

1 Constructivism and realism are themselves contested terms and certainly not everyone (and not even we, in a more extended discussion; see Dowling, 2009) would oppose them in quite the way that we are doing here.
2 Or visit virtually; Geertz ends with a discussion of Ruth Benedict's wartime study of Japanese culture produced at a time in which she could not, of course, visit Japan; as Geertz notes 'Benedict, who actually hardly went anywhere either, also wrote, as Swift said that he did, "to vex the world rather than divert it." It would be rather a pity were the world not to notice it' (Geertz, 1998, p. 128).

10 Opening and closing the account

1 We see nothing wrong with semicolons, by the way, and try to use them constructively; some readers, however, seem to find their use irritating and pretentious. You will need to make your own choice between the semicolon and the full stop.

11 The practitioner and educational research

1 And, of course, Gödel's inconsistency theorem has questioned the closure even of mathematical systems.
2 In the earlier works cited the expression *social activity theory* was used; this has been changed to *social activity method* in Dowling (2009).

Annotated bibliography

We have listed a number of books that we and/or our students have found to be useful. The short comments we have provided are intended to give some indication of why we feel a particular book to be interesting.

We have not included any journal articles. It is within journals that some of the most vigorous methodological debate takes place. There are some journals, such as the *International Journal of Qualitative Studies in Education*, that are dedicated to the exploration of methodological issues. Journals that are principally concerned with the publication of research reports, such as the *British Education Research Journal*, also publish papers of methodological interest from time to time. We recommend that everyone carrying out research should become familiar with the journal collection in their library or online.

The annotated bibliography has been divided into two sections. The first gives a short selection of general research methods books. Each of these attempts to give a comprehensive introduction to educational or social research. The second part of the bibliography contains more specialised books. We have included both recent texts and older works that we feel continue to be relevant and, we hope, stimulating.

General research methods books

Bell, J. (1999). *Doing Your Research Project: A Guide for First-Time Researchers in Education and Social Science*. 3rd edition. Buckingham: Open University Press.

A clearly presented and straightforward guide to designing, conducting and producing accounts and reports. The process is laid out sequentially and practical advice is given at every stage. In attempting to cover so much in a short book, superficial treatment of techniques and issues is inevitable.

Bryman, A. (2008). *Social Research Methods*. 3rd edition. Oxford: Oxford University Press.

Provides comprehensive coverage of approaches to research in the social sciences in an accessible manner, with numerous examples drawn from relevant empirical studies (some from educational research). Particularly strong on the relationship between quantitative and qualitative approaches and the development of mixed-methods research. Regularly updated, so a good source for insight into contemporary approaches.

Cohen, L., Manion, L. and Morrison, K. (2007). *Research Methods in Education*. 6th edition. London: Routledge.

> A useful reference book. Covers a wide range of approaches to educational research. Good on research design. Provides a reliable source of information on approaches such as personal construct theory that are given little space in other introductory research methods texts. Kept up to date with material on topics such as internet-based research and the use of geographical information systems. With so much to cover, the accounts given can only act as starting points.

Gilbert, N. (Ed.). (2008). *Researching Social Life*. 3rd edition. London: Sage.

> This collection of papers provides an accessible introduction to the conduct of small-scale qualitative and quantitative research. Includes the design of questionnaires, the measurement of attitudes, interviewing and ethnographic work. Not specifically aimed at educational researchers but a useful introductory text nonetheless. Different approaches to research are exemplified by accounts of three contrasting research studies.

Robson, C. (2002). *Real World Research: A Resource for Social Scientists and Practitioner-Researchers*. 2nd edition. Oxford: Blackwell.

> A very thorough and comprehensive introduction to conducting small-scale research. The author has a clear image of what he sees as constituting worthwhile research. Provides good, clear, practical advice on specific data collection techniques and approaches to the analysis of qualitative and quantitative data. Good sections on interviewing, on observation and on the analysis of quantitative data. Not aimed specifically at educational researcher. Has a distinct bias towards psychological research.

Specialised books

Adelman, C. (Ed.). (1981) *Uttering, Muttering: Collecting, Using and Reporting Talk for Social and Educational Research*. London: Grant McIntyre.

> The papers in this collection focus on talk in educational and other settings. The accounts of research given cover interviewing adults in the context of institutional case studies (Simon) through to the exploration of forms of speech in teacher–child interaction (Wells). In the appendix to the latter paper there is an example of a set of transcription conventions.

Antaki, C. (Ed.). (1988). *Analysing Everyday Explanation: A Casebook of Methods*. London: Sage.

> A collection of papers illustrating a wide range of approaches to the analysis of explanations. Each paper contains an outline of the theoretical perspective from which the research is carried out, an example, in qualitative mode, of analysis of a fragment of data and an evaluation of the approach adopted. This format draws attention to the need to address both the theoretical field and the empirical setting when designing and evaluating research.

Bannister, D. and Fransella, F. (1986) *Inquiring Man: The Psychology of Personal Constructs*. 3rd edition. London: Croom Helm.

Thorough and readable introduction to personal construct theory and the use of repertory grids.

Baym, N.K. and Markham, A.N. (Eds). (2008). *Internet Inquiry: Conversations about Method*. London: Sage.

Collection of essays, with responses, by key researchers in the field exploring questions of central theoretical and practical importance in the design and conduct of internet-based research. Specifically concerned with qualitative research, and with issues that are of particular concern in internet research. Includes consideration of gender, privacy, defining the boundaries of a project, the analysis of online and offline data and the assessment of the quality of internet research.

Bazeley, P. (2007). *Qualitative Data Analysis with NVivo*. London: Sage.

Practical introduction to the management and analysis of qualitative data using one of the most popular qualitative data analysis programs.

Barthes, R. (1973). *Mythologies*. London: Paladin.

First published in French in 1957, this short book provides examples of Barthes's form of semiotic analysis. Barthes takes as the objects of his analysis a range of popular cultural phenomena, from the world of wrestling to the brain of Einstein. The final chapter outlines Barthes' method, paying particular attention to the concept of myth.

Becker, H.S. (1986). *Writing for Social Scientists: How to Start and Finish Your Thesis, Book or Article*. Chicago: University of Chicago Press.

A practical book about academic writing that is actually interesting to read. Becker takes a serious sociological interest in both the producers of academic texts and their readership.

Bernstein, B.B. (2000). *Pedagogy, Symbolic Control and Identity: Theory, Research Critique*. Revised edition. Lanham, MD: Rowman & Littlefield.

Bernstein directly addresses the research potential of his thesis. Part One provides an exposition of his mature work. Part Two clearly lays out the distinctive approach to research that has characterised the empirical work of Bernstein and his colleagues for over three decades. Chapters 5 and 6 deal specifically with the movement between the theoretical field and empirical data and the development of network analysis.

Black, T.R. (1993). *Evaluating Social Science Research: An Introduction*. London: Sage.

Provides a thorough guide to reading quantitative research in the social sciences and education.

Bliss, J., Monk, M. and Ogborn, J. (Eds). (1983). *Qualitative Data Analysis for Educational Research*. London: Croom Helm.

An introduction to the use of networks in the analysis of qualitative data. Includes a number of short papers in which researchers give accounts of the process of analysis. In most cases the networks are not theoretically derived and tend to provide a means for the organisation rather than analysis of data. The paper by Holland is a notable exception.

Bogdan, R. and Biklen, S.K. (1992). *Qualitative Research for Education: An Introduction to Theory and Methods*. Boston: Allyn & Bacon.

Comprehensive coverage of the process of conducting a qualitative research study in education. Chapter on data analysis draws on examples of data from research studies and is particularly useful on the process of coding.

Bryman, A. (1988). *Quantity and Quality in Social Research*. London: Unwin Hyman.

A careful consideration of the relationship between qualitative and quantitative approaches to social research. The author argues that the practices of researchers should be taken into account in addressing the qualitative/quantitative distinction and that the epistemological polarisation of approaches that often characterises debate in this area is not fruitful.

Burawoy, M., *et al.* (1991). *Ethnography Unbound: Power and Resistance in the Modern Metropolis*. Berkeley: University of California Press.

Collection of ethnographic research by graduate students attending Burawoy's participant observation course at Berkeley. The introduction and conclusion by Burawoy place the empirical studies in a distinctive theoretical and methodological context. Participant observation is viewed as exemplifying 'what is distinctive about the practice of all social science' (p. 3).

Burgess, R.G. (Ed.). (1986). *Key Variables in Social Investigation*. London: Routledge & Kegan Paul.

A valuable discussion of important conceptual issues in the design of research. Each paper takes a particular variable common in social research (gender, for instance) and explores the movement from concept to indicators. The contributors are all experienced empirical researchers. The bibliographies provide good starting points for further reading.

Carr, W. and Kemmis, S. (1986). *Becoming Critical: Education, Knowledge and Action Research*. London: Falmer.

A well-argued critique of naive approaches to action research. Drawing on critical theory, the authors advocate an alternative basis for the development of practitioner research in education.

Clandinin, D.J. and Connelly, F.M. (2000). *Narrative Inquiry: Experience and Story in Qualitative Research*. San Francisco: Jossey-Bass.

An accessible and reflective exploration of narrative forms of enquiry by two educational researchers. Includes advice on all aspects of the research process in including carrying out fieldwork and writing research accounts.

Clegg, F. (1983). *Simple Statistics: A Course Book for the Social Sciences*. Cambridge: Cambridge University Press.

Straightforward introduction to statistics and quantitative analysis. Useful for beginning researchers looking for a non-threatening introduction to basic concepts. By necessity lacking in detail and limited in scope.

Coffey, A. and Atkinson, P. (1996). *Making Sense of Qualitative Data*. London: Sage.

An accessible account of the process of qualitative analysis. Focuses mainly on ethnographic work. Using examples from their own research, the authors illustrate the movement from data to an analytic account. They compare the coding of qualitative data with forms of narrative analysis. Useful sections on writing research accounts and reports and the use of information technology.

Croll, P. (1986). *Systematic Classroom Observation*. London: Falmer.

Provides a guide to systematic observation as a research technique in classroom settings. Includes advice on the use of observation schedules and examples from the ORACLE study.

Connolly, P. (2007). *Quantitative Data Analysis in Education: A Critical Introduction Using SPSS*. London: Routledge.

Introduction to statistics and quantitative analysis using data and examples from education. Contains instruction on and exercises using SPSS.

Crossley, M. and Watson, K. (2003). *Comparative and International Research in Education: Globalisation, Context and Difference*. London: RoutledgeFalmer.

Of interest to researchers who are carrying out work with an international or comparative component. Addresses key issues in the conduct, dissemination and and use of comparative research, and stresses the importance of cultural and contextual sensitivity in educational research.

Delamont, S. (2001). *Fieldwork in Educational Settings: Methods, Pitfalls and Perspectives*. 2nd edition, London: Routledge.

The early chapters focus on the reading and writing of research accounts and reports and the judgement of quality in qualitative research (and specifically ethnographic work). The latter part of the book traces the progress of the research project from the choice of a topic to writing an account.

Denzin, N.K. and Lincoln, Y.S. (Eds). (2005). *The SAGE Handbook of Qualitative Research*. 3rd edition, Thousand Oaks, CA: Sage.

A collection of forty-five specially commissioned papers covering a wide range of issues and approaches to qualitative research. Includes papers on particular perspectives on inquiry (e.g. feminist approaches), specific ways of approaching research (including grounded theory, ethnography and the use of case studies), methods for the collection of data (including observational techniques and interviewing) and modes of analysis (including semiotic analysis, the interpretation of personal experience and the use of information technology). Each paper has an extensive bibliography.

Dey, I. (1993). *Qualitative Data Analysis: A User-Friendly Guide for Social Scientists*. London: Routledge.

Dey views the analysis of qualitative data as an iterative process of coding, classifying and connecting. Data is broken down into bits that are categorised, linked and combined to produce an analytic account. He illustrates the process, which includes a form of network analysis, using extracts from a Woody Allen comedy routine. The approach is specifically related to the use of information technology in the analysis of qualitative data, but the techniques described are also appropriate for researchers who are not using a computer.

Dowling, P.C. (2009). *Sociology as Method: Departures from the Forensics of Culture, Text and Knowledge*. Rotterdam: Sense.

In this book, Dowling develops his Social Activity Method (SAM) that was first introduced in *The Sociology of Mathematics Education: Mathematical Myths/Pedagogic Texts* (1998; London: Falmer Press). The later work extends SAM as an organisational language and *constructive description* as a general approach to the analysis of diverse of texts, sites, and technologies, ranging from works of art to film, to websites, to classrooms, and so on. The work is potentially of value to readers concerned with thinking about the nature of research and the practicalities of analysis. In two of its chapters, the book also presents a fundamental critique of the work of Basil Bernstein and that in the field of the sociology of knowledge that has been inspired by him.

Dowling, P.C. (1998). *Mathematical Myths/Pedagogic Texts: The Sociology of Mathematics Education*. London: Falmer.

This work provides the general methodological basis for the position that is being taken in *Doing Research/Reading Research*. In particular, it elaborates the approach of constructive description and Social Activity Method (referred to as social activity theory in this work). It also represents an example of a combination of qualitative and quantitative approaches in the semiotic and content analysis of educational texts, in this case, in the area of mathematics.

Elliott, J. (2005). *Using Narrative in Social Research: Qualitative and Quantitative Approaches*. London: Sage.

Addresses both conceptual and practical issues in the design and conduct of narrative research, including the collection and analysis of narrative interviews, the ethics of narrative research, working with longitudinal data and quantitative narrative research. Equally strong on qualitative and quantitative research, and considers the relationship between approaches. Provides a guide to some of the major longitudinal quantitative data sets.

Elliott, J. (1991). *Action Research for Educational Change*. Milton Keynes: Open University Press.

Provides an introduction to Elliott's particular approach to action research. Elliott takes the view that action researchers set out to investigate activity within a specific setting with the express intention of improving practice within it. This places action research at the heart of the development of professional practice. This book includes practical advice for practitioners intending to carry out action research projects.

Feyerabend, P. (1975). *Against Method: Outline of an Anarchistic Theory of Knowledge*. London: Verso.

This work has been influential in debates on the epistemology of the sciences. See also the item by Kuhn.

Fielding, N.G., Lee, R.M. and Blank, G. (Eds). (2008). *The SAGE Handbook of Online Research Methods*. London: Sage.

Comprehensive collection of papers covering both qualitative and quantitative online research. Includes consideration of research design, data 'capture' online, online surveys and ethnographic research online.

Foddy, W. (1993). *Constructing Questions for Interviews and Questionnaires: Theory and Practice in Social Research*. Cambridge: Cambridge University Press.

Clear, detailed and practical consideration of the process of question design. Deals with both open and closed question and considers factors that impact on the validity and reliability of data arising from questioning.

Foucault, M. (1970). *The Order of Things: An Archaeology of the Human Sciences*. London: Tavistock.

This is a very important work in debates in the general area of the epistemology of the human sciences. It does, however, place heavy demands on the reader both in terms of knowledge and understanding of philosophical work and in respect of the sophistication of its own arguments.

Gitlin, A. (Ed.). (1994). *Power and Method: Political Activism and Educational Research*. London: Routledge.

The contributors to this collection of papers directly engage with the relationship between political activism and educational research. The approach is multidisciplinary and a variety of positions, including feminist and gay and lesbian perspectives, are explored. Conventional views of the relationship between the interests of the researcher and and those of the researched are problematised and alternatives proposed.

Greene, S. and Hogan, D. (Eds). (2005). *Researching Children's Experience: Approaches and Methods*. London: Sage.

A collection of papers focusing specifically on issues and approaches to research involving children. Includes consideration of ethics, interviewing, focus groups, narrative analysis and naturalistic observation. One paper considers creative approaches to research that are particularly apt for research into children's experience.

Hammersley, M. (1992). *What's Wrong with Ethnography?* London: Routledge.

Hammersley raises questions about the forms of ethnographic research for which he himself has been an active advocate. Very useful in the development of criteria for the judgement of one's own and other people's research (Chapter 4 is particularly helpful in this respect).

Hammersley, M. and Atkinson, P. (1995). *Ethnography: Principles in Practice.* 2nd edition, London: Routledge & Kegan Paul.

Thorough consideration of ethnographic approaches to social research. Provides much in the way of practical advice (including the management of field relations, collecting accounts and recording, organising and analysing data) well as tackling epistemological questions (such as those raised by naturalism and other realist positions). Includes consideration of the ethics and ethnographic research.

Hart, C. (1998). *Doing a Literature Review: Releasing the Social Science Research Imagination.* London: Sage.

Covers all stages in the process of reviewing literature, from identification of sources, through managing and organising references to development of an argument and the writing of the review.

Hodge, R. and Kress, G. (1988). *Social Semiotics.* Cambridge: Polity.

This book provides a very readable introduction to semiotic analysis and includes a range of examples of semiotic analysis of very diverse texts. The particular approach taken shifts the focus of semiotic analysis towards an interest in social structure.

Irvine, J., Miles, I. and Evans, J. (Eds). (1979). *Demystifying Social Statistics.* London: Pluto Press.

Introductory statistics books understandably focus on the strengths of quantitative approaches. The authors of the papers in this collection raise numerous questions about the history, foundations and applications of statistical analysis (for instance, in questioning the development of tests of statistical significance) and the use of statistics (for instance, the production, analysis and use of opinion polling).

Kuhn, T.S. (1970). *The Structure of Scientific Revolutions.* 2nd edition, Chicago: University of Chicago Press.

This has been a very influential book in debates on the epistemology of science. Although its focus is clearly on the natural sciences, it has also been widely cited in discussion on the nature of social science. See, also, the item by Feyerabend.

Kvale, S. (2007). *Doing Interviews.* London: Sage.

A thorough exploration of interviews as a source of data in qualitative research. Covers all stages in a research project from design through to writing and presenting outcomes. Particularly useful in considering how the quality of interview data is judged, and explores notions of validity, reliability and generalisability in relation to interview-based research.

Lareau, A. and Shultz, J.J. (Eds). (1996). *Journeys through Ethnography: Realistic Accounts of Fieldwork*. Boulder, CO: Westview Press.

A collection of insightful narrative accounts of the process of carrying out ethnographic-based research studies (inspired by Whyte's appendix to *Street Corner Society*).

Lewins, A. and Silver, C. (2007). *Using Qualitative Software: A Step by Step Guide*. London: Sage.

Practical text with copious examples, covering the processes of managing, exploring and analysing qualitative data using information technology. Includes consideration of the process of coding data, writing and using maps and diagrams in exploring data. Gives detailed explanations and examples of the use of three widely used programs.

Lincoln, Y.S. and Guba, E.G. (1985). *Naturalistic Inquiry*. London: Sage.

Thorough consideration of the possibilities of conducting naturalistic research. Includes practical advice on appropriate forms of data collection, analysis and reporting of results. Includes a critical discussion of causality and the social sciences.

Lofland, J. and Lofland, L. (1984). *Analysing Social Settings*. 2nd edition, Belmont, CA: Wadsworth.

Concise introduction to techniques for the in-depth exploration of specific social settings. Provides advice on the collection and analysis of data. Focuses particularly on the use of intensive interviewing and participant observation. Includes advice on making fieldnotes.

McCulloch, G. (2004). *Documentary Research in Education, History, and the Social Sciences*. London: Routledge,

Wide-ranging and thoughtful guide to using documents in research with a strong emphasis on education. Deals with the gaining access to and analysis of a range of forms of documentary data, including official records, archives, print media, letters, autobiographies and diaries.

Marsh, C. and Elliott, J. (2009). *Exploring Data*. 2nd edition, Oxford: Polity.

An accessible introduction to the analysis of quantitative data. Provides numerous examples and exercises. Focuses on the development of an understanding of the logic of quantitative research and of the construction of causal explanations. This updated edition includes instructions on the use of SPSS.

Maynard, M. and Purvis, J. (Eds). (1994). *Researching Women's Lives from a Feminist Perspective*. London: Taylor & Francis.

An exploration of the conduct of social research from a feminist perspective. The contributors draw on examples from their own research in the exploration of a range of epistemological, political and operational issues.

Miles, M.B. and Huberman, A.M. (1994). *Qualitative Data Analysis: An Expanded Sourcebook*. 2nd edition, London: Sage.

The authors outline a number of ways of analysing qualitative data, with a strong emphasis on diagrammatic forms of representation. They also address means of drawing and verifying conclusions. A useful reference book.

Oppenheim, A.N. (1992). *Questionnaire Design, Interviewing and Attitude Measurement*. New edition, London: Pinter.

Comprehensive guide to the design and conduct of survey- and interview-based research studies. Consideration is given to analytic and descriptive surveys and to standardised and exploratory interviews. Includes specific advice on pilot studies, the wording of questions and the development of attitude scales. Also covers data processing and statistical analysis.

Outhwaite, W. and Bottomore, T. (Eds) (1994). *The Blackwell Dictionary of Twentieth-Century Thought*. Oxford: Blackwell.

A concise and comprehensive introduction to a range of epistemological positions. More of an encyclopedia than a dictionary, many of the entries are by leading academics in the field (the entry for realism, for instance, is written by Roy Bhaskar).

Pole, C. and Morrison, M. (2003). *Ethnography for Education*. Buckingham: Open University Press.

Explores the potential of ethnography for research in educational contexts and provides practical advice on the design and conduct of ethnographic-style studies.

Potter, J. and Wetherell, M. (1987). *Discourse and Social Psychology: Beyond Attitudes and Behaviour*. London: Sage.

Begins with a review of various approaches to the analysis of accounts (including semiotic approaches and ethnomethodology). Building on this the authors explore the possibilities offered by discourse analysis to social psychological research. They outline a ten-step process for the analysis of discourse.

Powney, J. and Watts, M. (1987). *Interviewing in Educational Research*. London: Routledge.

Practical guide to interviewing. Includes guidelines for practice and advice on transcription.

Pryke, M, Rose, G. and Whatmore, S. (2003). *Using Social Theory: Thinking through Research*. London: Sage.

This collection relates to a masters course, 'Human Geography, Philosophy and Social Theory', offered by the Open University. The chapters recruit a dazzling array of philosophers and social theorists – from Richard Rorty, to Jacques Derrida, to Luce Irigaray, to Isabelle Stengers, to Benedictus de Spinoza and more – to 'think through' three phases of research – 'asking questions', 'investigating the field' and 'writing practices' – exploring the implications of constituting word and world in particular ways. There is no assumption of prior knowledge of any of the philosophers, but the chapters achieve accessibility without dumbing down. Though the authors are all geographers, this collection will certainly be of value to educational researchers having an interest in doing some serious and productive thinking about the nature of what it is that they are doing.

Rose, G. (1982). *Deciphering Sociological Research*. Basingstoke: Macmillan.

Rose provides a structured approach to reading sociological research, which will also be of interest to beginning educational researchers. The book contains useful chapters on concepts and indicators, sampling, and an introduction to quantitative analysis. The book also includes a number of sociological research reports that have been reprinted so that the reader can try out Rose's approach to 'deciphering'.

Scollon, R. and Scollon, S.W. (2004). *Nexus Analysis: Discourse and the Emerging Internet*. London: Routledge.

Presents an approach to research on computer-mediated communication, new media and the internet that draws on discourse analysis and semiotics. The text contains a number of examples from the authors' own research,

Scott, J. (1990). *A Matter of Record: Documentary Sources in Social Research*. Oxford: Polity.

Discusses the nature of social research and considers the place and status of documentary evidence. Provides guidance on the treatment of official documents (e.g. census material), the products of the mass media (e.g. newspapers) and personal documents (e.g. diaries).

Sikes, P. and Potts, A. (Eds). (2008,). *Researching Education for the Inside: Investigations from Within*. London: Routledge.

A collection of papers exploring practitioner research on aspects of their own professional practice. Considers the particular issues raised by insider research, including ethical issues and the management of the dual role of researcher and colleague in workplace settings.

Silverman, D. (2006). *Interpreting Qualitative Data: Methods for Analysing Talk, Text and Interaction*. 3rd edition, London: Sage.

Offers an approach to the analysis of various form of sociological data (including observations, texts, interviews and transcripts). Considers questions of validity and reliability and the practical relevance of sociological research.

Strauss, A.L. (1987). *Qualitative Analysis for Social Scientists*. Cambridge: Cambridge University Press.

Corbin, J. and Strauss, A. (2008). *Basics of Qualitative Research: Grounded Theory Procedures and Techniques*, 3rd edition. London: Sage.

Both books give descriptions of the grounded theory approach to conducting social research and analysing qualitative data. The first book details the process with copious examples and gives a flavour of the training seminars run by Strauss. The later book gives a sequential account of the process of conducting research in this style. This includes explication of various forms of coding of data, theoretical sampling, the development of theory and writing a report or thesis.

Stringer, E.T. (2007). *Action Research in Education*. 3rd edition, London: Sage.

Practical guide covering all stages in the design, conduct and dissemination of action research.

Vaus, D.A. de. (2001). *Surveys in Social Research*. 5th edition, London: Routledge.

Gives detailed consideration of the design of survey research and the analysis of quantitative data. Addresses the need to clarify the relationship between concept and indicator variables, describes various forms of sampling and details issues in the construction of questionnaires. Includes consideration of the use of cross-tabulations and alternative means of bivariate analysis.

Walford, G. (Ed). (1991). *Doing Educational Research*. London: Routledge.

Formal research reports rarely give a clear picture of the mechanics of conducting a research study. In order to give the beginning researcher some insight into this process, thirteen educational researchers give narrative accounts of their research. Provides necessary reassurance that there are always contingencies to be addressed and compromises to be made in the operationalisation of a research design or strategy.

Wengraf, T. (2001). *Qualitative Research Interviewing: Biographic Narrative and Semi-structured Method*. London: Sage.

Thorough and conceptually sophisticated guide to interview-based research. Extensive use of examples and data extracts to illustrate key issues in the design of the study, the conduct of the interview and the analysis of data.

Whyte, W.F. (1955). *Street Corner Society: The Social Structure of an Italian Slum*. 2nd edition, Chicago: University of Chicago Press.

Whyte, W.F. (1993). *Street Corner Society: The Social Structure of an Italian Slum*. Fiftieth anniversary edition. Chicago: University of Chicago Press.

The main part of the book is an account of an early urban ethnography which has been very influential. Both editions include an appendix, revised in the later edition, which reflects on some of the methodological issues involved in the study, including the validity of the use of key informants. The fiftieth anniversary edition also includes new sections in which Whyte responds to come of his critics.

Williamson, J. (1978). *Decoding Advertisements*. London: Marion Boyers.

This book provides a large number of examples of the semiotic analysis of mainly visual texts. It also includes some discussion of anthropological, psychoanalytic, semiotic and sociological work that is involved in the theoretical field within which the analysis takes place.

Wolcott, H.F. (2001). *Writing Up Qualitative Research (Qualitative Research Methods)*. 2nd edition, London: Sage.

Short, practical and interesting guide to writing.

Wright, D.B. (1997). *Understanding Statistics: An Introduction for the Social Sciences*. London: Sage.

Considers the foundations of statistical theory (including discussion of probability, levels of measurement and forms of sampling) and introduces a range of forms of statistical analysis of quantitative data. These include methods of hypothesis testing, comparison of means, regression, correlation and the comparison of proportions. Provides numerous examples and exercises.

Young, R. (Ed). (1981). *Untying the Text: A Post-Structuralist Reader*. London: Routledge & Kegan Paul.

Good introduction to post-structuralist approaches to the analysis of texts (including semiotic analysis). Papers by Foucault and Barthes are of particular interest.

References

ANC (1994). *A Policy for Education and Training*. Johannesburg: ANC.

Barber, M. (1996). *The Learning Game: Arguments for an Education Revolution*. London: Gollancz.

Barthes, R. (1972). *Mythologies*. London: Jonathan Cape.

Basset, E.H. and O'Riordan, K. (2002). 'Ethics of Internet Research: Contesting the Human Subjects Research Model.' *Ethics and Information Technology*. 4. pp. 233–247.

Baym, N. (2000). *Tune in, Log on: Soaps, Fandom, and Online Community*. Thousand Oaks, CA: Sage.

Becker, H.S. (1953). 'Becoming a Marihuana User.' *American Journal of Sociology*. 59. pp 235–242.

BERA. (2004). *Revised Ethical Guidelines for Educational Research (2004)*. British Educational Research Association. Available at www.bera.ac.uk/publications/pdfs/ETHICA1.PDF.

Bernstein, B.B. (1996). *Pedagogy, Symbolic Control and Identity: Theory, Research Critique*. London: Taylor & Francis.

Bier, M.C., Sherblom, S.A. and Gallo, M.A. (1996). 'Ethical Issues in a Study of Internet Use: Uncertainty, Responsibility, and the Spirit of Research Relationships.' *Ethics and Behaviour*. 6(2). pp. 141–151.

Bourdieu, P. (1977). *Outline of a Theory of Practice*. Cambridge: CUP.

Bourdieu, P. (1990). *The Logic of Practice*. Cambridge: Polity.

Brown, A.J. (1993). 'Participation, Dialogue and the Reproduction of Social Inequalities.' In Merttens, R. and Vass, J. (Eds). *Partnerships in Maths: Parents and Schools*. London: Falmer, pp. 190–213.

Brown, A.J. (1994). 'Exploring Dialogue between Teachers and Parents: A Sociological Analysis of IMPACT Diaries.' Presented at Research into Social Perspectives on Mathematics Education, Kings' College, University of London. Available from the author.

Brown, A.J. (1999). 'Parental Participation, Positioning and Pedagogy: A Sociological study of the IMPACT Primary School Mathematics Project.' *Collected Original Resources in Education*, Vol. 24, No. 3, 7/A02–11/C09.

Brown, A.J. and Dowling P.C. (1993). 'The Bearing of School Mathematics on Domestic Space.' In Merttens, R., Mayers, D., Brown, A.J. and Vass, J. (Eds). *Ruling the Margins: Problematising Parental Involvement*. London: University of North London Press, pp. 39–52.

Burawoy, M., Burton, A., Ferguson, A. A., Fox, K. J., Gamson, J. Gartrell, N. Hurst, L.,

Kurzman, C., Salzinger, L., Schiffman, J., and Vi, S. (1991). *Ethnography Unbound: Power and Resistance in the Modern Metropolis*. Berkeley: University of California Press.

Clegg, F. (1983). *Simple Statistics: A Course Book for the Social Sciences*. Cambridge: Cambridge University Press.

Coates, J. (1993). *Women, Men and Language: A Sociolinguistic Account of Gender Differences in Language*. 2nd edition, London: Longman.

Cohen, L., Manion, L. and Morrison, K. (2007). *Research Methods in Education*. 6th edition, London: Routledge.

Corbin, J. and Strauss, A. (2008). *Basics of Qualitative Research: Grounded Theory Procedures and Techniques*. 3rd edition, London: Sage.

Corson, D.J. (1992). 'Language, Gender and Education: A Critical Review Linking Social Justice and Power.' *Gender and Education*. 4. pp. 229–254.

Danet, B. (1998). 'Text as Mask: Gender, Play, and Performance on the Internet.' In Jones, S. (Ed). *Cybersociety 2.0: Revisiting Computer-mediated Communication and Community*. Thousand Oaks, CA: Sage, pp. 129–158.

Davies, B. (2003). *Shards of Glass: Children Reading and Writing beyond Gendered Identities*. 2nd edition, Cresskill, NJ: Hampton Press.

Donaldson, M. (1978). *Children's Minds*. Glasgow: Fontana/Collins.

Dowling, P.C. (1995a). 'A Language for the Sociological Description of Pedagogic Texts with Particular Reference to the Secondary School Mathematics Scheme *SMP 11–16*.' *Collected Original Resources in Education*. **19**.

Dowling, P.C. (1995b). 'Discipline and Mathematise: The Myth of Relevance in Education.' *Perspectives in Education*. **16(2)**. pp. 209–226.

Dowling, P.C. (1996). 'A Sociological Analysis of School Mathematics Texts.' *Educational Studies in Mathematics*. **31**. pp. 389–415.

Dowling, P.C. (1998). *Mathematical Myths/Pedagogic Texts: The Sociology of Mathematics Education*. London: Falmer.

Dowling, P.C. and Brown, A.J. (2007). 'Pedagogy and Community in Three South African Schools: An Iterative Description.' Available at: http://homepage.mac.com/paulcdowling/ioe/publications/Chapter%207.pdf.

Eckert, P. and McConnell-Ginet, S. (2003). *Language and Gender*. Cambridge: Cambridge University Press.

ESRC. (2005). *Research Ethics Framework*. Swindon: ESRC. Available at: www.esrc.ac.uk/ESRCInfoCentre/Images/ESRC_Re_Ethics_Frame_tcm6–11291.pdf#search=%22research%20ethics%20framework%22.

Ensor, P. (1995). 'From Student to Teacher: Continuity or Rupture.' Presented at the Kenton Educational Association Conference, Grahamstown, October. Available from the author at the School of Education, University of Cape Town.

Evans, T.D. (1988). *A Gender Agenda: A Sociological Study of Teachers, Parents and Pupils in their Primary Schools*. Sydney: Allen and Unwin.

Fish, S. (1995). *Professional Correctness: Literary Studies and Political Change*. Cambridge, MA: Harvard University Press.

Flanders, N. (1970). *Analysing Teacher Behaviour*. New York: Wiley.

Galton, M., Simon, B. and Croll, P. (1980). *Inside the Primary School*. London: RKP.

Garfinkel, H. (1967). *Studies in Ethnomethodology*. Englewood Cliffs, NJ: Prentice-Hall.

Geertz, C. (1973). *The Interpretation of Cultures*. 2000 edition, New York, Basic Books.

Geertz, C. (1988). *Works and Lives: The Anthropologist as Author*. Cambridge: Polity.

Glaser, B.G. (1992). *Basics of Grounded Theory Analysis: Emergence versus Forcing*. Mill Valley: Sociology Press.

Glaser, B.G. and Strauss, A.L. (1967). *The Discovery of Grounded Theory: Strategies for Qualitative Research*. Chicago: Aldine Publishing Company.

Goddard, A. (1989). *The Language Awareness Project Years 4 and 5 (Key Stage 2): Language and Gender Pack One*. Lancaster: Framework Press.

Goffman, E. (1990). *The Presentation of Self in Everyday Life*. Harmondsworth: Penguin.

Hamilton, D. and Delamont, S. (1974). 'Classroom Research: A Cautionary Tale.' *Research in Education*. 11. pp. 1–15.

Herrera, C.D. (1999). 'Two Arguments for "Covert Methods" in Social Research.' *British Journal of Sociology*. 50(2). pp. 331–343.

Hine, C. (2005). *Virtual Methods: Issues in Social Research on the Internet*. Oxford: Berg Publishers.

Holmes, J. and Meyerhoff, M. (2003). *The Handbook of Language and Gender*. Oxford: Blackwell.

Homan, R. (1980). 'The Ethics of Covert Methods.' *British Journal of Sociology*. 31(1). pp. 46–59.

Kelly, G.A. (1969). *Clinical Psychology and Personality: The Selected Papers of George Kelly*. Edited by B.A. Maher. New York: John Wiley.

Kozulin, A. (1990). *Vygotsky's Psychology: A Biography of Ideas*. New York: Harvester/Wheatsheaf.

Kress, G. (1993). 'Against Arbitrariness: The Social Production of the Sign as a Foundational Issue in Critical Discourse Analysis.' *Discourse and Society*. 4(2). pp. 169–191.

Lawler, R.W. (1985). *Computer Experience and Cognitive Development: A Child's Learning in a Computer Culture*. Chichester: Ellis Horwood.

Likert, R. (1932). 'A Technique for the Measurement of Attitudes.' *Archives of Psychology*. 22(140). pp. 1–55.

Luria, A.R. (1976). *Cognitive Development: Its Cultural and Social Foundations*. Cambridge, MA: Harvard University Press.

Malinowski, B. (1922). *Argonauts of the Western Pacific*. London: RKP.

Mellar, H., Bliss, J., Boohan, R., Ogborn, J. and Tompsett, C. (Eds). (1994). *Learning with Artificial Worlds: Computer Based Modelling in the Curriculum*. London: Falmer.

Merttens, R. and Vass, J. (1990). *Sharing Maths Cultures*. London: Falmer.

Merttens, R. and Vass, J. (Eds). (1993). *Partnerships in Maths: Parents and Schools*. London: Falmer.

Miles, M.B. and Huberman, A.M. (1994). *Qualitative Data Analysis: An Expanded Sourcebook*. 2nd edition, London: Sage.

Mills, S. (2006). 'Book Review: *The Handbook of Language and Gender*. Janet Holmes, Miriam Meyerhoff (Eds), Blackwell, Oxford, 2003, 759 pp., £85.' *Journal of Pragmatics*. 38. pp. 297–300.

Nunes, T., Schliemann, A.D. and Carraher, D.W. (1993). *Street Mathematics and School Mathematics*. Cambridge: Cambridge University Press.

Oakley, A. (1976). *Housewife*. Harmondsworth: Penguin.

OPCS. (1980). *Classification of Occupations.* London: HMSO.

Oppenheim, A.N. (1992). *Questionnaire Design, Interviewing and Attitude Measurement.* New edition, London: Pinter.

Patt, M.B. and McBride, B.A. (1993). 'Gender Equity in Picture Books in Preschool Classrooms: An Exploratory Study.' Paper presented at the Annual Meeting of the American Educational Research Association, Atlanta, GA, 12–16 April.

Pauwels, A. and Winter, J. (2006). 'Gender Inclusivity or "Grammar Rules OK"? Linguistic Prescriptivism vs Linguistic Discrimination in the Classroom.' *Language and Education.* **20**(2). pp. 128–140.

Perret-Clermont, A.-N. (1980). *Social Interaction and Cognitive Development in Children.* New York: Academic Press.

Piaget, J. (1932). *The Moral Judgement of the Child.* London: RKP.

Piaget, J. (1953). *The Child's Conception of Number.* New York: Humanities Press.

Riessman, C.K. (1993). *Narrative Analysis.* London: Sage.

Robson, C. (2002). *Real World Research: A Resource for Social Scientists and Practitioner-Researchers.* 2nd edition, Oxford: Blackwell.

Roethlisberger, F.I. and Dickson, W.T. (1939). *Management and the Worker.* Cambridge, MA: Harvard University Press.

Ryle, G. (1968). 'The Thinking of Thoughts: What is *Le Penseur* Doing.' Available at http://lucy.ukc.ac.uk/CSACSIA/Vol14/Papers/ryle_1.html.

Schön, D. (1983). *The Reflective Practitioner: How Professionals Think in Action.* London: Temple Smith.

Silverman, D. (2006). *Interpreting Qualitative Data: Methods for Analysing Talk, Text and Interaction.* 3rd edition, London: Sage.

Somekh, B. (1995). 'The Contribution of Action Research to Development in Social Endeavours: A Position Paper on Action Research Methodology.' *British Educational Research Journal.* **21**(3). pp. 339–355.

Stake, R.E. (1988). 'Case Study Methods in Educational Research: Seeking Sweet Water.' In Jaeger, R.M. (Ed.). *Complementary Methods for Research in Education.* Washington, DC: American Educational Research Association, pp. 253–278.

Steedman, A., Unwin, C. and Walkerdine, V. (1985). *Language, Gender and Childhood.* London: RKP.

Strauss, A.L. (1987). *Qualitative Analysis for Social Scientists.* Cambridge: Cambridge University Press.

Silva, T.T. Da (1988). 'Distribution of School Knowledge and Social Reproduction in a Brazilian Setting.' *British Journal of Sociology of Education.* **9**(1). pp. 55–79.

Taylor, T.L. (2006). *Play between Worlds: Exploring Online Game Culture.* Cambridge, MA: MIT Press.

Thorne, B., Kramarae, C. and Henley, N. (1983). *Language, Gender and Society.* Rowley, MA: Newbury House.

Thrift, N. (2003). 'Practising Ethics.' In Pryke, M., Rose, G. and Whatmore, S. (Eds). *Using Social Theory: Thinking through Research.* London: Sage.

Van Den Hoonaard, W.C. (2003). 'Is Anonymity an Artifact in Ethnographic Research?' *Journal of Academic Ethics.* **1**. pp. 141–151.

Warschauer, M. (1996). 'Comparing Face-to-Face and Electronic Discussion in the Second Language Classroom.' *CALICO Journal.* **13**(2). pp. 7–26.

Weber, M. (1968). *Economy and Society.* New York: Bedminster Press.

Walden, R. and Walkerdine, V. (1985). *Girls and Mathematics: From Primary to Secondary Schools*. Bedford Way Paper no. 24. London: Institute of Education, University of London.

Whiteman, N.E. (2006). 'Ethical Stances in Internet Research.' Available at: http://homepage.mac.com/paulcdowling/ioe/studentswork/whiteman2006.pdf.

Whiteman, N.E. (2007). 'The Establishment, Maintenance and Destabilisation of Fandom: A Study of Two Online Communities and an Exploration of Issues Pertaining to Internet Research.' PhD thesis, Institute of Education, University of London. Available at: http://homepage.mac.com/paulcdowling/ioe/studentswork/whiteman(2007).pdf.

Whiteman, N.E. (in press). 'Homesick for Silent Hill: Modalities of nostalgia in fan responses to Silent Hill 4: The Room.' (2008) In Taylor, L. and Whalen, Z. (Eds). *Playing the Past: History and Nostalgia in Videogames*. Nashville TN: Vanderbilt University Press, p. 32–49.

Whiteman, N.E. (forthcoming). 'Learning at the Cutting Edge? Help-seeking and Status in Online Videogame Fan Sites.' *Information Technology, Education and Society*.

Willis, P.E. (1977). *Learning to Labour: How Working Class Kids Get Working Class Jobs*. Aldershot: Gower.

Witmer, D.F., Colman, R.W. and Katzman, S.L. (1999). 'From Paper-and-Pencil to Screen-and-Keyboard: Toward a Methodology for Survey Research on the Internet.' In Jones, S. (Ed). *Doing Internet Research: Crticial Issues and Methods for Examining the Net*. Thousand Oaks, CA: Sage.

Woods, P. and Merttens, R. (1994). 'Parents' and Children's Assessments of Maths in the Home.' In Merttens, R. and Woods, P. (Eds). *IMPACT: Papers Presented at the Annual Meeting of the American Educational Research Association*, London: The IMPACT Project, University of North London.

Wright, D.B. (1997). *Understanding Statistics: An Introduction for the Social Sciences*. London: Sage.

Young, R. (1992). *The Southern Illinois Working Papers in Linguistics and Language Teaching, Volume 1*. Carbondale, IL: Southern Illinois University Linguistics Department.

Zuber, S. and Reed, A.M. (1993). 'The Politics of Grammar Handbooks: Generic "He" and Singular "They".' *College English*. 55(5). pp. 515–530.

Index

absolute zero 21
abstraction: abstract classification 25; research problem as 146–7
access and gatekeeping 37–8
account of research, organisation of 162–6
action research: ethical dimension 39–40; interrogation mode 144, 158–9
Action Research for Educational Change (Elliott, J.) 181–2
Action Research in Education (Stringer, E.T.) 187
Adelman, C. 177
African National Congress (ANC) 168
Against Method: Outline of an Anarchistic Theory of Knowledge (Feyerabend, P.) 182
Amazon 55
Analysing Everyday Explanation: A Casebook of Methods (Antaki, C., Ed.) 177
Analysing Social Settings (Lofland, J. and Lofland, L.) 184
analysis, units of 28
anonymity 38–9
Antaki, C. 177
anthropological research 49–50
application of interrogation mode 150–4, 158–60
approaches to research 6–7, 10–11
archiving software 64
art, technique of 164
association 152; cause and, distinction between 141–2; chi-square measure of 129–32
assumptions about readership 90–1
Atlas.ti 106
Attenborough, David 171
attitudes, exploration of 75–7
Australian Education Index 14
authorities: authority relations 79–80; authority strategies 103–5; within theoretical field 145

Bannister, D. and Fransella, F. 178
bar charts 114–17
Barber, M. 168
Barthes, Roland 178; semiotic analysis 92–3
Basics of Qualitative Research (Corbin, J. and Strauss, A.) 186
Basset, E.H. and O'Riordan, K. 33
Baym, N.K. and Markham, A.N. 178
Bazeley, P. 178
Becker, Howard S. 27, 178
Becoming Critical: Education, Knowledge and Action Research (Carr, W. and Kemmis, S.) 179
beliefs, exploration of 75–7
Bell, J. 176
Benedict, Ruth 175n2
Bernstein, Basil B. 2, 101, 178
best fit, line of 134
bias 30; biasing description 93–5; interrogation mode 148, 151; quality in analysis 88, 94; unintentional bias 30
Bier, M. *et al.* 32–3
Black, T.R. 178
The Blackwell Dictionary of Twentieth-Century Thought (Outhwaite, W. and Bottomore, T., Eds.) 185
Bliss, J., Monk, M. and Ogborn, J. 178–9
bluesquirrel.com 64
Boas, Franz 10
Bogdan, R. and Biklen, S.K. 179
books, library collections of 12
Bourdieu, Pierre 17n1, 174n1
Brazil 3, 50–1, 169
Bristol Online Survey (BOS) 77
British Education Index 12, 14
British Educational Research Association (BERA) 33–4, 36
British Library Direct 16
britsoc.co.uk 165
Brown, A.J. and Dowling, P.C. 70, 169
Brown, Andrew J. 70–1, 81, 97–100, 101,